THE HOLY FAMILY AND ITS LEGACY

THE HOLY FAMILY

AND ITS LEGACY

Religious Imagination from the Gospels to *Star Wars*

Albrecht Koschorke

TRANSLATED BY

Thomas Dunlap

COLUMBIA UNIVERSITY PRESS • NEW YORK

COLUMBIA UNIVERSITY PRESS
Publishers Since 1893
New York   Chichester, West Sussex

© 2000, Fischer Taschenbuch Verlag GmbH, Frankfurt am Main
English translation copyright © 2003 Columbia University Press

Library of Congress Cataloging-in-Publication Data
Koschorke, Albrecht, 1958–
    [Heilige Familie und ihre Folgen. English]
    The Holy Family and its legacy : religious imagination from the Gospels to Star Wars /
Albrecht Koschorke ; translated by Thomas Dunlap.
        p.   cm.
    ISBN 0–231–12756–1 (alk. paper)
    1. Jesus Christ—Family.   2. Family—Religious aspects—Christianity—History of doctrines.
3. Family—Europe—History.   I. Title.

BT313.K6813 2003
232.92—dc21

2003053123

Columbia University Press books are printed
on permanent and durable acid-free paper.

Designed by Lisa Hamm
Printed in the United States of America
c 10 9 8 7 6 5 4 3 2 1

CONTENTS

My interest in the Holy Family goes back to an afternoon in December 1992 when I found myself unable to tell the Christmas story to my then three-year-old son. Children can be relentless, and my answers to his persistent question of who Jesus' father really was must have been incoherent. I began to think about the fact that a problem lies at the heart of Christian patriarchy: the position of the father in this religion remains ambiguous, with consequences that extend far beyond the Christmas story.

However, my scholarly examination of this problem, which is now accessible to an English-speaking audience, could not be anything but fragmentary. Anyone who proposes to study Western culture from the perspective of the Christian family myth faces a task that is all but insurmountable, given the breadth of the topic. That is true in nearly every field: theology, history, art history, psychohistory, sociology of the family, anthropology, and—last but not least—literature.

If there is anything that can justify such an effort in spite of these daunting odds, it is the fact that there appears to be no single study of the complex of the Holy Family, which is fraught with such extraordinary cultural meaning. To be sure, the number of works that touch on the topic is vast. But to my knowledge, no reasonably systematic analysis of the symbolic and sociocultural valences of the Holy Family has ever been published.

This study journeys, for the most part, along stages on a European path. Throughout, special emphasis is placed on the German-speaking tradition, which reflects my own intellectual background, but also on the importance of such authors as Martin Luther and Sigmund Freud to the history of the family in the Western tradition. A study with a stronger focus on U.S. history would no doubt have to begin with the Puritan Revolution of the seventeenth century and probe into the legacy for family policy left behind by the Pilgrims and later waves of immigrants—down to Nathaniel Hawthorne's *Scarlet Letter*, a text of great significance for the literary aftereffects of the Holy Family. However, that would be material for another book. For the American edition, I have added a chapter on the virulence of the Christian family myth in the *Star Wars* films.

Another difference between the United States and Europe is perhaps more significant. The broader argument of the book rests on the experience of an extensive loss of meaning of religious traditions, especially Christian traditions.

It would appear that this is a specifically European experience—just as the very notion of a world-encompassing process of secularization rests on premises drawn from a nineteenth-century European philosophy of history, premises that are not necessarily shared by the rest of the world. For example, in spite of a strict separation of church and state, the United States has not witnessed a real laicization of its public space, as any U.S. coin will confirm. To that extent, the complex interrelationships among family, politics, and theology will appear different, in some respects, from an American point of view than they do in this book, which was conceived primarily with an eye on Europe.

A. K.

PART I Dispositions

I

AROUND THE YEAR ZERO

The Christian calendar has a birth anomaly: it lacks the number zero. In the year 525, Abbot Dionysus Exiguus set out to devise a precise method for determining the date of Easter. Much to his chagrin, he had to rely on a chronology derived during the reign of Diocletian, the Roman emperor infamous for his persecution of the Christians. Dionysus began by calculating the date of Christ's birth. That date furnished the starting point for a new method of counting time, one that no longer referred to the chronology of the Roman Empire but to the arrival of the Christian Messiah: the year of his birth became year 1 of the Christian era.

That decision was perfectly logical within the context of Dionysus's time. The number zero did not come into use until the High Middle Ages, under Arab influence, and it faced an uphill struggle before gaining acceptance. Moreover, for theological reasons alone it would have been impossible to mark an event as momentous as the incarnation of God with a symbol for nothingness, a neutral cipher. The redemptive power of Christ's birth could be expressed only by the number that was the positive starting point for all other calculations: the holy number of unity and wholeness, the number of the beginning, the golden number—1.

Dionysus's method of temporal reckoning was slow to spread. Throughout most of the Middle Ages, there was a profusion of regional and shorter-lived methods of dating. The biblical time frame, which went all the way back to the creation of the world by God, remained authoritative when it came to dating larger eras. At this time, therefore, Christianity and Judaism still shared a historical horizon. That began to change in the modern period (after 1500), which saw the growing custom of incorporating even pre-Christian dates into the Christian era by counting backward from the birth of Christ. At this point, however, it was no longer possible to insert a zero. (An attempt by Jacques Cassini to do so in 1740 was unsuccessful.) Beginning in the seventeenth century, the general rule was to have the first year of the Christian era preceded by the year 1 B.C. (before Christ). An event that was the *beginning* of redemptive history—Christ's birth—became an event in the *middle* of time, but this was possible only at the price of an arithmetical incongruity.

As a result of this temporal structure—because zero is missing at the threshold of the Christian era—the entire construct of subsequent decades and centuries is out of alignment, departing by a year from the decimal system. That is why the "real" start of the new millennium, regardless of the official celebratory calendar in Rome and throughout the world, occurred at midnight on December 31, 2000.

Extending the established reckoning of years into the time *before* the birth of Christ had far-reaching consequences. For one thing, it liberated chronology from the shaky beliefs in creation, which could no longer be reconciled with progress in science. By breaking free of the Bible-centric world era, the way was opened for a secular temporal order. A uniform method of reckoning had been created, one that spanned cultural spheres and had no temporal boundaries. Paradoxically, this secularizing step entailed, in purely arithmetical terms, a strengthening of Christocentrism. "It is one of the ironies of history," Hans Maier has noted, "that the method of temporal reckoning that places Christ at the center of time finally triumphed during the Enlightenment—in other words, in the very period that sought to free itself from Christian traditions in many spheres of life."[1]

But the practice of counting backward from the birth of Christ has another important effect. By transcending the chronology of the Hebrew Bible, it succeeds—mathematically, so to speak—in expunging the prehistory of Christianity, its *Jewish* origins. This method of temporal calculation fulfills precisely the program of theologians who interpret biblical events as leading up to the arrival of the Christian Messiah and who regard the Hebrew Bible as the prefiguration of the New Testament.

Henceforth, every date incorporated the notion that the occurrences of the pre-Christian world all move toward the order-creating, key event of Christ's birth and are conceivable only from the vantage point of this gravitational center. In a sense, the Christian method of counting the years, which transcended Europe to become the world standard, sends out two vectors in opposite directions: looking ahead and back, they assign a historical place to every event. And they do so from a central point that is more than a mere transitional location on the time continuum: for Christ's birth takes place *within time* and is simultaneously the *hinge of time* as such and therefore outside its order. It is situated where the positive and negative number sequences meet without transition, in the very fold of the temporal universe to which everything that has been and is yet to come is inclined—an insertion from the outside that, simply based on the method of reckoning, lays claim to having no worldly temporal origin.

ב

FAITH AND CODE

Anyone who uses the current worldwide method of temporal reckoning is acting out Christian articles of faith without being aware of it. The legend of Christ's birth may be no less remote and incidental to someone than the myth of Europa, a king's daughter whom Zeus, in the guise of a bull, abducted and who later gave her name to an entire continent. The history of names, of ciphers, of the customary categories of language and reckoning is replete with such initial coincidences. All cultural signs have an etiological dimension, and these etiologies consist of thick sedimentary layers of forgotten reasons and constraints that have ceased to have meaning in the shopworn, conventional ways in which these signs are used. But that is not the critical point. Even things that one does not know about possess real power. Power is not a question of *belief* in reality; it adheres to the ways in which reality is *coded*.

At first glance, a theme like the Holy Family seems antiquarian in this day and age. Even if there are still many professed believers, the Christian West has entered a post-Christian era. Two thousand years after the birth of Christ, the process that is dissolving the traditions of society's fundamental religious imprint is accelerating at a breathtaking pace. This trend has long since spread from the city to the countryside, from the educated classes to the less educated classes, from the young to the old, from progressive to conservative circles, from affluent to poorer nations, and, not least, from Protestantism to Catholicism. The secularizing process is being driven by structural change in many spheres. I am talking about the dissolution of premodern ways of life, the decline in the meaning of human suffering (from work, disease, pain, and death), the waning of the consciousness of sin as the backdrop to religious hopes of redemption, and, finally, the dismantling of collectively binding exemplars in general. The Christian calendar, which once imposed its rhythm on life week by week and year by year, has largely fallen into desuetude—except for a few holidays, religious remnants in a nonreligious culture.

Even where individuals are active churchgoers, the real religious component of church life is in decline. The churches, too, are turning into service organizations: in part for charitable purposes, in part merely for ceremonial purposes. One can call this trend the *folklorization* of faith. There is a lot of hand-wringing about the excessive commercial exploitation of holidays such as Christmas and Easter, the only ones still rooted in social custom. As it is, there are many who, while standing aloof from ecclesiastical life, regard the waning of the religious dimension with a certain nostalgia. Among nonparticipants, that feeling is even linked to a kind of anxiety about an impending calamity.

In a certain sense, Christianity has once again become what it was at the outset: one sect among many in a cultural sphere in which all conceivable religious practices can be tried and combined in a syncretistic manner. There are striking parallels between the present, post-Christian era and the first centuries A.D. in the Mediterranean region.

Given this plethora of circumstances unfavorable to Christian tradition, the question invariably arises: Why should we concern ourselves with the Holy Family? And why do biblical themes as such appear to enjoy a certain popular currency? Numerous works on the life of Jesus have been published over the past few years.[1] Mary, too, is a topic of remarkable public interest.[2] A few years ago there was even a biography of the Holy Spirit.[3] Nor is the Devil absent from this cast: not as a member of the Holy Family, of course, but intimately linked with it as the enemy of God and the tempter of his Son, who eventually triumphs over him.[4]

There are two answers to these questions. First, it would appear that an interest in cultural history has survived the religious ties. Precisely because the Christian faith is no longer experienced as a serious life option by most people, its component parts have become available both as accessories—one need only think of the angelic fashions of a few years back, the large crosses that are part of punk accoutrements, and the entire Catholic kitsch of pop culture—and as the object of intellectual curiosity: the beginning of the new millennium provided an occasion for retrospective glances and stocktaking.

Second, one might doubt that the influence of religious patterns of thought and life has, in fact, vanished without a trace, as it would seem it has when a family today gathers awkwardly around a Christmas tree and tries to sing a carol of which even the elders know only the first verse by heart. After all, it is possible that the path by which religion is mediated is not—or at least not primarily—a belief referred to as "living faith" in sermons and at church conferences. If that is indeed the case, we need to shift our attention from the outward appearance of postreligious society to the *deep structures of its imagination.* Perhaps such structures exert their influence without registering in a person's awareness. That again raises the question of how a religion such as Christianity has influenced elementary social codes and may be doing so still.

This approach can sharpen our interest in a topic like the Holy Family. How is it that this family (or certain aspects of it) exercised the collective imagination to such a degree that it became the most prominent subject in Western painting? Why do Mary-like mothers and Jesus-like sons play such a prominent role not only in the late Middle Ages or during the Counter-Reformation but also during the Enlightenment, in the nineteenth century (with its faith in science), and even today in movies such as *Terminator* and the *Star Wars* series, to the point where one can count them among our society's leading cultural stereotypes? And lest one forget the paternal side (this is where the story gets truly complicated): What does the figure of the Father-God, who sends his Son among humans and lets him sacrifice himself for them, have to do with the social and familial institutions of male-dominated society in its Western incarnation?

Anyone who raises these kinds of questions is less interested in the truth or refutability of historical facts than in the *logic of cultural phantasms*. If one starts from the hypothesis that a constellation of individuals such as the Holy Family not merely is a legendary, incidental grouping—one that can be demystified in one way or another by historical research—but possesses the power of an exemplar, and as such is a constant and malleable reference point for far-reaching psychosocial developments, then specific theological questions become relevant even for staunch nontheologians. In that case, it would not be enough to highlight the inconsistencies, contradictions, and manipulations of the biblical tradition and its theological afterlife (even though such an analysis, correctly done, is surely not without interest). And it would be completely insufficient to label as mere theological and ideological hairsplitting the mysteries that the intellectual elites of the Christian centuries pondered with an intensity and a meditative concentration no longer accessible to us. Rather, one must ask from where these enigmatic biblical figures derive their peculiar and apparently irresistible attraction, what *social substance* they possess, and what kinds of transformations they have undergone in the course of their long history.

Given the vastness of the theme, this book can do no more than sketch an answer. Many intermediate stages in the long accretive process of Christian symbolism and many internal divergences will have to be neglected; the overarching overview invariably comes at the expense of individual sedimentary layers in the theological development of Christianity. This is especially true for the early Christian period—that is to say, the era when the new faith took shape. It is impossible to do justice to that epoch in an essay that, for the sake of brevity, bases many aspects of its arguments on the "results" of a developed Catholic dogma.

3

POSITIONS I: JESUS AND HIS FATHERS

In purely mathematical terms, two thousand years of Christianity means two thousand years of the Holy Family. Christ's birth, with which our system of temporal reckoning begins, took place within the bosom of his family. At its *core*—which, to be sure, is given shape only by the traditional telling of the story—this family consists of three persons: father, mother, and son. It is important to review the various familial positions. First of all, son, not daughter. Christianity is a religion of the son. Whatever else that means, it certainly excludes daughters from the central religious figuration. Moreover, it is an *only* son—at least the only son of *God*. The Gospels tell of brothers and sisters of Jesus, a situation that has led to theological complications. The most popular explanation insists that these siblings were the children of Joseph's first marriage, which means they are only half siblings. Actually, they are not even half siblings since Joseph, as everyone knows, is not considered Jesus' physical father. Joseph is thus Jesus' stepfather, so to speak, and that would make his brothers and sisters stepsiblings. None of this, however, made its way into the depictions of the Holy Family. Only John the Baptist is occasionally placed alongside Christ as the second child; more rarely still, Anne and Joachim, according to nonbiblical tradition Mary's parents, round out the image of the Holy "clan." Yet all these persons remain secondary iconographic figures, and they fall victim to the increasingly intimate characterization of the family picture in modern times.[1] The pictorial tradition concerns itself chiefly with a three-person household.

It should already be apparent that the Holy Family is a constellation with a difficult and diffuse context: in its tradition-shaping form, it had to be cleansed of contrary indications in the Gospels themselves. It is impossible to ignore the textual traces attesting to the fact that Jesus hailed from a household in Nazareth with many children. Matthew recounts how Jesus returned to his hometown and taught in the synagogue there. The people were amazed and asked: "Where does he get this wisdom from, and these miraculous powers? Is he not the carpenter's son? Is not his mother called Mary, his brothers James, Joseph, Simon, and Judas? And are not all his sisters here with us? Where, then, has he gotten all this from?" Matthew continues: "So they fell foul of him, and this led him to say, 'A prophet will always be held in honour, except in his home town, and in his own family.' And he did not work many miracles there: such was their want of faith" (13:54–58).[2]

Hessian Master, altar wing panel, ca. 1410. Parish church, Rauschenberg.

Jesus is reluctant to be reminded of his birth family. When he is around them, his miraculous powers fail. The Evangelists record his displeasure; but they—and the exegetical tradition that follows—are out to make the offspring of an ordinary Jewish family into the one and only chosen Son of God. Their efforts were crowned with great success in the Christian pictorial imagination. In all of Western art there is, to my knowledge, not a single painting showing Jesus in the midst of his brothers and sisters. Everything revolves around the one familiar core configuration: father, mother, and son.

This brief discussion has already touched on the problem of paternity. The Holy Family, after all, is not a real family. According to Christian belief, Joseph and Mary, the holy parents, did not beget Jesus by sexual procreation. The angel Gabriel announces to Mary the birth of her son. His name is derived from the Hebrew construction *Gavri-El*, which means "God is my husband."[3] The name of the angel already contains the message he announces to Mary: "You shall conceive and bear a son, and you shall give him the name Jesus" (Luke 3:1). To which Mary responded: "'How can this be? . . . I am still a virgin.' The angel answered, 'The Holy Spirit will come upon you, and the power of the Most High will overshadow you, and for that reason the holy child to be born will be called Son of God'" (1:34–35).

The mystery of the virginal conception, which plays such a preeminent role in Christianity, has repercussions for the position of the father. Fatherhood is divided into two or even three sources: first, Joseph as the human foster father; second, God as the father in heaven; and, third, the Holy Spirit as the emanation from God, by whom Mary, as we read in Matthew, "was with child" (1:18).

Repeatedly, legend and painting have depicted the Holy Family as an intimate community filled with tender affection, playing a crucial role in allowing an ideal of familial intimacy to take shape in the first place, and take hold in everyday life. Still, a kind of fissure runs through this constellation: human fatherhood competes with a different, heavenly, transcendental fatherhood. It has not occasioned enough surprise that Christianity, as a patriarchal religion, was not able to cast the role of father in an unambiguous way. Instead, it offers two divergent models that cannot be connected without conflict:

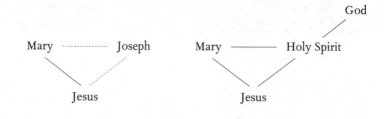

4

POSITIONS II: MARY AND THE TRINITY

The relationship diagram of the Holy Family superimposes two triangles that differ with respect to the position of the father. Inscribed within the triangles is thus a hidden foursome—in the form of a divergence, an opening, an element that renders the situation dynamic. And that is not all: a third triangle comes into play, disrupting the economy of the first two. For the enigma of divine paternity touches on another mystery that forms one of the core notions of Christian dogma: the mystery of the Trinity:

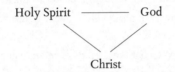

Trinity refers to the substantial unity of three persons: God, Christ, and the Holy Spirit. It forms a triangle that is no triangle; rather, it is directed against the process of triangulation itself by undermining the very act of drawing boundaries between persons. This makes the relationship model of the Holy Family even more complicated, especially when one considers the position of the mother.

In this system of overlapping and interweaving triangular relationships, Mary, the mother of Jesus, has multiple attributions. First, she functions as the companion and ward of her husband, Joseph, as is very clear from the Christian Christmas ritual and numerous pictorial representations. Mary and Joseph journey from Nazareth to Bethlehem, find shelter in a stable, guard their child, and escape the designs of King Herod by fleeing to Egypt—all nuclear-family stories.

In reality, though, Joseph does not fulfill his patriarchal role, and Mary, as the chosen maid of God, establishes a privileged relationship to a *higher* paternal principle. She conceived her child by the Holy Spirit, not by the earthly man at her side. In colloquial terms, one could say that she is God's wife: the mother of the Son of God. However, God—in Trinitarian fashion—is unified into a single essence with Christ (his son) and the Holy Spirit. And that is why Mary is not only the bride of God, but also the mother of God, and it is as such that she is venerated, especially in Orthodox and Catholic Christianity. Given the Trinitarian unity of God the Father and Christ, Mary's status as bride *and* mother of God means that she is both mother and bride to her own son. What we are dealing with here is not merely some arbitrary theological combination. In particular, Christian theology has explored this relationship with great intensity, and it has become the source of a mystical experience of faith. Especially in the Middle Ages, one finds Mary repeatedly linked to her son, Jesus, as a bride.

If one were to lay out all the possible combinations of the three triangles in which the Holy Family is situated, one would arrive at some baffling results. Here it shall suffice to indicate the range of themes that emerged in the Christian tradition itself. They include the notion that Mary encounters in her only child the incarnation of the heavenly Father and thus simultaneously her bridegroom. This dogmatically attested consequence of the doctrine of the Trinity has surely contributed to the special importance that attaches to the mother–son axis in the Christian idea of the family; in particular, it has exerted considerable influence on female religiosity.

It must be said, however, that these kinds of relationships do not occur in the realm of naturalistic gender relations. Rather, they belong to a *logic of spirituality*, a logic whose essential quality is the *absence of sexuality* and in which customary gender attributions fail. Built into the imagined order of Christianity is also the possibility of transcending and exchanging sexual identities. In imitation of Mary, every believer, male or female, can experience himself or herself as the bride of Christ. Jesus, for his part, is at times endowed with maternal attributes and venerated as a mother.[1] Sometimes the accident of language determines the gender marking. In Hebrew, the Holy Spirit would be *ruach* and thus feminine; the Greek Bible uses the neutral noun *pneuma* for *ruach*; only the Latin *spiritus sanctus* makes it grammatically masculine.[2] The theologians, however, understood the Holy Spirit as the expression of the love between God and Christ and in this way preserved female traits within it. Thus the Trinity with which Mary is linked as a bride does not simply represent a "male cartel." It contains within itself many nuances of meaning, and in this way it participates in modeling the relationship between spirituality and masculinity.

5

FROM THE JEWISH BIRTH FAMILY TO THE
CHRISTIAN DESTINATION FAMILY

The account in the Gospels is transparent when it describes situations that seem plausible for Palestine at the beginning of the Christian era. Jesus, one of many children from a simple craftsman's family, founds a kind of itinerant sect, preaches, teaches, heals, exorcises evil spirits, and performs magical cures—deeds that meet with disapproval from his family and former neighbors. His parents are Joseph, a Jewish craftsman, and Mary (Miriam in Hebrew), a simple, uneducated woman. But this is not the narrative level that concerns the Gospel writers. Above what one might call the empirical circumstances of his origins they superimpose another, *sacred* structure of relationships. Jesus now appears as the Son of God, who has chosen Mary as the mother of the Messiah and has dispatched the Holy Spirit to her. The motif of the Holy Family cuts across both levels: the Jewish birth family, which, however, has been truncated by the elimination of the rest of the clan; and the Christian destination family, a triangle composed of God the Father, the virginal mother, and the Son sent among humankind as the Messiah.

One is compelled to note in this setup a break with Jesus' descent, a break as radical as one could possibly imagine. First, Jesus was not conceived sexually. His human father is not his real father; Jesus will turn his back on this human father and submit to the disposition of his heavenly father, a submission that will lead to his death on the cross. Second, he will trigger an unexpectedly powerful antifamily mass movement. His followers will leave their homes, search out the solitude of the desert as ascetics, and take monkhood and ecclesiastical celibacy upon themselves in order to follow his teachings.

While his closest family members have very little understanding of who he is, Jesus, for his part, does not treat them very kindly. He disavows and repudiates them. His behavior at the wedding in Cana shows that even toward his own mother he violates the commandment of showing respect for one's elders, which was strictly observed in Judaism. When Mary informs him that there is no wine left, Jesus answers: "Your concern, woman, is not mine" (John 2:4).[1] This contrasts sharply with the loving intimacy that the later Western pictorial tradition imparts to the birth scene. The Gospel writers, whose stories serve to establish the Christian religion of the Son, emphasize the founder's *rebellion* against the order of the family.

Jesus preaches, attracting many followers as well as enemies. Matthew writes: "He was still speaking to the crowd when his mother and brothers appeared; they stood outside, wanting to speak to him. Someone said, 'Your mother and your brothers are here, outside; they want to speak to you.' Jesus turned to the man who brought the message and said, 'Who is my mother? Who are my brothers?'; and, pointing to the disciples, he said, 'Here are my mother and my brothers. Whoever does the will of my heavenly Father is my brother, my sister, my mother'" (12:46–50).

A nearly identical account is found in the Gospel According to Mark (3:31–35). On one side are his natural kin, whom Jesus does not admit into his presence and whom he does not recognize as his family. On the other side is his *true family*, the disciples, the faithful, the brothers and sisters in God. Jesus leaves no doubt that he repudiates the principle of family loyalty in favor of a spiritual principle, that of community with the disciples and believers. He is switching from a natural to a spiritual affiliation, from his father's house to his status as the Son of God. "If anyone comes to me and does not hate his father and mother, wife and children, brothers and sisters, even his own life, he cannot be a disciple of mine" (Luke 14:26).

A tremor of apocalyptic fury runs through these sayings:

You must not think that I have come to bring peace to the earth; I have not come to bring peace, but a sword. I have come to set a man against his father, a daughter against her mother, a son's wife against her mother-in-law; and a man will find his enemies under his own roof. No man is worthy of me who cares more for father or mother than for me; no man is worthy of me who cares for son or daughter; no man is worthy of me who does not take up his cross and walk in my footsteps. By gaining his life a man will lose it; by losing his life for my sake, he will gain it. (Matthew 10:34–39)

To recapitulate, Jesus, the scion of the Holy Family, which has exercised the Western pictorial imagination to such an extraordinary degree, presents himself as the radical destroyer of familial bonds. I am here not talking about merely a few marginal episodes that were later pushed into the background. Quite the contrary: it was precisely in this regard that Jesus inspired the emergence of a tradition. For his followers, whether during his lifetime or in subsequent centuries, would, in fact, sever all affiliations to family, clan, place, and ethnic group to establish new, spiritual communities: communities of faith—monastic or otherwise—that cut across the conventional system of social obligations.

Francesco Vanni, altar of the Immaculate Conception, 1588. San Salvatore, Montalcino.

All this is connected to the transformation in the code of fatherhood. Jesus cannot say the things he says as the child of a craftsman from Nazareth: he demands and does scandalous things; indeed, he shakes to the very core the cohesion of society at the time, a cohesion grounded in blood kinship and clan affiliation. But he is not speaking as the craftsman's son; he is speaking as the Son of the Father in heaven. He himself carries out what he demands from his disciples: repudiating the genealogical order of humankind to institute a new line of descent derived from God.

In antiquity and in the world of premodern Europe, the family has, in essence, two functions. (To be precise, one would have to speak of *clan* and *kinship group*. The family in the narrower, biological sense that we know of is a recent historical phenomenon. The word "family" did not establish itself until the modern period.) First, it is the *locus of legitimate sexual procreation*. A man and a woman enter into marriage to procreate and raise their offspring. This function, however, does not stand alone; it works to fulfill the second, overarching function: continuing the genealogical line. It is not about the mere fact of procreation; it is about the procreation and continuation of one's own line. A genealogical bond links the generations since the beginning of the world, and it will continue to the end of time. A person without a family tree has no descent and no future. He lacks a name (for all names are, first and foremost, genealogical markers) and an identity. He has no place in a society whose distinctions rest on categories of kinship.

Not until one becomes fully aware of this can one recognize what kind of anomaly the Holy Family represents. It will not fulfill its genealogical mission either in the present or in the future—at least not in the conventional, physical sense of genealogy. In Western consciousness, Jesus Christ is celibate. He turns his back on the realm of familial procreation and replaces it with a bond to God and with discipleship. In the process, discipleship, in its most important functions, is identical to brotherhood—notwithstanding the fact that a few women are among Jesus' most faithful followers. Membership in the brotherhood destroys loyalties of kinship. It establishes its own, initially largely egalitarian, structures much the same way as the life of the early church had a communist tinge. The two ideals of Christian asceticism—celibacy and poverty—are directly related. Common to both is the fact that they interrupt the process of genealogical transmission. The suspension of sexuality is joined by the suspension of property—that is to say, of family property that is supposed to be inherited along kinship lines. Against the backdrop of the expectation that the Kingdom of God is imminent, both ideals destroy the continuation of earthly affairs.

6

THE MAN JOSEPH AND MONOTHEISTIC RELIGION

A Marginalized Figure

Mary's importance, especially in the sphere of Catholic piety, is beyond question. Joseph, however, has suffered quite a different fate. In a reversal of the usual biographical scheme, he owes his semi-shadowy existence solely to the woman at whose side he stood. He represents a companion figure about whom we are given only sparse information, and at a certain point that information ceases entirely, without any further comment. In addition, he is a figure who has long been the laughingstock of Western popular culture.

Western art pays him heed only marginally as an additional figure, a third person beside the mother–child dyad that is the focus of artistic attention. We find him as the protector of the small family to which he does not belong. In the scenes of nightly veneration, he is the one holding the lamp. The medieval mind envisaged him as an old, frail man so as to make his abstinence appear plausible. That image, however, did not necessarily do much to enhance his reputation. At times it places him in iconographic proximity to the type of the lecherous and foolish old man, whose lust is inversely proportional to his ability to satisfy it.

The inversion of age is joined by that of gender, for the legend has the aging Joseph, in the background of the scene, perform emphatically inferior and—according to traditional convention—female tasks: cooking porridge and washing diapers. (Incidentally, it should be noted that Western culture in general was unable to develop a code of conduct that kept paternal interaction with babies free of ridicule.)

In an essay on cultural history, Gabriela Signori has written:

In a sense, the late medieval male world—especially that of unmarried men, which was displaying its masculinity ever more ostentatiously with codpieces and tight leggings—could not look upon a man like Joseph with anything but contempt and mockery. Through his passive role in the act of procreation, he violated one of the chief rules of male honor. On this point the depictions of Joseph eventually intersected with the anticlerical literature of the time. For just like its counterimage, the lecherous cleric from merry tales and shrovetide plays, the example of Joseph reveals . . . that male asexuality could also be perceived as a threat. Clerics and holy men like Joseph, each in their own way, questioned the existing patriarchal gender hierarchy.[1]

But it is not only these sorts of problems of social integration that turn Joseph into a precarious figure. Church dogma, too, struggled to assign him a place. While Mary's virginal motherhood became a paradoxical core element of the Christian faith early on, the man at her side remained a multifaceted figure and had great difficulty freeing himself from the air of tragicomedy that attached to him. Patristics had its hands full trying to close the credibility gap that was forming around the Joseph figure—provoking countless efforts at filling the missing parts of the story with apocryphal and legendary material—against insinuations from Jews, pagans, and heretics.

According to one Jewish tradition, Jesus was the illegitimate son of the Roman soldier Panthera. With patent polemical intent, this story denounces Mary as an army whore; at her side, Joseph, a powerless, cuckolded husband, does not strike a favorable pose. But even the Christian Apocrypha depict Joseph as a man who had to be forced to accept his good fortune of being allowed to act as the guardian of the Virgin Mary. The second-century proto-Gospel of Jacobus has Mary grow up as a temple maid. At age twelve, we are told, she is publicly betrothed: the high priest hands a rod to each of the assembled suitors, and the chosen one will be revealed by a miracle that will manifest itself on his rod—a phallic ritual. News of the gathering of men finally reaches Joseph, a widowed carpenter: "And Joseph threw down his axe and went out to meet them."[2] He is given the last rod. The divine sign was not, as once with Aaron, the miraculous blossoming or greening of the rod; instead, "a dove came out of the rod and flew on to Joseph's head." In this way, the sign of the Holy Spirit is inserted into the fertility rite. Joseph does not fail to protest the strange decision: "I (already) have sons and am old, but she is a girl. I fear lest I should become a laughing-stock to the children of Israel."[3] It is only with harsh threats that the high priest prevails upon him to accept Mary.

At the Interface Between Judaism and Christianity

The canonical Gospels themselves are noticeably reticent when it comes to information about Jesus' foster father. Joseph is said to have been a pious man. Informed of Mary's pregnancy, he wishes to spare her public gossip and intends to dismiss her quietly (Matthew 1:19). In a dream, an angel announces to him the birth of the Messiah and makes him change his mind: "'Joseph son of David,' said the angel, 'do not be afraid to take Mary home with you as your wife. It is by the Holy Spirit that she has conceived this child'" (Matthew 1:20). His original decision already requires some explanation, for as a "righteous" *Jew*, Joseph should have followed the rules of Mosaic law, which stipulates that if a bride is guilty of sexual misconduct, she should be led before the gates of the city and stoned to death so as to "rid yourselves of this wickedness" (Deuteronomy 22:23–24).[4]

Joseph is thus violating the literal application of the law. This is not merely an anecdotal detail. His position as such is marked by a break with custom. The extraordinary events, of which he is a witness, wrest him from the path of tradition. Here one already sees opening up the discrepancy between the "letter" and the "spirit" of the textual tradition, a discrepancy that would later give rise to profound theological consequences. Through his tacit acceptance of this child, conceived in such a miraculous fashion, Joseph abandons the ground of Jewish orthodoxy. It appears as though Joseph himself, by virtue of his self-abnegation and refusal to take a stand regarding his male honor, is anticipating the Christian–Pauline endeavor of transcending the letter—which is rooted in the body—through the spirit.

Jesus' procreation severs the agnatic link—that is, the line of male blood kinship. Mary conceives not a mortal man, but the Holy Spirit; the Word of God itself becomes the seed in her—that, at least, drawing on the Gospel According to Luke, becomes the established theological interpretation. A staggering amount of ink has been shed over the question of the Annunciation and the mystery of the asexual conception. Yet this shift from physical to divine conception, this direct connection of the man Jesus to God, is possible only at the price of a rupture, a discontinuity. Jesus' status as the Son of God corresponds to the breach in agnatic filiation that takes place in Joseph's manhood. Mary's virginity is the blank spot that interrupts the chain of bodies and creates space for the linkage to the spiritual realm. Christian thinking—and, with it, the associated body–spirit dualism—has always been interested only in the second aspect, the connection with the logos, and not in the first, the wound, the rupture. Right up to Hegel and his Christology, it articulated a theory of *mediation*, largely ignoring the *disjunction* on which it was based.

The Genealogical Dilemma

One must realize what the interruption of the father–son succession means in the Jewish tribal order, which was organized along patrilineal lines. Male genealogy assigns the son a place, and if Jesus is not Joseph's son, he has no place within Jewish society. Linked to Joseph's thwarted paternity is a dilemma that Christian dogma was never able to resolve. In the Gospels, Jesus is given two—contradictory—genealogies, both of which are intended to prove his descent from King David. In fact, these genealogies relate to Joseph, not Jesus. The proof they are meant to deliver thus is valid only if based on the premise that there is an actual kinship between the two.[5]

What one is dealing with in this instance is a kind of conflict of goals in the accounts of the Gospel writers, which once again has to do with the point of fracture represented by the Joseph constellation. If Jesus is supposed to be the Messiah of the *Jews* foretold in the Hebrew Bible, he must be the offspring of the house of David in the only lineage of descent that matters—the male line. But if he is supposed to be the *Christian* Messiah, what matters is the report about the virginal birth and thus Joseph's exclusion from paternity, which means that the genealogies handed down in the Gospels cease to fulfill their legitimizing function. On the one hand, the Gospels are stories of prophecy fulfilled; they seek to attest that the prophecies of the Hebrew Bible have come true in the person of Jesus. On the other hand, they assert that he is not part of that tradition, an assertion personified in the nonpaternity of his Jewish father. The Gospels employ a gesture that trumps Judaism on the basis of its own tradition. But as the gesture unfolds, it flips back on itself and in the process renders its own premises null and void.

The church fathers already sought to resolve this contradiction by making Joseph into Jesus' adoptive father; this would have made Jesus a descendant of the Davidian line by dint of a *legal* paternity. But this answer is itself part of the problem it seeks to resolve. For the legal practice of adoption, which has a prominent place in Roman Law (where even natural paternity must be affirmed by a formal act of adoption), is utterly unknown in ancient Judaism.[6] The only arrangement in Jewish law for legitimating children as heirs was levirate marriage, wherein a man married his deceased brother's wife. This served not only to provide for the widow but also to protect the repository of the male seed from defilement. According to Ida Magli, this was "a very concrete procedure to prevent the sacredness of the essence from coming into contact with something foreign."[7]

Jewish rules of consanguinity were based on a painstaking supervision of the purity of semen and blood. While a person's religious affiliation depended on the mother, the right of access to offices and civic privileges was passed down in the male line, which is why questions of descent were subject to stringent control.

As a Jew, it would simply have been impossible for Joseph to adopt the son of Mary, his bride. Only from the vantage point of ancient Christian thought—that is, with a retroactive change in the premises on which it was based—was it possible for this familial construction to appear credible. A *petitio principi*, paternity *in the figurative sense*, meant to establish Jesus as the fulfillment of the redemptive hopes of the Hebrew Bible, had to be imputed to the Jewish man Joseph in what one might call an anticipation of the new times.

A Difference in Reading Cultures

The theological line of argumentation that relates the New Testament back to the Hebrew Bible suffers much the same fate as the genealogical argument. It must draw on means other than literalness. There have been lengthy disputes between Christian and Jewish scholars over the interpretation of various key passages in the Bible; for example, take the one in Isaiah that in the King James Version reads: "Behold, a virgin shall conceive, and bear a son, and shall call his name Immanuel" (7:14). Jewish biblical scholars have put forth lexical and grammatical considerations that undermine the connection between this prophecy and the birth of Jesus articulated by Christian exegetes on the basis of Matthew 1:22. To the chagrin of Christian authorities, the public disputations about this and other questions that were held in the Middle Ages were regularly decided by the rabbis in their favor.[8]

What lies behind such controversies are different theological reading cultures. On the Jewish side, one finds an insistence on a more precise historical and contextual setting of texts; on the Christian side, the development of virtuosic procedures of allegorical interpretation that allow the New Testament to be read as the fulfillment of the Hebrew Bible. Christianity engages in figurative reading in order to decontextualize and appropriate Jewish messianism. The allegorical approach is therefore the handmaid in an act of usurpation. The literal text would have made the Christian faith regress, as it were, to its Jewish circumstances of origin: it contained a permanent *threat* (personified in the Jews) to the message of salvation. That the Jews are incapable of spiritual emotion, and that there is something corrupting in this inability, is one of the more subtle anti-Jewish stereotypes that Christianity contains within itself.

It is impossible to overemphasize this fundamental contradiction within the formation of the Christian tradition. Jesus was a Jew, and the first Christians—followers of Jesus Christ—were Jews. Initially, Christianity was nothing more than a movement of renewal within Judaism. But from the perspective of Orthodox Judaism, the members of this small Galilean sect were *apostates*, individuals who had lapsed from the faith of their fathers. Jesus was locked in a constant quarrel with the representatives of Jewish orthodoxy—the Pharisees and the scribes. He exempted his disciples from rules (such as the strict observance of the Sabbath) that were holy in the eyes of his opponents. In the decades after Jesus' death, Paul, the Roman Jew whom many scholars of Christianity regard as the true founder of the new religion, carried on this clash with Mosaic law to the point where he even declared that ritual circumcision was unnecessary; in so doing, he was casting aside *the* central sign of corporeal affiliation with the Jews, the chosen people.

Apostasy from the faith of the fathers—that is the sign under which the young Christian community grew up. After all, even the historical Jesus had, in fact, fulfilled the commandment to honor one's father and mother in a way that the Jewish world in which he lived would not have understood. He had not recognized the man whom all regarded as his father, instead replacing the natural paternity with a religious–spiritual bond of fatherhood. Still, it was important to the Gospel writers to make it appear as though Jesus' words and deeds were the fulfillment of Jewish religious hopes. However, the only way one can successfully establish this claim—on both a genealogical and a theological level—is by asserting a conjoined reading of the New Testament and the Hebrew Bible, one that embeds Jesus' activities within the continuity of the Jewish faith. Revolt, denial, apostasy—these acts have to take on the form of prophecy fulfilled. In this regard, one could say that Christianity is the creation of the theological interpretation of its champions. The *only* way for Christianity to uphold the claim that it is the legitimate *heir* to the Jewish faith is by establishing and defending the *primacy of allegorical interpretation*. Only if the spiritual interpretation of the events recounted in the Gospels prevails has the Messiah truly come, is the "good news" true. At the beginning of the creation of Christian meaning stands the effort to trump the literal reading of Holy Scripture with a higher, more spiritual reading. The *expatriation* of Joseph and the expatriation of Jewish biblical exegesis are acts identical in meaning. Both are acts of turning away from one's own origins, be they genealogical or hermeneutical.

From the Christian perspective, though, the true message of salvation had to remain unknowable for the Jews. As far as Joseph is concerned, Mariological texts depict him in a figurative sense as someone who has difficulty reading. In speaking of Mary, a sermon falsely attributed to John Chrysostom uses the topos of the sealed book and goes on to elaborate:

Hear what the prophet says of this man and of the Virgin: a sealed book will be given to a man who knows the letters. Who is this sealed book if not the perfectly immaculate Virgin? By whom is it given? By the priests. And to whom? To the carpenter Joseph, a man who knows the letters, that is to say, who had been married once before; and he will say: I cannot read. But why can you not read, Joseph? I cannot read, he says, because the book is sealed. For whom is it being preserved? It is being preserved as a house for the creator of all things.[9]

One can recognize the sermon's reference to the apocryphal story of Mary being given as a wife in the Temple to the man chosen by a divine sign. The pseudo-Gospel has turned one of the phallically armed suitors for the nubile maid into the fiduciary guardian of the Virgin. Translated into the pictorial language of the sermon, it means that Joseph must protect the *unreadability of the book* by virtue of the task assigned to him by God and the priests. In this system of analogy, only the woman who can be addressed as a sexual being is readable. Here, too, Joseph represents the figure that still records the rupture that Christianity later seeks to render invisible by overlaying it with a hermeneutics centered on the logos.

Splitting the Father Function

The Joseph complex thus forms a dual focal point on the losing side of Western monotheistic religiosity. The earthly genealogy is severed and opens itself to a divine genealogy through a virginal birth and resurrection. What is also interrupted is a certain kind of readability in favor of the emergence of meaning. Henceforth, central elements will be culturally available only in the form of doubling: the father (Joseph/God), the man (physical exclusion/divine emanation), the phallus (as semen/word channel), descent (blood/spiritual kinship), the letter (unreadability of Mary/readability of the Gospel as *the* book). The question is: How has this circumstance inscribed itself—less so as a motif than in structural terms—into the texture of the grand narrative of the West?

After all, the Holy Family is not merely a religious phenomenon. It is one of the most important contributors of images in the history of art and thus in the iconography of the Western world as such—right up to the pop culture of our day. In this way, it has exerted a lasting influence on ideas about gender and family roles. One cannot understand the development of the institution of the family in the West without reference to this constant engagement with its New Testament model. Against this background it is significant that the European model family par excellence turns out to be an incomplete family marked by a complicated symbolic economy, a family rendered ambiguous by a dual paternity. Strangely enough, none of the great cultural theorists have shown any interest in this situation. Not even Freud—who in his essay "Moses and Monotheistic Religion" did attempt a comprehensive analysis of the father–son axis in the Christian faith as well—addressed this fact.

The history of Christian monotheism is, from the outset, a history of the splitting of the father function into an empirical and a transcendent part, into a present but powerless patriarchal authority and an absent one ruling from afar. This schism of fatherhood, linked to the separation—pregnant with cultural import—of sexual and spiritual love, was reflected at various times in different gender configurations. But it contains far more than an assignment of roles that was capable of being culturally assimilated (within certain boundaries). Through all the acts of historical adjustment, it represents *the* key mechanism in a system of power whose directives are issued in the name of the Father.

7

THE INIMITABLE MODEL

Measured by conventional criteria, the life of Jesus, in terms of its origins as well as its legacy, can be understood only as an *exceptional, holy event*. The difficulty lies in the fact that the exceptional constellation of the Holy Family simultaneously became a model constellation in the West. How does such an improbable construction of relationships become the exemplar of how the faithful should lead their lives? How can it invite emulation when such emulation is always doomed to fail under earthly conditions? Why does later Christian ideology of the family make use of a triangle of individuals that contains at its very core traits that are so distinctly *alien*—not to say *hostile*—to the family?

No matter how one tries to identify with any of its myriad forms, the Holy Family always resists a smooth translation into everyday life. It retains what seems to be an irresolvable remnant. And yet it invites imitation with great suggestive power. The fundamental reason for this interplay lies in a theological dogma that sets Christianity apart from its neighbor religions and imparts to it a special dynamism: the conviction that God entered the world and became fully and completely human, in essence and not just in form. By descending into the womb of a woman, God united the holy and the profane, transcendence and reproduction. Mary's virginal body is a place of exchange where the "word" becomes "flesh" and, conversely, the flesh transfigures itself.

Yet the transmutability of the Word of God and the human body, as vouched for by Mary's child, cannot be conceptually fixed once and for all. An element of unrest is inherent in it, continually impelling observers to come up with new formulations. The mystery of the *single* substance, the unity of man and God embodied in Jesus, provides merely the dogmatic brackets within which Western pictorial tradition changes in a peculiar way. While the religious imagination strives to clarify the relationships within the Christian primordial family by elaborating one side of that unity—the incarnation—the characteristics of the other side—divinity—intrude on this anthropomorphism with equal vigor and an alien and imperious air.

Human closeness and divine remoteness are exposed to a constant, mutual irritation. One could almost say that the Christian ur-family is *afflicted* by the sacred. Every one of its relational axes—through the constant repetition of the same numerical configuration of 2 + 1—is haunted and "disturbed" by a numinous power. The distant origin of the child irrupts into the relationship between Mary and her son; the holy marriage is thwarted by the wife's bond to God; Joseph's fatherhood is ruptured because two figures are cast in the father role. All this sets the Holy Family irrevocably apart from its human and earthly postfigurations. And yet it is precisely these anomalies that contain tremendous social energy. They reach deeply into the phantasmal substructure of familial processes and thus into the very process by which societies are constituted.

What I am talking about here is the way in which religious symbolism functions in general. It is clear that the sacred and the profane are intimately interrelated, without ever being able to overlap completely. But it is not necessary to follow the example of the faithful and regard this incongruity as reflective of a moral imperfection or ontological deficiency in earthly existence. On the contrary, this incongruity seems to be an essential condition for the cultural reach and power of what humans declare as holy. Religious symbols extend in two directions. One is toward social empiricism, the starting point for sequences of similarities or imitative activities. The other is a dimension of *otherness*, one that resists translation into the life of the world and therefore appears only in the form of paradoxes or riddles, of foreign bodies, to which, over time, a number of interpretations attach themselves that are inadequate, inexhaustible, and, in the final analysis, futile.

These religious symbols, whose function it is to depict and semantically regulate the tension between the sacred and the profane, carry within themselves once more this same tension. Behind their visible surface they conceal, so to speak, an arcane sphere that is imperceptible from the outside. On the side facing the world, symbols provide conceptual patterns that can be put to multiple use in the constant play of the collective imagination. At the same time, the hidden sphere preserves a *constitutive knowledge* that can never enter into the social production of meaning in more than an incomplete form since it forms the *boundary* of that production and creates the very *conditional structure* by whose rules it operates. In other words, stored in that sphere is the unavailable–sacred dimension of society itself, the *secret of its coding*. Religious symbols are navigational signs. They are involved in the basic rules of the social code. They function as half-visible, half-invisible border relays between the symbolic order (which all social articulations obey) and the realm of the imaginary (the intersubjective interior relationships that arise in the field of the main symbolic coordinates).

As far as the model character of the Christian ur-family is concerned, this would mean that, if correctly read, its "impossibilities" in particular should also contain information about long-term mechanisms for social guidance. This perspective shifts front and center that which is numinous, unapproachable, unfathomable, ruptured, and liminal about the Holy Family in order to draw from these dimensions inferences about the *transcendental mechanism* of Western society. It is not the case, however, that the "impossibilities" inherent in the sacred, exemplary events lessen their ability to connect with society. It is precisely the uncertainty principle, which keeps the myth of the Christian family suspended between the divine and human realms, that permits wide leeway for acts of appropriation and the transfer of meaning. The irruption of God into the arena of the family establishes a dense web of empirical–sacral relationship options. The internal relationships within the Christian family triangle are *overdetermined* in a way that makes possible a staggering multiplicity of symbolic assimilations. As a result, the Holy Family has become the core complex of a cultural symbolism that, over the course of two thousand years, has hardly left any combinatorial possibility unexplored.

8

COMBINATORICS I: THE MOTHER—SON AXIS

From Rebellion to the Return Home of the Dead Christ

Early representations portray the Madonna as a rigid majesty removed to cosmological dimensions. But this is only one extreme among the profusion of pictorial possibilities available to artists. In Jesus, Mary gives birth to a human child of flesh and blood. The *humanization of God*—a lengthy process in the history of iconography, from the majestic and severe depictions in late antiquity and Byzantine art to the sculptural corporeality of Renaissance painting[1]—goes hand in hand with the process of making Mary's motherhood increasingly a phenomenon of this world. This, in turn, opens the field to every nuance of a profoundly human mother–son relationship. Based on the doctrine of the incarnation, which was given its final formulation at the Council of Ephesus in 431 C.E., the supernatural dimension in the relationship between Christ and the Madonna appeared in an increasingly natural light, more suited to the human world.

Mary, who gazes on and worships her child with divine love; who cares for, cradles, and nurses him; who finds the young boy—feared to be lost—in the Temple, reproaches him, yet cannot help but feel amazed at the wisdom he displays in his conversation with the scribes; who must endure being rebuffed and denied by her grown son, to whom a male teacher, John the Baptist, has by now revealed his calling: all these episodes can be generalized beyond their personal connection with Jesus. They offer a biographical pattern that male psychobiographies in general can adopt. Transposed to this level, the stages in the life of the Christian Messiah can be read as stages in a process of detachment, which compels the grown son, filled by the sense of his spiritual mission, to alienate himself from his origins and his mother. Embedded within their primary religious text, the Gospels present something like a model of emancipation, and their power lies in the fact that they do not conceal the resulting conflicts—depicted here in exemplary fashion in the tensions between the family and the circle of disciples.

But that is not all. What one can reconstruct as the psychodynamic of Jesus' life on the basis of the Gospel narratives becomes, in the process of transmission,

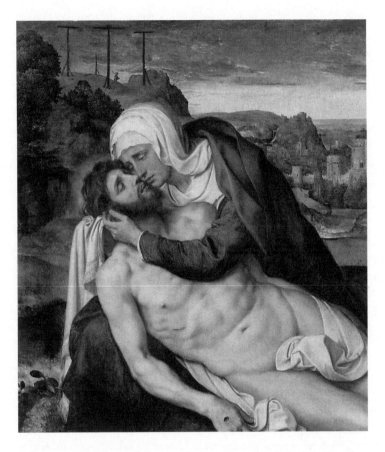

Willem Key, *Lamentation of Christ*, sixteenth century. Alte Pinakothek, Munich.

increasingly drawn into the force field of long-term historical currents. The depiction in the New Testament sources clashes with interpretative forces flowing in contrary directions, forces that are, in turn, guided by what is in this instance a collective psychodynamic. If the Gospels recount the development of the young man Jesus in the form of a process of detachment, the great Marian transformation of Christianity that began in the eleventh century turns the thrust of that process upside down. In so doing, it departs from the ground of the New Testament and supplements its account with a web spun from legendary additions and pictorial embellishments.

The theological basis for these maneuvers is exceedingly tenuous. Only a single passage in the Gospel According to John attests to Mary's participation in her son's Passion: "But meanwhile near the cross where Jesus hung stood his mother, with her sister, Mary wife of Clopas, and Mary of Magdala" (19:25). This lone mention becomes the starting point for a colossal, radical iconographic change. Against the backdrop of the altered, emotionalized piety of the High and late Middle Ages, artists and preachers were working on a *dramatization* of the death of Jesus that has left deep traces in the pictorial memory of the West. Ever since, the grieving onlookers at the foot of the cross have grouped themselves around a second main figure: the *mater dolorosa*—the mother of the slain Messiah, bent over in grief and dissolving in tears for her son.

The mother's grief is not a genuinely Christian motif, but is drawn from the stock of pagan religiosity. In connection with the life of Jesus, however, it takes on a meaning all its own. Read as the finale in a story of emancipation, the scenes at the cross become evidence that the process of detachment from the family has failed. Jesus dies in deepest desolation. The disciples have denied him; they have fled and are in hiding. Only Mary and a few women from her circle remain loyal to him. Not the death on the cross alone, though certainly the lamentation of Christ—which elevates his mother into the one who reestablishes the community of the believers—confirms iconographically the crushing of the confraternal rebellion. Jesus—who left his homeland in Galilee, denied his parents and siblings, and instructed his followers to emulate his example—returns to the place of his human origins as one defeated and crucified. His corpse is symbolically laid back into his mother's lap. The Jewish woman Miriam has overcome her rejection in the figure of the Christian Madonna *dolorosa* and has reincorporated her son. She takes on the traits of an archetypal *possessive mother* who drives her child into regression.[2] The mother–son dyad is restored—at the price of the son's death.[3]

Stabat Mater

The profound transformation engendered by this *rehabilitation of the mother* is strikingly reflected in the text of the "Stabat Mater," a thirteenth-century Marian poem variously attributed to Jacopone da Todi or Bonaventure that inspired some important musical settings through the centuries. Three different perspectives are successively laid out in the poem. It opens by depicting the scene at the cross and evokes compassion in the listener at Mary's suffering:[4]

Stabat Mater dolorosa	The sorrowful mother stood
juxta crucem lacrymosa	weeping by the cross
dum pendebat Filius.	on which her Son was hung.

In the second sequence, which begins with the ninth stanza, just before the middle of the work, the speaker directs his appeal to Mary herself:

Eja mater, fons amoris!	O Mother, fountain of love!
Me sentire vim doloris	make me feel the power of sorrow,
fac, ut tecum lugeam.	that I may grieve with you.

The author directs at the Mother of God the strange request to share in her sorrow so that he may gain access to Jesus through her intercession. The prayer intensifies to the point where the speaker also seeks to participate in the pain of the crucified, pleading with Mary to impress the wounds of Jesus deeply into his soul (stanza 11). Sunk in contemplation of the scene at the cross, the author thus expresses a twofold desire for grief: he wants to all but experience Mary's pain in his own body and in this way also feel the suffering of her son:

Fac me tecum pie flere	Grant that I may truly weep with you,
crucifixo condolere	to suffer with the Crucified,
donec ego vixero.	as long as I shall live.

Only in the final two concluding stanzas does the poem address Christ directly with a plea—and this, too, is done in the form of a mediation, "through his Mother" (stanza 19). Throughout the poem, the perspective on Christ's Passion comes from the gaze and feelings of his mother. The "Stabat Mater" conjoins two mimetic relationships. First, the speaker feels compelled to project himself into the mother's gaze as she looks upon her crucified son; Mary is to become for him a figure of entrance and access. He thus appropriates a female gaze, praying that he might feel as does her mother's heart. Second, he desires to take upon himself the *imitatio* of Christ's Passion, seeking redemption through participation in his martyrdom. But the mysticism of the wounds evoked in these verses has an unavoidable deeper meaning. Through his desire for suffering, the speaker identifies with precisely the person at whom the mother's sorrowful gaze is directed. He enjoys a kind of "benefit of suffering"—finding himself reflected in the mother's tender mourning, which attracts all attention to itself. A peculiar

Botticelli, *Pietà*, 1495. Alte Pinakothek, Munich.

solidarity links mother and son. The figure of the Father, who has commanded the sacrifice at the cross, does not appear in the "Stabat Mater." The Christian Passion has become an affair *within* the mother–son dyad—a suffering over which is spread the soft radiance of undivided maternal love.

Pietà

The reestablishment of the dyad dominated by the maternal gaze finds its consummate expression in the motif of the Pietà. Usually Pietà depictions show only Mary and Jesus, pushing the intimacy of grief to its final consequence. Some painters, among them Giovanni Bellini, openly brought out the analogy between the Madonna and Child and the Pietà: like the sleeping child, the body of the dead Christ rests gently while stretched out in the mother's lap, which is draped in a wide garment and spreads out like a kind of resting place. The proportions are distorted: the body appears smaller, boyish, and delicate as it nestles in an almost floating manner into the folds of cloth and the sheltering body of the mother. All this finds its highest perfection in the famous sculpture by Michelangelo,

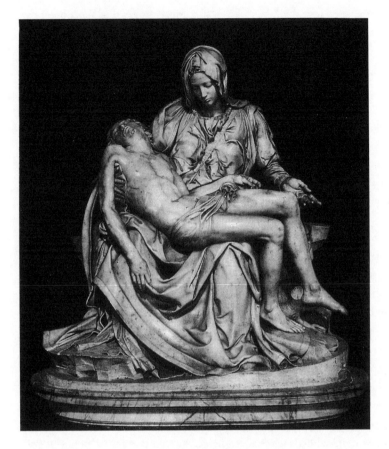

Michelangelo, *Pietà*, 1489–1499. St. Peter's Basilica, Rome.

which also endows Mary with a youthful beauty that abolishes the natural age difference between the two figures.

Since the fourteenth century, the Pietà has established an independent, powerful tradition that does not place front and center the messianic nature of the divine child or the rebellious strain of Jesus' later life. What flows into this tradition is the dark side of the Gospel narrative, the Passion. It articulates the profound desolation and abandonment to pain and suffering that constitutes one of the most important and puzzling resources of Christian piety. But the suffering does not get out of hand; it does not flare up: it is born and encompassed by the calm demeanor of the grieving mother—indeed, by signs of her acquiescence. The grief

conjoins maternal love with the idea of self-sacrifice. In this dual function of desolation and consolation, the Pietà motif becomes capable of being recast in multifarious ways. A specific cult of mourning, connected to a cult of the sacrifice, attaches itself to this motif.

There is hardly a story of male suffering in the European cultural sphere that
does not invoke parallels to Christ's Passion. (In fact, male narcissism rarely appears in this context without messianic overtones.) Evidently, the mother's
lament represents a formula of pathos that is indispensable as an intensifier—a
sounding board, so to speak—of the significance of male self-sacrifice. That extends right up to the European war memorials of the nineteenth and twentieth
centuries: despite their thoroughly official function, they make use of the visual
effect of a purely human and private bond of grief between the mother and the
lifeless body of the young hero.

Modern statecraft inherited and profaned the motif of the Pietà in two ways:
first, with respect to what it chooses to depict and, second, with respect to what
forms the unspoken margins of the depiction. For no matter how profound the
silence that surrounds the grieving mother and the body that has sunk into her
arms, no matter how intimately the curvature and folds of drapery of the two figures blend, an invisible observer is always attendant upon this scene of together-
ness. It is the one at whose command the sacrifice was made, in whose will the
mourning mother acquiesces; the one who imparts an element of devotion to
even her most bitter pain. The image of the male corpse, which dominates the
iconography of the West,[5] and the corollary image of the grieving Madonna or
its successor, the soldier's mother, are defined by a third, external, divine or godlike figure.

Incidentally, the unified Germany also adopted the image of the Pietà. Since
1993, the country has had a "Central Memorial," located in the "Neue Wache"
in Berlin. At the request of then chancellor Helmut Kohl, the templelike build-
ing (designed by Karl Friedrich Schinkel) houses an enlarged bronze sculpture
by Käthe Kollwitz, a Pietà from 1937/1938. In a very generalized formulation,
the memorial is dedicated to the "victims of war and tyranny." The fact that the
Christian symbol of the Pietà excludes a majority of the victims it is intended to
commemorate—the Jews—triggered vehement though futile public criticism.

But the calamity of the German policy of memorialization after the historical
turning point of reunification includes yet another misstep. In the First and Second World Wars, the grieving mother was virtually turned into a national icon,
a symbol of all those who willingly sacrificed themselves to war.[6] This tradition

played an important role in Käthe Kollwitz's life as well as in the genesis of her artistic work.[7] The memorial to the victims therefore employs creative devices that were already used by the perpetrators. Without acknowledging as much, the ritual of grieving enters into complicity with the forces whose victims it mourns. This effect challenges us to inquire into the beginnings of the pictorial tradition and ultimately into the role of the grieving mother of Christ.

Acts of Mystical Participation

Any description of the axis Jesus–Mary would be incomplete were one to limit it to only the mother–son relationship. After all, Christian spirituality conjoined the two figures simultaneously as bride and groom. This image can be applied both to individual piety and to the symbolism of collective formations. Mary can be a model of how to live—especially for female believers—not only by virtue of her motherhood but also through her status as a bride.[8] Christian virgins in late antiquity who were destined for the holy life were called "brides of Christ."[9] Nuns, daughters of Mary who profess the vow of celibacy in the convents, are similarly betrothed to Jesus; their consecration resembles a wedding feast.[10] Female mysticism of the late Middle Ages elaborated this spiritual–erotic relationship with Christ into an intense personal experience.

Mary became the ideal image of all those who were lovingly filled by the presence of God. She functions as an allegory of the Christian community, which, following a topos used by Paul and repeatedly invoked, enters into a mystical marriage with Christ. The key text for this notion is in the Letter to the Ephesians:

> Wives, be subject to your husbands as to the Lord; for the man is the head of the woman, just as Christ also is the head of the church. Christ is, indeed, the Saviour of the body; but just as the church is subject to Christ, so must women be to their husbands in everything. Husbands, love your wives, as Christ also loved the church and gave himself up for it, to consecrate it, cleansing it by water and word, so that he might present the church to himself all glorious, with no stain or wrinkle or anything of the sort, but holy and without blemish. In the same way men also are bound to love their wives, as they love their own bodies. (5:22–28)

With these statements, Paul laid the theological foundation for the unequal standing of the sexes—a move that prejudiced the Christian conception of marriage well into the modern era. At the same time, however, he molded a notion of social life whose reach can scarcely be overestimated. Love in the Pauline sense is not an emotional relationship between separate, mutually independent individuals. It does not rest on an interpersonal relationship in the modern sense. A man and a woman who unite in love form *one* body, an indissoluble entity composed of head and body. The love between Christ and the community of believers, which is intended to furnish the model for human love, is *partitive* instead of *relational*. When Paul calls the church the redeemed body of Christ, this female aspect does not confront the encompassing nature of Christ externally; rather, it has always been a part of it. The community relates to Christ not as one person to another but as the (lesser) part to the (sublime/majestic) whole. Love is the name for the inner state of the total communitarian body founded on Christ.

The *Sponsus–Sponsa* Motif

In the course of the Middle Ages there emerged an independent pictorial type in which Christ and Mary, as *sponsus* and *sponsa*, preside over the hierarchical structure of the spiritual and secular world in a nuptial communion. At times they are placed at the same height like a sovereign couple; in other versions, however, Mary appears smaller and subordinated to the central figure of the Redeemer. This pictorial complex includes the motif of the crowning of Mary: in a spiritual reversal of the natural flow of time, Christ, the sovereign of the world, elevates his mother to the position of Queen of Heaven at his side. He anticipates his own descent by selecting Mary as the woman who would bear him; Mary as the creature of her son—"Vergine madre, figlia del tuo figlio" (Virgin Mother, daughter of thy Son), as Dante proclaims.[11]

The mystical nuptial bond is a religious symbol in which several relationships and hierarchies intersect, are exchanged, exert reciprocal influence, and overlap. Not only does it function as a "nodal point" of spiritual meanings, but it also enacts institutional balances of power. In that way it becomes, in very general terms, an *organizational center of social synthesis*.

1. First, it makes possible the Pauline analogy of heavenly and earthly marriage, allowing the *sponsus–sponsa* depictions to refer back directly to the empirical balance of power between men and women and to be used to regulate gender norms. While it is certainly true that Christian allegory obeys its own internal genre rules, there is also always an interaction between it and sociohis-

Sponsus–sponsa, in Bede's commentary on the Song of Songs, twelfth century. Cambridge.

torical realities.[12] The patristic doctrine of marriage already borrowed exten-
sively from Mary's mystical marriage to God in order to assign men and women
their place in a divinely ordered world. Yet one cannot simply read the innumerable elaborations of the nuptial motif as the expression of relevant sociohistorical facts. They are influenced by many additional factors arising from dogmatic, ethical, legal, or ecclesiopolitical considerations.

2. Theologically, the *sponsus–sponsa* constellation enters into the textual
competition between the Jewish and Christian Bibles. For the topos of the mystical marriage cites the great erotic poem of the Hebrew Bible, the Song of
Songs, as it appropriates it spiritually and draws it into the context of the veneration of Mary. This is a wrenching exegetical leap, one that separates the notion
of love from all pleasures of the flesh and places it in service to the unappeasable

transcendental longing. The Hebrew hymn to the beauties of the body is turned into a celebration of purity and self-communion in God. But even the intimacy of this mystical union bears the stamp of the asymmetry of the genders: within the spiritual union, God maintains his primacy over the faithful soul surrendering itself to him.

3. This gradient is transferred to the collective worship of God. Whenever Mary is seen as a representative of the church community as a whole, she symbolically represents a special virtue of the *ecclesia*—its humility toward the heavenly groom. She is the recipient, the hearer of the words of the Lord, who does everything by virtue of divine power and nothing through her own being. Even when Mary, with these attributes, personifies the church as a whole, this allegorical combinatorics, which reached the height of its expression in the Middle Ages, does make internal differentiations. For the *sponsus–sponsa* model can be used to illustrate the institutional relationships between the ecclesiastical dignitaries and the church, and thus the Catholic conception of office as such. The bishop, sworn to celibacy, also contracts a marriage in the higher sense of the word: during his ordination, he becomes the *sponsus*, the groom and spouse of his church, to which he is now married, and as such he represents, like the pope himself, the role of Christ on earth.[13] The system of mystical participation created ambiguous role relationships: as members in the virginal *ecclesia*, ecclesiastical dignitaries assumed the feminine part; as the *sponsus* of their congregation, they assumed the masculine and dominant part.

4. Finally, the motif of the nuptial bond can provide a stage for the iconopolitical struggles between secular lordship and the papacy's claim to power. In this case, the interest of the church is different from what it was in the symbolic relationships mentioned earlier, for it is aimed at strengthening Mary's hierarchical position: "The image of the triumphant Virgin," writes Marina Warner, is a "symbol of the triumphant Church,"[14] while kingship and emperorship in the Middle Ages established their legitimacy on a Christological foundation.[15] Depending on the context of its use, the same symbol thus served highly divergent claims to power and legitimacy.

While this list makes no claim to being exhaustive, it can attest to an important function of the motif of the Virgin as *sponsa*. In its transfer to institutional pairings, this motif helps to initiate an all-encompassing Christian communitarianism. More specifically, it makes power relationships appear as love relationships; it recodes dependence as dedication and authority as devotion and solicitude. Out of a more or less violent coexistence of bodies, it gives rise to syntheses of a higher order held up by spiritual forces. The Christian theology of love not only affects institutional politics, but has a pacifying effect on the affective coherence of society as such.

Mothers bear children, ensuring the biological reproduction of the human race. The cycle of corporeality passes right through their bodies. And that is why the fact that the central mother–child axis of Christianity was simultaneously conceived as a nuptial, nonsexual love relationship has such profound importance. It lays the symbolic foundation for the process of *disembodying* social coherence. This disembodiment goes hand in hand with the creation of collectivities as *corporations*. The model of virginal union transforms corporeal relationships of dependence into an aggregate of mystical love relationships between mystical corporations that incorporate individuals only to the extent that they can be raised beyond the limits of their biological existence.

Among all Christian mortals, only Christ and Mary were allowed to transcend the boundary between heaven and earth. According to the Gospels, Jesus rose from the dead and ascended into heaven. The bodily assumption of Mary, which is based solely on legendary sources, established itself as an article of faith only much later. Its prerequisite was that Mary, like Christ, was declared to be free of original sin and thus free of the transience and corruption of the flesh. Despite massive resistance from within the church, in 1950 Pope Pius XII declared the dogma of Mary's bodily assumption. Christ and Mary are thus, according to Warner, "the only beings Catholics now believe to be in heaven in their bodies."[16] If there is *religious precision*, it reveals itself in this dual transfiguration. Jesus and Mary, the mystical couple that has spawned so many subsequent pairings, the powerful symbol of a spiritual corporeality already on earth, entered into heaven in corporeal spirituality.

9

COMBINATORICS II: THE SACRED MARRIAGE

The Purification of the Woman

Anyone who studies the way in which the marriage between Mary and Joseph has come down through the ages will encounter a phenomenon one could call the *contagious power of chasteness*. Christianity was not content with the article of faith that the Son of God was born as a result of a virginal conception. In the earliest period, the explanation offered for the mention of Jesus' brothers and sisters in the Gospels is that after the arrival of the Messiah the holy couple lived in a consummated marriage and had more children. But the notion of Mary's lifelong virginity began to spread as early as the middle of the second century. It was advocated by the founders of Christian monasticism, the church fathers Clemens and Origenes, and spread throughout the West as a result of their influence.[1]

But that is not enough: Saint Augustine's dogma of original sin calls attention to the theological necessity of also exempting Mary—who has a corporeal bond to the Son of God by virtue of giving birth—from the guilt of all humanity since the Fall. Since original sin is passed on through the chain of sexual reproduction, popular legends and theological arguments were soon spun around Mary's own birth. Anne and Joachim, Mary's parents according to legend, were also said to have conceived their child through a divine miracle. The logic of purity follows the logic of pollution, except that the direction is reversed. Sexual abstinence, the counterforce to original sin, spreads along the same line of matriarchal descent by which original sin spreads, infecting generation upon generation. According to a tradition within the order of Carmelite nuns, this work of purification even extends to the mother of Mary's mother: we are told that the conception of Saint Anne by Stollanus and Esmeria was attended by miraculous circumstances.[2]

In 381 C.E., the Second Council of Constantinople proclaimed Mary's perpetual virginity. In 390 Pope Siricius declared Mary "an inviolate virgin during the pregnancy and the birth of Christ." In 451 Mary was given the title of Ever Virgin, and the Fourth Lateran Council in 649 declared Mary's perpetual virginity a dogma of the church.[3] The late Middle Ages, the Counter-Reformation, and even the progressive nineteenth century expanded on and deepened the image of

Mary's pure, asexual motherhood. Based on controversial documentary evidence, in 1854 Pope Pius IX proclaimed Mary's immaculate conception by her mother, Anne, an incontrovertible article of faith.[4] Shortly thereafter, fourteen-year-old Bernadette Soubirous in Lourdes had a vision of a figure who identified herself as Mary the Immaculate Conception.[5]

There are good reasons why feminist writers, in particular, have examined the many facets of the cult of Mary over the past few decades. They have seen in it the key to a cultural history of the sexual and social disciplining of women by the Catholic Church. In fact, repressive tendencies are obvious in the shaping and re-shaping of this central Christian figure over the centuries. And yet one is not dealing with a monolithic process, let alone one that was *guided* over the long term by certain (male) actors. Sociostructural developments of this kind are not intentional; they produce long-term effects that none of the parties involved can predict.

In retrospect, the transformation of the figure of Mary presents itself as the rewriting and overwriting of an underlying model. First, this transformation works to *Christianize* Mary, to superimpose over the concrete Jewish environment of her life qualities as the Christian Queen of Heaven, the Chancery Clerk of God, the intercessor, the patron saint, or whatever else her attributes may be.[6]

Second, this process also superimposes a nonbiblical, pagan context. The motif of virginal birth is not unique to Christianity. Antiquity had countless virginal goddesses, most of whom were connected with agrarian cults.[7] Many ancient gods and heroes were born of virgin mothers. The emerging Christian religion came into direct contact with the cult of Artemis at Ephesus. In addition, the miraculous descent from a virginal mother created a mythological, typological kinship between Christ and Dionysus. Christianity thus adopted a common topos in order to highlight the divinity of the founder of its religion. In this way, it ensured that Jesus would be noticed in the crowded world of ancient religions, while at the same time imparting to the pagan motif its own, unmistakable handwriting.

Mary and the Pagan Mother Goddesses

As virginal mother, Mary inherited the qualities of the goddesses that predated patriarchy; yet it was only her radicalization at the hands of Christianity that turned the two predicates of virginity and motherhood into a paradox. For in the fertility rituals that gave rise to goddesses such as Hera, Aphrodite, Artemis in Asia Minor, Cybele, Ishtar, and Astarte, virginity is cyclically renewable and does not stand in contradiction to maternal fertility. This kind of virginity has very little to do with a moral virtue. The "love goddesses of the near east and classical mythology," Marina Warner has noted, "are entitled virgin despite their lovers, who die and rise again for them each year." For these goddesses, "sacred virginity symbolized their autonomy, and had little or no moral connotation. They spurned men because they were preeminent, independent, and alone, which is why the title virgin could be used of a goddess who entertained lovers. Her virginity signified she had retained freedom of choice: to take lovers or to reject them."[8]

In this context, "virgin" refers to a woman who is autonomous and not put in her place by marital monogamy. What characterizes her is not the absence of sexuality but its excess: an unrestrained desire of natural power that acts outside of male control and its rules of possession. The rise of ancient city-states, which entailed a change from an older, matrilineal kinship system to a patrilineal one, diminished the symbolic value of such untamed femaleness.[9] The character of female goddesses changed accordingly. Fertility and virginity became separated and now appeared as mutually exclusive qualities. The urban goddess Athena represented a new type of chaste, sexually untouched goddess whose links to older matriarchal cultures were being suppressed.

Yet even in this attenuated form, the divine attribute of virginity retains a potential threat to the fixed social order. "The title of virgin goddess," writes Carol Christ, "signifies both limitation and independence within a patriarchal context. The virgin goddess has lost her primordial power as Mother. But as virgin rather than wife, she remains independent of patriarchal marriage and the subordination it requires. In addition, as virgin she retains access to the wildness that would be considered inappropriate in the wife."[10]

Even in the domesticated form of Olympian mythology, the virgin goddess remains a goddess *without a master*. Her cool reserve conceals a dark, wild, untamable side. This applies to Greek Artemis even more so than to Athena, whose domestication was largely successful: as a huntress, Artemis roams the forests, the realm beyond the pacification of culture. All the greater is the resistance to acculturation that was put up by the opposing type within the emerging polarity between fertility and chastity—for example, by Aphrodite, who, as the goddess of love, the mother of Eros, and the unfaithful wife of Hephaestus, nevertheless bears the title of virgin. One must make oneself aware of the expansive and contradictory connotations of the Greek word *parthenos* to appreciate the change of meaning it underwent within Christian religiosity.

Outwardly, the virginal mother Mary shares some characteristics with her pagan competitors. She attracts the love of the ruling deity, as did Semele, the mother of Dionysus and lover of Zeus; she is worshiped as the nursing mother, like the Egyptian goddess Isis, who looks just like her in some of her representations;[11] she gives birth to a god who must die to renew the world and mourns him in an annually renewed cycle of grief, just like the great mothers of the agricultural cults had done before her. She can adopt attributes and mythological epithets whose Christian slant barely manages to conceal their pagan origins—as, for example, in the sisterly resemblance between Mary and Aphrodite that is palpable in spite of the fact that they are typological opposites. Such cultic legacies could even be expanded to include the abstinent man Joseph at her side, who fulfills a function similar to that of the chaste or even castrated priests of the ancient temple goddesses as the guardian of a realm in which sacred virgins are chosen for a life of marriage to the gods. Legendary traditions like the apocryphal story of Mary's betrothal in the Temple proliferate beyond Christianity's attempt at dogmatic closure and even establish bridges between mutually antagonistic religions.

In a certain sense, the Christian Virgin is similarly "masterless." Neither she nor her successors ever allow themselves to be completely subordinated to the masculinity on earth. They resist the marital ownership and the male desire for their bodies, countering such worldly claims of possession with a privileged proximity to the divine. Something of the old complicity with the supernatural powers persists in the cult of the Madonna—a legacy that repeatedly aroused suspicion on the part of men. Moreover, Mary's virginal motherhood not only elevates her above all mortals but also predestines her to being a mediator between the human and the divine realms. As such it was possible for her, at least within the Catholic world, to become the most important figure to whom religious acts were addressed. Nor should one forget that the worship of the nursing Mother of God, whose milk is a miraculous relic, at times relates directly to old fertility concepts; among Mary's many tasks is that of procuring the blessing of numerous offspring.[12]

And yet the relationship among virginity, motherhood, and transcendence in Christianity is very different from that in the pagan mother cults. This is so not only because over a period of nearly two thousand years the Catholic Church carried out, with radical seriousness, an ever more far-reaching desexualization of the mother figure, but for the simple reason that Mary was denied the status of a goddess. For dogmatic reasons, she was not permitted to move up to the same level as the Father, the Son, and the Holy Spirit. Looked at from the power relationships within the religions of antiquity, this was a clear demotion. The Madonna had to content herself with the theological rank of a mortal woman, no matter how blessed, elevated, and transfigured she was. The esteem that she and many other female saints enjoyed in the heavenly hierarchy was not much of a compensation.

This diminishment in rank of the Christian Mother of God also diminished her mythological reach. The pre-patriarchal type of the virgin goddess "is essentially one-in-herself. She is not merely the counterpart of a male god."[13] In contrast, Mary offers merely a "truncated image of the goddess."[14] Because she is cut off from sexuality as a primal, all-transforming, prerational, and pre-identitarian force, she is deprived of much of her ability to sustain a counterforce to the regime of the monotheistic father god. She thus loses the most important resource that was left even to the virgin goddesses of the Olympian generation: the connection with the *margin* of the world that had been seized by male divinities.

In Christianity, the status of being "masterless" is possible on only *one* level, as a withdrawal from the (sexual) obligations of this world. But as such, it represents nothing other than the prerequisite for service to a higher lord. Humility and devotion are the chief qualities of Mary and of all the Christian virgins following in her footsteps. Her earthly maneuvering space is enclosed within the hegemonic space of the heavenly patriarchy. Not even primordial time is still within the purview of the mother: God himself created his maid Mary in order to create himself. The Trinitarian construct embraces the primordial, world-creating dimension that mythological motherhood laid claim to for itself.

The growing importance of the mother image in the history of Christianity must be viewed against this backdrop. It has little or nothing to do with the revival of archaic aspirations of the mother cult. On the contrary, it expresses the tendency to force the figure of the masterless woman back into the framework of the patriarchal family structure. What Mary is not permitted to be as a woman, she is as a pure, untouchable mother. All the transcending power of her virginity flows into the veneration for her son—the Son who is one with the Father in heaven. The religious expropriation of woman finds its completion not in the opposing figure of the Father but in that of the Son.

Transformationism of the Sacred

Mary's paradoxical qualities have imposed on the holy marriage the burden of a latent, forever unresolvable gender tension. To be sure, Joseph is granted the role of head of the family, but his status of earthly preeminence cannot compete with Mary's privileged relationship to her child and thus to the divine. He lives in the half-shadow of the house; his nimbus is thinner and does not outshine it. It would seem that Joseph participates least in the potential of transfiguration that the Holy Family generates in the history of its cultural transmission.

The trait of being without a master, however, is subdued in Mary's nature: she entrusts herself to her husband's leadership on earth with the same humility with which she yields to God's decree. Hardly anything points to the fact that the model of the Christian ur-family could, in effect, be used to break open or even invert the manifest hierarchy of the genders.

When it comes to the question of what kind of real-life orientation the model of Mary provides, her paradoxical dual status as Virgin and mother broadens into the paradox of the religious *imitatio* as such. Two powerful, mutually irreconcilable traditions spring from the figure of Mary. One elevates a life of chastity into the highest ideal and, over the centuries, devises various forms and institutions for it. The other connects to the Christian cult of motherhood and creates, from this perspective of Marian iconography, pictorial models for a woman's life. The first gravitates toward ways of life outside the family, whereas the second, later, tradition develops within the familial sphere. At best, the two strains can be united only by means of compromise solutions. An institution has been erected on the boundary between them: marriage, understood as the locus of the physical union of man and woman.

It is by way of marriage that societies guarantee their continued physical existence. This function clashes with the chastity prerogative in Christian teachings. As long as Christians formed a minority, that conflict was only latent. This changed as Christianity began to appropriate an increasing degree of secular authority, eventually rising to become the sole religion.

From Saint Augustine up to the High Middle Ages, the problem of marriage—a theological and consequently also a legal problem—was treated as a core element of the church's social ethics. In the process, the discussion alternated between two models: the Hebrew Bible commandment to "be fruitful and multiply" and the ideal of sexual abstinence that could be derived from the Gospels. From the standpoint of that ideal, the church, as an institution devoted to holiness, has nothing to do with a fleshly matter such as marriage. But from the perspective of the commandment to be fruitful, marriage is a way of life ordained by God—even if it is no more than an unavoidable concession to humanity's sinful nature. This dilemma still attaches itself to the solution on which the theologians eventually settled: that of elevating marriage to a sacrament. The state of Christian matrimony blends the sacred and the profane, adherence to God's will and sin. The church, which seeks to exert moral influence on the modalities of humankind's reproduction, is compelled to incorporate into its rites the very place where original sin is propagated and transmitted.

The model of the holy parents played a significant role in the debates that turned marriage into a sacrament—not despite but *because* of the model's unattainability. It is unattainable because it can be used to attest that all lower unions of the flesh are deeply flawed and thus deserving of betterment. In this way, the church was able, as it were, to fence in *the* reproductive center of the social body and surround it with its own norms, while depriving it of its symbolic potency. In so doing, it was participating in a long-term process one might describe as the *de-carnalization of the social dimension*, whose radical consequences, beyond the realm of the church's influence, are only now becoming fully apparent.

This de-carnalization traditionally starts with the female gender. The closure of woman reaches its high point in the body of the Madonna.[15] The exorcism of the female sex not only claims biographical victims but also creates a broad psychopathological syndrome; much has been written about the path that leads from the Madonna to the hysterical woman. Yet the succession to Mary finds its greatest momentum not in the separation of the two character strands that flow from the Virgin and mother but in what is, in the final analysis, an impossible *convergence*. For the Christian endeavor of purification has consequences even for mothers who follow the model of Mary. They can participate in the quality of purity in their own way: either by preserving a chaste soul and submitting to their husbands without feelings of lust, as medieval confessors prescribed, as a way of at least approaching the unattainable ideal of chastity; or by using tools—placed at their disposal—for giving their motherhood a higher, spiritual interpretation. The bourgeois female image of the eighteenth and nineteenth centuries, which elevated an asexual motherhood into the gender norm, still bears the imprint of the cult of Mary.

And yet the legacy of the Holy Family is not entirely privative. By dissolving the eternal cycle of sex—lust, violence, possession, and death—it encourages a sublimated understanding of marital and familial relationships. In this way it can offer women, at least under favorable sociohistorical conditions, a certain space free from external compulsions. The proximity to the sacred that Christianity accords to woman, the *excess* of her motherly role beyond its purely biological function, provides some kind of counterweight to the sacrifices demanded of her. Intentional or not, Christianity assigns women a high symbolic rank. Within the system of this faith, woman embodies the *place where holiness enters into the profane world*. It is through her that the entire semantic transformation of the supernatural into the natural takes place; she is the paradoxical place where the antithetical sides of religious symbolism are supposed to merge into one. On her falls the burden of *realizing* the unfulfillable model of the New Testament—on the long road from the Holy Family to the sanctification of the family.

10

COMBINATORICS III: THE FATHER—SON AXIS

The Near and Distant God

Christianity moves between two visions of the divine. According to Bernhard Lang, "God may be experienced as majestic and superior, or as familiar and loving: as God the Father, or Christ the Son."[1] This allows the religion to respond flexibly to diverse situations of faith without provoking a dogmatic crisis every time. Within the continually redrawn boundaries of orthodoxy and heterodoxy, Christian symbolism is also astonishingly "multioptional" with respect to the father–son axis.

The first Christians lived with the sense of the *close presence* of God. "First-century Christianity," writes Lang,

> which venerated a lowly Christ who had died the death of criminal, provided a strong contrast to the solemn sacrificial cult celebrated at the Jerusalem Temple and the pagan temples of the Greco-Roman world. Christ had been resurrected by the divine Father; however, the resurrection had not removed him from the community of believers. Christ was present in a tangible way in ecstatic rituals and magical meals. The heavenly Father, by contrast, remained in the background; yet, even he could be drawn into closeness, because Christians felt they shared Christ's high degree of intimacy with the Father, for they considered themselves to be his children.[2]

Yet the growing distance between laity and clergy, the erection of an ecclesiastical hierarchy, the assumption of certain powers by the church, and, finally, the alliance between the church and the empire favored a different image, one that accentuated the majesty of the Father in heaven. Drawing on ethnology, Lang distinguishes between the "learned tradition" of the theologians and the "little tradition" of popular piety: the former emphasizes God's numinous remoteness, thereby strengthening the clergy's position as intermediaries; the latter concentrates on "Christ's real, effective presence" in the Eucharist and in miraculous faith.[3] Time and again, the clerical tradition's tendency to elevate God was subverted by movements whose adherents were looking for a direct, brotherly, and amicable relationship to God. Sometimes this led to serious struggles and even schisms within Christianity, though it did not destroy the faith's religious foundation itself, which was sufficiently broad in its conception to make room for both views of God.

Whether one imagines the gentleness and mercifulness of the Savior who entered into human suffering or timidly admires the magnificence of the one who created the world and is enthroned above it also makes a difference with respect to the metaphors that are used in articulating these visions. Christian allegory makes liberal use of the conventional gender stereotypes to describe a person's qualities without regard to purely biological factors.[4] In this context, loving care has a maternal connotation, as a result of which the Christ who humbles and sacrifices himself out of love for humanity takes on female traits, while God's reign of ordering and judging is linked to masculine attributes.[5] *Humanization* translates allegorically as *feminization*. Various reform movements—especially the Cistercians in the twelfth century under the leadership of Bernard of Clairvaux—were characterized entirely by a mystical motherliness, one that shaped not only the relationship to God but also the orchestration of the emotional life within the hierarchy of the order.[6]

The spectrum of Christian images of God thus also deals, implicitly or explicitly, with models of secular authority. In the final analysis, what is at stake is the question of whether and to what extent the ruled are permitted to see the ruler as a being like them; whether they may, on the basis of a common nature, *participate* in him or whether they will be confronted by the insurmountable *otherness* of the ruler. These kinds of debates already accompanied Christianity's rise as the state religion of the Roman Empire. No matter how godlike and majestic the emperor appeared, no matter how absolute his claim to power, he still had to possess the quality of mercy.

"Appeals to the shared humanity of an emperor and those he ruled had deep roots in the political thought of the ancient world," writes Peter Brown in his study *Power and Persuasion in Late Antiquity: Towards a Christian Empire,* noting that Christian theology endowed this appeal with a new foundation: "The emperor was to show *sunkatabasis,* condescension, to his subjects, as the rich stooped to hear the cry of the poor and as God himself had once stooped to join himself, through his Incarnation, to the impoverished flesh of the human race."[7] In a theological dialectic, Christology made it possible to conceptually combine the two sides of the imperial expression of power into one. Brown continues:

> The early Byzantine icon of Mary as Mother of God, with the infant Christ seated in majesty in her lap, as if still bound to her womb, receiving, as a gentle reminder of human kinship, the touch of her hand upon his knee, was an image that conjured up a poignant wish for solidarity. If God and humanity could be seen to be bound together in so intimate a manner, by the shared flesh of the Virgin and her child, then the invisible thread of fellow feeling for a shared human flesh that linked the emperor to his subjects and the rich to the poor might yet prove as strong. In this way, the Christological controversies of the fifth century centered obsessively on the nature of the *sunkatabasis*, the awesome condescension of God in stooping to identify himself with the abject poverty of the human condition. [8]

Against this background, one can gauge the explosiveness of the discussions about Christ's divine and human nature that took place at the councils of the fourth and fifth centuries (Nicaea, Constantinople, Ephesus). And even a difficult theological construct like the Trinity revealed its political significance. The *difference* within the Christian father–son axis makes it possible to connect the conditions of earthly lordship to the divine model; the majesty of the emperor and his representatives absorbs some of the glow of the heavenly majesty. From this perspective, Christian theology is able not only to assert the supernatural origins of power but also, in so doing, to legitimate the entire graded structure of *social distinctions*. The *unity* of the Father and the Son, however, also guarantees the coherence of the political body, the "mystical solidarity"[9] between the ruler and those he rules, between the divine and earthly polarities in the system of power.

The fact that this unity, in turn, has a name that opens it to cultural semiotics—the name Holy Spirit, interpreted by the theologians as God's *loving* self-understanding—also allows one to make statements about the nature of the creative and uniting forces within the social body. In pagan religions, these forces were frequently represented by a mother goddess. That was done in full awareness of the fact that a society's survival rested on a foundation of sexual fertility, on the natural basis of power to give life. Christianity divides the function of maternal love and fertility into two components, as it were: the Holy Spirit and the human Virgin Mary. In both, the feminine has been reduced to the point where it becomes a mere vehicle of God's self-understanding within the father–son relationship.[10]

The Divine and Human Father

In societies with patrilineal kinship systems, the theological notion that father and son are, in the end, the same—that the father returns in the son and the mother forms merely the corporeal vessel of that return—is by no means implausible. From this perspective, the Christological model can be instrumentalized, to a certain degree, for family politics—as, for example, in the age of the feudal revolution, which implemented an exclusive line of succession from the father to the first-born son.[11] However, these kinds of "applications" end at the demarcation line between divine and human fatherhood. The Christian identity of the Son with the Father does not establish a genealogical continuum but breaks it. Whoever follows Christ in acknowledging his Father in heaven must regard himself as an orphan in his earthly life. All contrary language rules notwithstanding, he no longer has any parents and relatives. He only appears to bear the signs of fleshly resemblance to those who consider him their kin, remaining, in the words of Isaac of Stella, "a stranger and pilgrim in this place down below."[12]

There thus emanates from Christ, into the Middle Ages and far beyond, an appeal that constitutes a blatant and provocative objection to the order of the family. Still, religious typology also found the ways and means to combine divine and human concerns in this sphere, and to render them comparable in spite of their incommensurability. For there is a visual relationship between the heavenly Trinity and the trinity of the Holy Family. It is supported by the identity of the Son in the two trinitarian schemes. As far as the position of the father is concerned, Joseph appears as God's earthly placeholder, and in this roundabout way he is able—even if incompletely—to participate in the mystical unity between the divine Father and Son. The third term of this comparison places Mary and the Holy Spirit into a structural equivalence—a fact that once more demonstrates the difficult and tension-filled relationship within her division of functions.

The two fathers of Christ were linked to each other not only in formal terms. Patristics established a typological relationship between them. Saint Ambrose did not believe it was mere coincidence that "His father was a carpenter. For by this image, He shews that His Father is He Who as Fashioner of all established

IESV matris deliciæ,   Paternæ decus gloriæ.
  Tu matri libas oscula,   Tu spes ad te clamæntium
  Tu patri das solatia.   Salus et mundi pretium.
       Hieronymus Wierx fecit et excud. Cum Gratia et Priuilegio. Buschere

Hieronymus Wierix, *The Holy Path of Life*, ca. 1600. Antwerp. The heavenly and the earthly trinity intersect in the figure of Christ.

the world. . . . For although the human may not be compared with the Divine, yet the image is sound, because the Father works with Christ's fire and Spirit, and like a Good Woodsman of the soul, hews off our vices."[13] The artisan Joseph offers a symbol of the creator of the world, the *deus faber*, in miniature. Saint Ambrose's commentary on Luke, which moves Joseph's humble and industrious life into the redemptive realm, has left its traces in art history.[14] Successful efforts to upgrade the figure of Joseph, which began at the end of the Middle Ages, picked up on the words of the church father. Even if the kind of typological biblical interpretation practiced by Ambrose was gradually becoming less influential, the illustrations and writings of the early-modern period agree with him insofar as they emphasize that industriousness as such is pleasing to God and thus possesses a redemptive quality. They transpose the allegorical redemptive connection of Joseph's work into a changed religiosity, one that was increasingly dominated by the work ethos of early capitalism.

Thus the complex of motifs of the Holy Family also offers room for movements that countered the monastic escape from family in the name of Christ. Even the distance between Jesus' divine Father and his earthly father is variable. This has a direct bearing on Joseph's fitness as a paternal role model and thus on the question of the extent to which human fatherhood can be reconciled with the dominion of the heavenly Father, which established the patriarchal world order in the first place. The degree of this patriarchal concord is partly determined by a *symbolic politics* that deals with several competing father authorities and can either play them off against each other or allow them to mutually strengthen each other.

Moreover, typologically Joseph stands not only for God but also for Christ in what at first glance appears to be a confusing convergence of roles—as the chaste husband of the Virgin Mary. For Christ, too, is linked to his mother, Mary, by a nuptial bond; this connection likewise is not physical but mystical in nature. This idea was given an institutional embodiment with respect to the figure of Mary as *ecclesia*. It is only natural to situate the priest, who bonds with the ecclesiastical community represented by Mary, as Joseph's successor. Like Joseph, he is the *visible* husband of the bridal church, whose *invisible* husband is Christ himself.[15]

II

THE DISSOLUTION Of DISTINCTIONS

The gravitational field of the Holy Family dissolves all distinctions, without which no kinship system can exist. If the function of religious symbolism lies in its ability to unify divergent meanings and combine them into a single symbol, in this case that would amount to the complete collapse of the nomenclature governing the familial universe. The boundary between licit and illicit relationships—a strict boundary guarded by implacable taboos—dissolves. Taxonomic terms that are separated by a wide chasm in their profane usage become identical. Yet this dissolution of distinctions and differentiations is not experienced as threatening. It does not strike the fear of anomie into believers. On the contrary, the play and counterplay of unrelated categories goes hand in hand with an immense feeling of exultation. It triggers an ecstatic torrent of words, a supernatural enthusiasm of powerful expressiveness. Christian religiosity attains its highest fervor precisely at that point where it encounters this shifting fluidity of its own distinctions.

A splendid example of such an ecstatic state of linguistic exception is provided by the fourth-century writer Ephrem the Syrian, who composed a series of hymns about the incarnation of Christ. One of the hymns is dedicated to the "wondrous mother of Jesus":

> Our Lord, no one knows
> how to address Your mother. [If] one calls her "virgin,"
> her child stands up, and "married"—
> no one knew her [sexually]. But if your mother is
> incomprehensible, who is capable of [comprehending] You?
> *Refrain: Praise to You for Whom, as Lord of all, everything is easy.*
> For she is Your mother—she alone—
> and Your sister with all. She was to You mother;
> she was to You sister. Moreover, she is Your betrothed
> with the chaste women. . . .
> A wonder is Your mother: the Lord entered her
> and became a servant; He entered able to speak
> and He became silent in her; He entered her thundering

and His voice grew silent; He entered Shepherd of all;
a lamb he became in her; He emerged bleating.
The womb of Your mother overthrew the orders.[1]

And Mary sings a hymn in praise of her child:

What can I call You, a stranger to us,
Who was from us? Shall I call You Son?
Shall I call You Brother? Shall I call You the Bridegroom?
Shall I call you Lord, O [You] Who brought forth His mother
[in] another birth out of the water?
For I am [Your] sister from the House of David,
who is a second father. Again, I am mother
because of Your conception, and bride am I
because of your chastity. Handmaiden and daughter
of blood and water [am I] who You redeemed and baptized.[2]

"What can I call you": mother, sister, bride, maid, and daughter; or son, brother, bridegroom, lord, and creator? A series of kinship titles usually separated by
rules of irreconcilability find themselves joined in intimate proximity in a bright
tone of harmony. Speech becomes intoxicated by the ease with which such incompatible and paradoxical continguities can be created. Where the sacred is
close, the order of names falls into a state of metonymical flux. One label blends
with another, with its secondary or contrary meaning. All participate in all the
others, are exchanged, permit themselves to be transposed, yield to one another.

Ephrem's hymn consists of a grand celebration of the unification of signifiers.
One could almost say that it becomes the scene of a Christian version of the
Dionysian Oneness. Yet this exuberant Oneness does not take place in a physical but in a mystical bacchanalia. After all, Christianity sets itself apart precisely
because of its revulsion toward the sexual promiscuity of the pagan gods. In his
polemical tract against Celsus and in his work *The True Doctrine*, Origen argues
that neither God nor the angels were even remotely guilty of "what Kronos did
to Uranus or what Zeus did to his father," or of behaving "like 'the father of gods
and men' when he had sexual intercourse with his daughter."[3] The writings of
the church fathers are full of attacks on the incestuous and blasphemous subject
matter of pagan mythology—and filled with the certainty that the followers of
Christ were immune to such temptations.

The worship of the ancient divinities could also take place in a ritualized play of symbols. The polytheism of the Mediterranean and oriental cultures created a pantheon that was translatable from one language to another and from one cultural sphere to another. The gods and goddesses of the sun and the moon, of fertility and all the other cosmic phenomena, could absorb a thousand different names. Whoever addressed them followed a practice of naming (*epiklesis*) that, according to Jan Assmann, "was characteristic of the religiosity of that time: invoking the gods by the names the various nations gave them."[4] Isis in particular, the nursing mother of Horus, whom some religious scholars regard as the true precursor to Mary, attracted this multiplicity of names. In the syncretism of Greco-Egyptian cults, she was considered the universal, cosmos-embracing deity. "Isis," writes Assmann, "neither makes nor demands distinctions; she abolishes all existing ones."[5] That is why she is called "'the one of the ten thousand names'; she is the ultimate point of reference for all the names of the gods."[6]

But in Ephrem and the Christian hymnists who preceded or followed him, we are dealing with something very different. Mary is not a goddess but a woman. As the *only member* of her sex who becomes the recipient of God's grace, she cannot be venerated through a multilingual chain of names and cultural forms of different backgrounds. The polytheistic tradition of *epiklesis* is foreign to the innermost nature of the Christian faith. Moreover, Mary's chief characteristic lies not in promiscuity but in virginity. And it is precisely her virginity that turns Mary into a multifarious creature with an unlimited capacity for interconnection, to the point where classificatory signs begin to "dance." In the middle of the dance floor one finds an omission, a nonoccurrence, a white spot. As Marie-Odile Métral has argued, the *virtual dimension* of her virginity—which is not periodic but eternal and inviolable—makes it possible to transcend in mystical acts "the prohibition against incest with the father (God) and the brother (Christ) . . . the prohibition against being wife *and* lover."[7] She concludes: "Virginity is, paradoxically, a behavioral mode that affords more room to Eros than does marriage. It symbolically transcends the incest prohibition. It unites with the Father and in so doing fulfills a desire that is free of any obligation of procreation."[8] This leeway given to an Eros that has been unleashed under the banner of virginity spreads over all the relationships that can be connected to the central constellation of Christ's conception.

Gregory of Nyssa already informs us that it is not only Mary who is virginal, for this grace is also perceived in connection with the incorruptible Father. Indeed, it is a paradox to find virginity in a Father who has a Son whom He has begotten without passion, and virginity is comprehended together with the only-begotten God who is the giver of incorruptibility, since it shone forth with the purity and absence of passion in His begetting. And again, the Son, conceived through virginity, is an equal paradox. In the same way, one perceives it in the natural and incorruptible purity of the Holy Spirit. For when you speak of the pure and incorruptible, you are using another name for virginity.[9]

The attribute of virginity is diffused in all directions. It crosses the gender barrier and creates a *third* gender beyond the polarity of man and woman. It is even capable of transcending the boundary between Mary's human existence and the divine Trinity. The greatest triumph of virginity lies in its ability to create a bridge between heaven and earth. In this capacity, the love of the Virgin overlaps in a surprising way with the Platonic Eros. Gregory continues:

> [B]y reason of its lack of passion it exists with the whole of other-worldly nature and associates with the superior powers. . . . Therefore, since the power of virginity is such that it resides in heaven with the Father of spiritual beings, and takes part in the chorus of the supramundane powers, and attains to human salvation, and since, by itself, it brings God down to a sharing in human life and lifts man up to a desire of heavenly things, becoming a kind of binding force in man's affinity to God, and since it brings into harmony by mediation things so opposed to each other by nature, what power of words could be found to equal the grandeur of this marvel?[10]

Virginity means love: love for God. Through its power of connection, it makes all human beings into sons of the Mother of God and thus *brothers of God*—a kinship title whose impossibility almost takes away the breath of those who utter it.[11] Divine chastity speaks no other language than that of the union of love. In the thirteenth century, Saint Bonaventure could refer to Mary as "the bride of God, the chamber of the entire Trinity and the special bed of the Son."[12] The female mystics of the twelfth and thirteen centuries—chief among them Mechthild of Magdeburg—gave expression to this topic in their own nuptial visions.[13]

The multiple meanings of kinship that accrued around the circumstances of the Christian ur-family became incomprehensible and lost their mystical meaning

only with the *despiritualization* of religious content that began with the Reformation. These meanings were now infused with a different, cruder subtext harking
back, one might say, to paganism. One of Freud's contemporaries was Oskar
Panizza, whose tirades against the figure of Mary were driven by a true rage
against Catholicism, especially the papacy.[14] Like a distorting mirror, Panizza
holds up the literal meaning of these kinship combinations to the combinatorial
enthusiasm of the exegetes:

> In the great Roman *family of gods*: God the Father, God the Son, the Holy Spir-
> it, Mary, St. Anne, and the pope, one sees immediately from the sum of the epi-
> thets, from the relationship spreading out in every direction, who is the true cen-
> ter of the system, from which direction most of the rays emanate. Only with
> horror do I cite the following honorific titles, which throw sufficient light on the
> strange, polytheistic, incestuous relationships of this Catholic family: *St. Anne* is
> *God's grandmother, mother of Mary, mother-in-law of the Holy Spirit. —Mary:*
> *daughter of God the Father, daughter of St. Anne, wife of God the Father, daughter*
> *of the Trinity, mother of the Son, sister of the Holy Spirit, bride of the Holy Spirit,*
> *wife of the Holy Spirit, confidante of the Trinity, substantively unified with the Trin-*
> *ity,* the *fourth person of the Trinity. —God the Father: father of the son, father of*
> *Mary, husband of Mary. —Christ* gets away with two epithets: *Son of God, Son of*
> *Mary. —The pope: Christ's vicar, God on earth, Vice-God, knows God's mysteries,*
> *speaks on familiar terms with Christ, opens the heavens, is the Son of God, om-*
> *nipresent on earth.* —We believe that the Germans should have nothing to do with
> this rat's nest of relationship and should keep their hands and conscience pure.[15]

We need not agree with Panizza's attack, carried out in the spirit of German
Protestantism, to become aware of two problems it touches on. The first concerns
the *driving forces* concealed behind this metonymical web of all these intercon-
nectable titles of kinship and office. Is what finds expression here a language of desire that springs from a realm beyond the prohibitions that constrain the life of
regular mortals? Is the sublime language—which finds no contradiction in categories such as "mother," "daughter," "bride," "lover," "father," and "son"—
merely a displaced way of articulating a desire for the forbidden? Is Christianity,
in fact, grounded in a—merely spiritually concealed—idea of the "primal" sexual incest?

This raises the second question, which concerns the *function* of such a confusing play with signifiers. If religious symbols cut across the taxonomy of kinship,

does that mean they are working against the social order? Does the sacred create *disorder*, importing confusion into society's scheme of classifications? And how could such a dysfunctionality be compatible with the *normative* effects of the model of the Holy Family?

Once again, we are dealing with the "Janus-faced" structure of religious symbolism. One aspect of its nature is evidently that it dissolves *boundaries*— transcending all existing commandments, norms, determinations, logic, and identities. This is where it participates in religion's *promise of freedom*. However, this symbolism creates its own inclusions and exclusions, commonalities and differentiations, cohesions and disjunctions. In other words, into the cultural framework it inscribes new "wish maps," with new liminal effects. The process of decoding is followed by a process of recoding on the basis of its own no less imperious rules. In the Christian universe of faith, this locus of passage, this moment of the asymbolic, of the gap between the two codes, has assumed positive form in the tabula rasa that is the body of the Virgin Mary, which, released from the gender order, can create relationships and connections between everybody and everything.

PART II Theories

If the central figuration of Christianity consists of triangles, and if the functionality of triangular relationships rests on the fact that the third factor both unites and separates the other two, Christian symbolism endows *unity* with a remarkable preponderance over the countervailing force of *alterity*. The dogmatic construction of the Trinity as well as the medieval *unio mystica* between the mother and the identical Father-God/Son cause the triangulations they form to collapse on themselves, so that no remnant of otherness remains between the vertices of the triad.

Structurally the collapse of any and all distinctions between persons within the structure of the family corresponds to the notion of incest as described in more recent psychoanalytic theory: "[T]he incestuous transgression," writes Juan Eduardo Tesone,

> consists not only of a physical exchange, but is above all the omnipotent desire to occupy all places simultaneously: to be simultaneously father, mother, son, and daughter. As [Pierre] Legendre has said . . . the desire for incest is the desire for omnipotence, that is to say, it signifies the desire for the impossible. The law prohibiting incest exists precisely to set a limit to this absolute desire. God and the Holy Family do not know incest . . . since God lacks nothing. Incest leads to a confusion of places, and consequently to a confusion of genders and generations. The incestuous family expresses the fact that it lacks the acceptance of otherness. The equation of such a family reads $1 + 1 + 1 = 1$ and not $1 + 1 + 1 = 3$.[1]

The equation $1 + 1 + 1 = 1$ can be read as a mathematical expression of the dogma of the Trinity. Nevertheless Tesone, invoking Pierre Legendre,[2] argues that God does not know incest because it is incompatible with his nature to experience a lack of sex. One could specify further: God does not know the *desire* for incest because the triangles of relationships of which Christ is a part have *always* fulfilled the desire for fullness and wholeness, for a "confusion of places" and the "confusion of genders and generations." God, Christ, and the Madonna—once exegesis had transcended the relationships of the Jewish ur-family of the New Testament—have been one since time immemorial. Similar to the scenario in the incestuous family, Mary's virginity opens up a transitional and multiple structure that makes it possible "to occupy all places simultaneously: to be simultaneously father, mother, son, and daughter."

According to the psychoanalytical model, the Oedipus complex erects a barrier against the incest desire. This model is based on the tension between desire and prohibition. By contrast, the Christian familial triangle could be interpreted as a figuration that *fulfills* the desire for wholeness, unity, and the dissolution of boundaries to a high degree—at the price of sexual abstinence and passion. One might say that both models describe familial triads with implosive tendencies. But they each obey their own unique grammar and create divergent foundations for self and otherness. Not least, they encourage the telling of different stories—be they theological, theoretical, or therapeutic in nature.

12

THE FAMILY NOVEL OF RELIGIONS

Jesus and Judas

Jacobus de Voragine (born around 1230), a Dominican monk and later arch-bishop of Genoa, acquired lasting fame though his collection of the lives of the saints and stories of the apostles and martyrs. His work, a compendium of the historical and popular traditions of the Christian West, circulated rapidly and was translated into numerous languages. One might call it a best-seller if that term were not incongruous with reference to the medieval culture of manu-scripts. Entitled *Legenda aurea* (The Golden Legend), the book was a remark-able success in Europe for centuries.

One of the legends deals with the apostle Matthias, one of the twelve apostles of Jesus. He was not among the original twelve, however, but took the place of Judas after the latter had committed suicide over his betrayal of Jesus. This of-fered the author an opportunity to insert the story of Judas.

Jacobus, drawing on what he calls an "admittedly apocryphal history," claims that Judas was the son of Ruben and his wife, Cyborea. "One night, after they had paid each other the marital debt, Cyborea fell asleep and had a dream that she related, terrified, sobbing, and groaning, to her husband. She said: 'I dreamed that I was going to bear a son so wicked that he would bring ruin upon our whole people.'"[1] In time, when the birth of a son confirmed her fears, the parents decided to put him into a basket, which they set adrift on the sea. The basket was carried to the shores of an island called Scariot. (One here encoun-ters Jacobus de Voragine's notorious penchant for weaving popular etymologies into his stories.)

As it happened, the queen of the island was out for a walk on the beach and saw the basket. Being childless, she decided to take the child in and declare it her own offspring. "The child, of course, was brought up in royal style. Not long af-terward, however, the queen conceived of the king and gave birth to a son." Soon there was bad blood between the two sons, the real and the adopted one, espe-cially since Judas was displaying his evil nature. As one can imagine, the episode ends badly: Judas kills his stepbrother and flees to—of all places—Jerusalem.

In Jerusalem, Judas becomes manager in the household of Pilate—which, from the perspective of pious Christians, again attests to his bad character. And now the events escalate. One day Pilate is looking out of his palace into a neighbor's orchard and is seized by a longing for the apples he sees there. He dispatches his manager to steal them. But the orchard belongs to none other than Ruben, Judas's father. Ruben catches the apple thief in the act but does not recognize his son; Judas, in turn, knows nothing of his true birth. An altercation ensues in which Judas kills his own father: "As daylight faded and night came on, Ruben's body was found and it was thought that he had been overtaken by a sudden death. Pilate awarded all Ruben's belongings, including his wife Cyborea, to Judas." Eventually the whole affair comes to light, and the author has considerable trouble offering up a believable account of Judas's remorse and his acceptance into the band of Jesus' apostles, given all the crimes he had committed, which would be followed by those recounted in the biblical story. In fact, Jacobus de Voragine himself is not at all convinced by what he recounted of the life of Judas prior to his apostleship: "So far, however, what we have set down comes from the aforesaid apocryphal history, and whether it should be retold is left to the reader's judgment, though probably it is better left aside than repeated."

The Judas legend obeys a very transparent plan. Its intent is to heap all evil on the head of the eventual betrayer of Christ. Beginning with his mother's ominous premonitions, the medieval reader and listener is presented with a life full of horrors. The various elements that make up the story are also easily identified: exposure in the reed basket and adoption by the island queen are taken from the Moses story; the murder of the king's real son repeats Cain's murder of his brother, Abel, the first murder in the history of humankind; and the episode of the apples echoes the story of the expulsion of Adam and Eve from paradise. Finally, patricide and incest with his own mother have no biblical models, but here, too, the subtext is instantly identifiable: Judas is modeled after the Greek tragic hero Oedipus.

Judas's life story is composed of a series of evil deeds. One should add that he also incurs guilt as the treasurer of the band of apostles by committing fraud and embezzlement. And yet Judas does not represent merely an anecdotal villain who has become the object of the Christian art of inventive storytelling. He is nothing less than the *personification of evil* in God's universal plan of redemption. When he hanged himself out of remorse over his final and greatest misdeed— the betrayal of the Messiah—his body "'burst asunder in the middle and all his bowels gushed out.' Thus his mouth was spared defilement since nothing came out through it, for it would have been incongruous that a mouth which had touched the glorious lips of Christ should be so foully soiled."

Judas is Christ's satanic antagonist, a kind of mirror image. His nature is evil, while Jesus brings salvation to humankind. Every element of his *vita* can be decoded in the sense of this dichotomy. While the angel brings Mary the good news that she has conceived, Judas's mother has an ominous dream vision. While Jesus' parents recognize his miraculous nature through various signs of grace, Judas's parents are so fearful of the curse revealed to them that they expose their own child. The episode on the island of Scariot consists of a straightforward contrafactum of the Moses story: instead of growing up to become the ruler's favorite, Judas becomes the murderer of the king's real son. Finally, with the theft of the apples in the garden, Judas *repeats* the Fall instead of atoning for it, as Jesus does. So much for the "contrariness" of the mirror image. But a mirror image means not only opposition but also similarity. In what way would Judas be similar to the Savior?

To answer this question, one must reflect on the intimate rendering of the mother–son dyad in the Christian pictorial imagination. First the dead man Jesus returns to Mary's protective womb. Then, following his resurrection, he lives with his mother in a state of heavenly matrimony. One could speculate that medieval believers were already aware of the danger that this privileged relationship might be given an incestuous interpretation in a physical sense and that, as a result, the figure of Jesus might be overlaid by a guilt-burdened, tragic figure like Oedipus in Greek mythology. Against this background, the Judas story in the *Legenda aurea* can be seen as an attempt to shift an element that is inherent in the Holy Family but culturally highly menacing onto the Christian Savior's antagonist, to transfer it to the figure who represents his symmetrical negation.

While this interpretation is speculative, it does provide an explanation as to why Christian mythologists were eager to heap the crime of Oedipus—which is quite alien to the context of the story—on Judas's catalog of sins beyond his betrayal of Christ, which led to Jesus' arrest in the garden of Gethsemane. In this sense, the *Legenda aurea*'s strategy of providing narrative relief leads us—contrary to the intent of its inventor—onto the trail of an Oedipal interpretation of the New Testament Passion.

Freud: Patricide and Filial Sacrifice

There is only a single work in which Sigmund Freud deals in detail with contexts that touch on the issues surrounding the Holy Family: his late work *Moses and Monotheism*. To properly assess this study, one must take into account its time frame. Unlike most of Freud's other works, *Moses and Monotheism* has a long and extended creative history, as is clearly apparent from the various prefatory comments, insertions, expressions of misgivings, and additions that give this book a scattered and disjointed appearance. The first part appeared in 1937, while the third part was finished in 1938, following Freud's emigration. A book about Judaism and Christianity at that very time could be nothing other—explicitly or implicitly—than a book about the Nazi regime and anti-Semitism. The assumption of power by the Nazis, the annexation of Austria, the persecution of psychoanalysis as a "Jewish" movement, and Freud's flight from Vienna—"the city," Freud wrote," which from early childhood, through 78 years, had been a home to me"[2]—destroyed the belief in progress of the liberal bourgeoisie to which Freud belonged. Freud was forced to admit that there was evidently something in religion that survived the process of enlightenment and that, without having a place in the official consciousness of the culture, reached across a great distance to entangle human beings in their past.

Freud revisited the question of religion repeatedly following the publication of his work *Totem and Taboo* (1912–1913). This subject matter was for him a natural place of inquiry because he found at work within it the same mechanisms that operated in the individual psyche—mechanisms he traced back to intrafamilial socialization. Starting from this premise, it was easy to draw conclusions from the father problem, which stands at the center of psychoanalytical theorizing, back to the figure of the Father-God, and vice versa.

Freud's later work *Moses and Monotheism* was also based on this system of analogy, which presupposes that collective—meaning primarily religious—developments are comparable to psychopathological developments within the individual psyche. Looking back at his book *Totem and Taboo*, he wrote: "From then on I have never doubted that religious phenomena are to be understood only on the model of the neurotic symptoms of individuals, which are so familiar to us, as a return of long forgotten important happenings in the primeval history of the human family, that they owe their obsessive character to that very origin and therefore derive their effect on mankind from the historical truth they contain."[3]

Moses and Monotheism consists of a series of essays that appear as a sequence of chapters in later editions. Marshaling linguistic and other evidence, in the first chapter Freud seeks to prove that Moses, the founder of the Jewish nation and religion, was himself not a Jew but an Egyptian. Freud was drawing on the scholarship of his time, though he did use and weigh it selectively in support of his thesis.

THE FAMILY NOVEL OF RELIGIONS   67

The second chapter revolves around the question of how the Jewish belief in a single God could emerge out of Egyptian polytheism. Freud argues that Moses was a high-ranking Egyptian under Pharaoh Ikhnaton and passed the latter's monotheistic beliefs on to the Jews. The core of the Jewish religion thus lies in the religion of Aton, which itself was only a brief episode in Egypt. According to Freud, the ritual of circumcision was also Egyptian in origin.

However, the books of Moses give evidence of a dual tradition: one using the name Jahweh for God; the other, the name Elohim. Freud infers from this the existence of two originally independent cults. He characterizes Jahweh as a "rude and narrow-minded local god, violent and blood-thirsty," whereas he recognizes in Elohim the higher-ranking divinity of the Aton religion. According to his scheme, these were separate traditions that were "fused" only after the fact.[4] The Exodus from Egypt took place under the banner of the sole, transcendent God that the religious founder Moses had introduced to the Jews; only later did the Jews succumb to the more primitive and more physical Jahweh faith and date it back to the time of the Exodus.

According to Freud, the history of Judaism thus consists of two phases, two beginnings, whose differences the later redaction of the Hebrew Bible texts sought to cover up. Yet this harmonization did not take place without conflict. Between the first faith, transcendent and monotheistic, and the second, characterized by nature religion, there is, Freud believes, a decisive break. That break was the *murder* of the Egyptian Moses. Freud based himself on Ernst Sellin, the historian of religions, who advanced this spectacular theory in the early 1920s.

Perhaps this is the place to inject a word or two about the historical credibility of Freud's assumptions. It became clear soon after the publication of the essay that Freud's edifice—which he constructed with great rhetorical skill out of more or less vague but mutually supporting hypotheses—was not accepted in scholarly circles. In effect, the book was considered fanciful or dubious. Incidentally, Freud was never really flustered by research and studies contradicting his theories. Josef Hayim Yerushalmi notes: "It is said that when someone once told you that Sellin had abandoned his theory that Moses had been murdered by the Hebrews, you merely replied, 'He was right the first time.'"[5]

Although there have been recent attempts to rehabilitate Freud's construction—for example, the Moses book by the Egyptologist Jan Assmann[6]—it appears to be unsalvageable with respect to its historical substance. Paradoxically, however, Freud's account, so clearly erroneous in some of its central assumptions, retains a radiance and persuasive power that have placed it far ahead of competing and "truer" versions, and to this day the gap has not been closed. All this sheds light on the mechanism of discourse in psychoanalysis as such. One could say that it is more interesting and rewarding to question Freud's theory than it is to verify other, better-supported theories.

That holds true especially when it comes to the third chapter of *Moses and Monotheism*. Freud starts all over again by recapitulating his theory of a double origin of the Jewish religion. He follows this with the question of how the reinstallation of the strict monotheistic Father-God came about, why the memory of him and the memory of his murdered emissary Moses was able to persist so tenaciously throughout the prophetic tradition and eventually emerge victorious over the Jahweh cult.

With regard to the redaction of the Hebrew Bible, Freud argues that "the priests, in the account they represent, desired to establish a continuity between their own times and the Mosaic period. They attempted to deny just that which we have recognized to be the most striking feature of Jewish religious history, namely, that there was a gap between the Mosaic law-giving and the late Jewish religion—a gap filled in at first by the worship of Jahve and only later slowly covered over."[7] For this shift from one phase to another—repressed but incontrovertible—Freud offers an explanation that presents the history of the Jewish people as a collective psychic history analogous to the individual psychic development of a neurotic. In both cases, he finds a scheme that passes through the stages of "Early Trauma—Defence—Latency—Outbreak of the Neurosis—Partial return of the repressed material."[8] In both cases—the people and the exemplary (meaning male) neurotic that Freud has in mind—the crux is the conflict with an overbearing father figure. One is dealing with the desire to commit murder and the act itself, with repression and a growing, eventually unmanageable, feeling of guilt. In short, what unfolds is an Oedipal drama.

The murder of Moses, which Freud makes the basis of his subsequent deductions, stands in the shadow of another murder that was the subject of *Totem and Taboo*: the murder of the primeval father, *the* founding trauma of every culture, which was simultaneously the birth of the patriarchal conception of God. From this latest point on, Freud's combinatorics become dizzying.

Totem and Taboo appropriates Darwin's hypothesis of the primal horde. According to Freud, the leader of the horde, the *ur-father*, possesses the absolute monopoly of power and access to sex. As a result, the young men who hover about the horde—and especially the females—are driven out. "One day"[9] the brothers who had been driven out of the horde come together and kill the father, after which, following the custom of the time, they devour their victim in an "attempt to assure one's identification with the father by incorporating a part of him."[10] But this act of liberation and empowerment exacts a high price: it burdens the perpetrators with a sense of guilt that cannot be assuaged and even continues to grow over the course of time.

This guilt feeling produces two consequences. First, it instills in the brothers the mechanism of "deferred obedience."[11] They now impose on themselves most of the sexual restrictions that the father had previously imposed on them. This is the origin of the incest taboo and the law of exogamy. Second, the memory of the murdered ur-father becomes enlarged and transfigured. This is the origin of the patriarchal notion of God. Freud finds this primeval event preserved through time as a ritual act in the totemic phase of culture, as described by ethnologists around 1900, which is characterized by marriage and food taboos, on the one hand, and by the ritual consumption of the totem, on the other. Jewish monotheism is in his eyes a late "return of the one and only father deity whose power was unlimited."[12]

From here, one can draw further connections to the Christian religion. For one, Freud believes that the Christian father cult has also retained visible traces of the totemic ritual and thus of the murder of the primeval father, to which he traces it back. He notes that "more than one author has been struck by the close resemblance between the rite of Christian Communion—where the believer symbolically incorporates the blood and flesh of his God—and the Totem feast, whose inner meaning it reproduces."[13]

However, another connection is even more far-reaching. According to Freud, the Jewish people are burdened by a double trauma. Like all humankind, they are descendants of the murderers of the primeval father. But the murdered and deified ur-father returned to them, and they *repeated* the original deed through their murder of Moses. Although they tried to repress this second deed as well, they suffered the same fate as the neurotic, who, after a period of latency, is confronted with the return of the repressed experience. All the more so because the Jews see themselves as bound in a special and exclusive way to the one and only Father-God, whose chosen people they claim to be. Yet it is precisely in their role as God's favorite children that the Jewish people are dominated by a special ethical severity. Proof of their exclusive bond to the father lies in the fact that they are punished with particular severity; in a masochistic cycle, the punishment in turn binds them in even greater obedience and feelings of guilt to the fatherly–divine law.[14]

Against this backdrop, it is no coincidence that Judaism became the scene for an act of atonement with world-historical consequences: Christ's death on the cross. The Christian religion of atonement, which starts with this crucifixion, *fulfills and transcends* the Jewish guilt imperative. Here Freud's essay arrives at one of its most dense and suggestively irresistible passages:

> The restoration to the primeval father of his historical rights marked a great progress, but this could not be the end. The other parts of the prehistoric tragedy also clamoured for recognition. How this process was set into motion it is not easy to say. It seems that a growing feeling of guiltiness had seized the Jewish people—and perhaps the whole of civilization of that time—as a precursor of the return of the repressed material. This went on until a member of the Jewish people, in the guise of a political-religious agitator, founded a doctrine which—together with another one, the Christian religion—separated from the Jewish one. Paul, a Roman Jew from Tarsus, seized upon this feeling of guilt and correctly traced it back to its primeval source. This he called original sin; it was a crime against God that could be expiated only through death. Death had come into the world through original sin. In reality this crime, deserving of death, had been the murder of the Father who later was deified. The murderous deed itself, however, was not remembered; in its place stood the phantasy of expiation and that is why this phantasy could be welcomed in the form of the gospel of salvation (Evangel). A Son of God, innocent himself, had sacrificed himself—and had thereby taken over the guilt of the world. It had to be a Son, for the sin had been murder of the Father. . . .
>
> That the Redeemer sacrificed himself as an innocent man was an obviously tendentious distortion, difficult to reconcile with logical thinking. How could a man who was innocent assume the guilt of the murderer by allowing himself to be killed? In historical reality there was no such contradiction. The "redeemer" could be no one else but he who was most guilty, the leader of the brother horde who had overpowered the Father. Whether there had been such a chief rebel and leader must—in my opinion—remain uncertain. . . . If there was no such leader, then Christ was the heir of an unfulfilled wish-phantasy; if there was such a leader, then Christ was his successor and his reincarnation.[15]

Freud proceeds with the instruments of a veritable criminal line of argumentation. The punishment must match the guilt. The person who is punished is the one who carried out or intended to carry out a crime. Thus if the ritual of punishment is found in the Son's sacrifice, the primeval crime that is being punished must have been the murder of the Father—or at least the *desire* for murder, for it is in principle impossible to distinguish between the wish impulse and the completed deed in the calculations of the unconscious.

What separates Christians from Jews is therefore the *admission* and the *restitution* of the primeval crime of patricide. Freud writes:

> The poor Jewish people, who with its usual stiff-necked obduracy continued to deny the murder of their "father," has clearly expiated this in the course of centuries. Over and over again they heard the reproach: you killed our God. And this reproach is true, if rightly interpreted. It says, in reference to the history of religion: you won't *admit* that you murdered God (the archetype of God, the primeval Father and his reincarnations). Something should be added, namely: "It is true, we did the same thing, but we *admitted* it, and since then we have been purified." [16]

Marcuse: Christian Revisionism

The Passion story, interpreted through psychoanalytic categories, leaves behind a conflicting legacy. Although Christ does take upon himself the primeval guilt of humanity, it continues to exist in the form of original sin. Although the followers of Christ—chief among them Paul—inherited the Jewish religion of guilt, the subsequent development would show that in the process they displaced most of the guilt onto the Jews and prepared the ground for a deeply rooted *Christian anti-Judaism*. Finally, the power relationship between Father and Son was never clarified, as Freud himself noted:

> The way in which the new religion came to terms with the ancient ambivalence in the father–son relationship is noteworthy. Its main doctrine, to be sure, was the reconciliation with God the Father, the expiation of the crime committed against Him; but the other side of the relationship manifested itself in the Son—who had taken the guilt on his shoulders—becoming God himself beside the Father and in truth in place of the Father. Originally a Father religion, Christianity became a Son religion. The fate of having to displace the Father it could not escape. [17]

The social theorist Herbert Marcuse, a cult author of the sixties generation, tried to extract an antiauthoritarian point from this ambivalence. What Freud, entirely in keeping with the old doctrine of guilt, called the "fate of having to displace the Father," took on for Marcuse the perspective of a struggle for liberation on the part of the sons. In his book *Eros and Civilization*, first published in 1955, he reaccentuated the psychoanalytical approach by arguing that "the life and death of Christ would appear as a struggle against the father—and as a triumph over the father. The message of the Son was the message of liberation: the overthrow of the Law (which is domination) by Agape (which is Eros). This would fit in with the heretical image of Jesus as the Redeemer in the flesh, the Messiah who came to save man here on earth."[18] Marcuse turns Jesus into the leader of the rebellion of the generation of sons, a rebellion under the banner of *love* against the *law* of the father. Except that the redeemer of the flesh on earth does not have the last word. The church theologians reinterpret his act of liberation and bring the rebellious Son back into the Father's sphere of authority. In the words of Marcuse: "Then the subsequent transubstantiation of the Messiah, the deification of the Son beside the Father, would be a betrayal of this message by his own disciples—the denial of the liberation of the flesh, the revenge on the redeemer. Christianity would then have surrendered the gospel of Agape-Eros again to the Law; the father-rule would be restored and strengthened."[19] The rebel, who devoted himself to the project of sexual liberation, was integrated—as junior boss, as it were—into Christianity, Inc., which has been flourishing for nearly two thousand years. The Father, according to Marcuse, had the last word; his regime was shared with partners, not overturned. Just as the Christian cult of the saints constituted a concession to the polytheism of the converted peoples,[20] the construction of a divine Trinity softened the strict monotheistic conception of God of the Mosaic religion. This, too, was a historically variable "compromise formation," to use a Freudian expression.

In some way, these theories carry on the psychodrama of the religions. They read the Christian generational conflict (if that is what one can call it) into their own respective time. However, in the process they also expose themselves to the risk of taking over the blind spots of their own contemporary context. One blind spot in the Freudian reconstruction is particularly glaring: it concerns the object of dispute for whose sake the conflict is being carried out.

The question is this: Where is the mother in this game of men? In constructing his hypothesis, Freud eventually loses sight of her altogether.[21] Let us not forget that the brothers once rebelled against the father to gain control over his woman/women. The thesis of the primeval patricide projects the Oedipal triad—whose great constants are the son's incestuous urges and the resultant sexual competition between father and son—back into primeval times. Where does this sexual aspect appear in the founding story of Christianity, which Freud, after all, sees as the reversal of the murder of the primeval father? Is Mary the possession contested by the Father-God and the Son-God? If so, who carried the day? Although, to put it bluntly, it is not the Son who murders the Father but the Father who kills the Son, is it not the case that the theologians subsequently immortalized the post-mortal love relationship between the Son and the Mother? Does not Christianity, in this respect as well, relate a split and ambivalent story by allowing the Son to take possession of the Mother, but only at the price of giving up his life, his body, his flesh, by inextricably fusing incest and sacrificial death? Is it possible to see the figure of the Pietà as a specifically Christian compromise solution to a primal religious Oedipal drama?

Yerushalmi: The Hostile Brothers

Numerous clues make it appear very doubtful that the Oedipal model is applicable to the constellation of the Holy Family, not only because the majority of Christian theologians would protest against such an interpretation (much as they would also oppose, with good exegetical arguments, the interpretation of the Eucharist as a veiled totemic meal). The Oedipal scenario also brings with it a whole series of presuppositions that are, in turn, historically conditioned and therefore possess limited applicability.

The most important of these presuppositions is the one that projects all relationships onto a fundamental pattern of sexual attraction. In other words, it isolates some kind of sexual substrate and declares it to be the *inner truth* of human interpersonal existence—with the consequence that all expression that is not directly sexual can be conceived of only as derivative stages of this basic pattern. Now, the Holy Family is characterized precisely by the *omission* of the sexual dimension, and the real essence of Jesus' teachings lies in opening up a new—spiritual—bond between humankind and God and among humans. The psychoanalytic retranslation of the spiritual dimension into the sexual dimension would revoke this critical cultural step of Christianity with a single stroke, so to speak. It views through its own lenses the momentous spiritual urge of the classical world around the time of Christ's birth, to which Christianity owes its birth and diffusion. And these lenses, as one could readily show, were an optical creation of the nineteenth century.

As result, there has been no dearth of attempts to relate Freud's essay on Moses not so much to the time about which it purports to speak but rather to the birth of psychoanalysis and to the background of Freud's own life. Freud as a Jew writing about the guilt feelings and the father complex of Judaism— what would be more natural than to recast this into the complex "Freud and his father"?

A book by that title was, in fact, published by the family sociologist Marianne Krüll.[22] The original German subtitle reveals her central thesis: "The Creation of Psychoanalysis and Freud's Unresolved Bond to His Father." This thorough study is not the only attempt to relate Freud's speculations about Judaism to his own background and to psychoanalysis as a "Jewish" science. The book *Freud's Moses* by Josef Hayim Yerushalmi also deals with the man Sigmund Freud; his relationship to his father, Jakob, who was still connected to Judaism by bonds of religion; and the imperatives of his own religious tradition. Yerushalmi also engages in some historical reflections concerning the emergence of Christianity out of the faith of the fathers. He does that in a—necessarily one-sided— "conversation" with the founder of psychoanalysis, for whom he expresses respect in spite of all his reservations and objections. This "conversation" he entitled "Monologue with Freud":[23]

> I wonder if it ever occurred to you that the very opening of Christian Scripture (chapter 1 of Matthew) is a "family romance" far more blatant than the one you perceived in the Book of Exodus, and that this was to have untold consequences for both Christians and Jews through ages to come. Here, in a transparently retroactive attempt to legitimize the messiahship of Jesus, he is given a mythical genealogy as a direct descendant of King David, this royal pedigree being the sine qua non for the Messiah in Jewish tradition itself.[24]

The new religion was first faced with the challenge of establishing itself among the many religious currents in the Mediterranean world. It had to free itself from the stigma of illegitimacy and endow itself with "a noble and venerable lineage. This it could accomplish only by appropriating the history and hence the antiquity of Judaism itself." That this process did not take place without undisguised hostility toward the older faith is revealed in the writings of the church fathers, which openly *disinherit* the Jewish people in favor of Christianity. Yerushalmi to Freud: "The Christian appropriation of the sacred history and chosenness of the Jews involves, necessarily, an aggressive displacement of the Jews themselves with all the intensity of a fierce struggle over a royal succession or a bitter contest over an inheritance. This dimension seems to have eluded you." For

Yerushalmi, this gives rise to a very different Oedipal constellation from the one Freud had in mind:

> In your *Moses* you provided a creative and stimulating application of the Oedipus complex to the problem of Judaism and Christianity, both as repetitions of the primeval patricide and as emblematic of the character of each of the two religions. But I think you did not carry your Oedipal analysis far enough. Christianity is a "Son-Religion," to use your apt phrase, not only because it deified the Son but because, both historically and theologically, it is an offspring of Judaism and therefore stands in an Oedipal relationship to Judaism itself. Thus, despite the figurative Christian claim to spiritual antiquity, the Jews are the "Old" Israel, the Christians the "New," the former possess the "Old Testament," the latter the "New." In each instance the "New" supplants the "Old" just as the Son usurps the Father.

But even this reinterpretation of the notorious Father–Son rivalry in Freud cannot fully grasp the conflict between Christians and Jews. To do that, one must superimpose several "family romances," for both systems of faith, after all, refer to one Father-God and are in the same position with respect to him. Yerushalmi thus has them appear on the stage of world history as two hostile brothers:

> At the same time, in their relationship to God the Father, Judaism and Christianity are both son-religions, each inevitably claiming its exclusive legitimacy at the expense of the other, for if one be true the other must be false. Hence, if it is to serve as a useful analytical tool in probing the deeper meaning of Judaism vis-à-vis Christianity, we must further complicate the Oedipus complex. We should take into account not only the rivalry of the son with the father, but the rivalry between the sons. "Over whom?" you may well ask. (Curiously, desire for the mother, so significant in your account of the Oedipal conflict of the individual, disappears along with the wives of the Primeval Father in your account of the history of religion.) Who, then, at the juncture we have reached, is the mother? I would simply and brazenly answer—the Torah, the Teaching, the revelation, the Torah which in Hebrew is grammatically feminine and which is midrashically compared to a bride. It is over possession of her that Christianity, the younger son, came to challenge, not so much the Father as Judaism, the elder son. For this struggle "sibling rivalry" is perhaps too tame a phrase. Psychologically (and alas, all too often even historically) we are talking about fratricide.

Not Oedipus but Cain, except that this time the younger brother becomes the perpetrator. "This guilt, repressed and denied," Yerushalmi goes on, altering Freud's derivation of the anti-Judaism of the church, "is a fratricidal one, the guilt of having usurped the birthright of which Christianity is never completely secure so long as the Jews, obstinately refusing to acknowledge the usurpation, remain as a witness and a reproach." For this model, Yerushalmi can draw on patristic sources, especially Saint Augustine. What is especially important, however, is the fact that Yerushalmi not only seeks to dissolve the classical Oedipal fixation of Freud's theory, but also puts forth a suggestion for identifying the female element he believes is the object of the quarrel between the unequal brothers Judaism and Christianity. The contest is over the *teachings*, which means that it is precisely not about sexual but spiritual possession.

Anyone whom this strikes as too esoteric can substitute a different feminine element for the female part contested by the rivals. That would be an entity that, though composed of human beings, is transpersonal: the *community*. If Jesus and, after him, the apostles convert Jews into Christians by way of teaching and missionary work—and the first Christians were, after all, Jews; only later did the young sect open itself up to pagan converts—they are tearing from the bosom of the Jewish faithful the believers won over to the new faith in order to turn them into members of the rapidly growing Christian community.

The people of Israel considered themselves the bride of God since Hebrew Bible times. The sign of this relationship is *circumcision*, the sacrifice of the foreskin, a ritualistic act akin to castration and, in this respect, an effeminizing ritual.[25] Although the Christians soon broke with the law of circumcision, they did so only to replace the Jewish "external mark in the flesh" with the "true circumcision . . . of the heart, directed not by written precepts but by the Spirit," as Paul put it in the Letter to the Romans (2:28–29)—that is to say, to replace it with a cut that went much deeper inwardly. They did not dissociate themselves from the laws of the blood covenant to make human beings into utterly single and separate beings, but to spiritualize them and allow them to enter into a renewed community with Jesus Christ. In this spiritual community, the faithful as *community* are feminine in nature.

Every soul to whom God grants admission is feminine according to its role. Yet even the collectivity of the community, the community of faithful souls, is personified as a bride. It already appeared this way in the teachings of Paul, and the church fathers elaborated further on this thought. One sees once again how difficult it is to transpose unambiguous gender attributes to the complex relationships

Nicolas of Verdun, *Circumcision of Christ*, Verdun altar, 1181. Joseph approaches the child with the knife and the cloth to perform the Jewish rite of circumcision.

of participation within the Christian *ecclesia*. From a gender perspective, Christian men are, so to speak, doubly coded: first, in analogy to Christ as the head, that is, as the male part in a love relationship; second, as members of the community, which assumes the role of the obedient woman toward the Christian God. As an individual person, the man is male; as part of the community of the faithful, he must yield to God like a woman.

There is much one could say about the symbolic dimension of male collectives assuming female traits—which exerted its influence right up to the mass collectives of the modern era. Here, at any rate, it carries with it a certain confusion if one recalls Freud's Oedipal triad and identifies as the object of contention between Jewish father-religion and Christian son-religion not merely a woman but a male-dominated collective. The confusion seems to increase with Yerushalmi's observation that the rivalry between Judaism and Christianity also articulates itself as a rivalry between an older and a younger brother, as competition for the place of honor of the most-loved child.

Unexpected help comes, of all places, from the camp of the Christian theologians. In his fruitful speculations about the birth of the Christian religion out of the Jewish father complex, Freud could no longer name with any plausibility the *object* of the generational conflict—the desired Mother. He lost sight of her entirely in the clash of the male protagonists. One can supply this missing link. Its Christian name is Mary. And here I am referring not to Jesus' biological mother but to the Mary of the theologians. Common to all the "replacements" for the contested female object—be they the soul of the believers, the entirety of the community, or the reception of the true doctrine—is that they can be represented allegorically by the Mother of Christ and his brothers in faith. Thus the Oedipal scheme, which Freud employed as a universal key in his theory of religion, makes sense only if one spiritualizes it in turn. As a sexual schematic, it comes up empty. Paradoxically, it can be completed only if one moves *beyond the natural gender.*

13

Girard: Beyond Violence

René Girard, perhaps the most important contemporary theorist of religion, also developed his ideas through a critical engagement with Freud. Girard agrees with the founder of psychoanalysis on one point: the assumption that culture has violent origins. He sees human societies dominated by the cycle of violence. Violence triggers counterviolence, a vicious cycle that, as the old institution of the blood feud shows, is by its very nature never-ending. Girard believes that human beings have a tendency to behave *mimetically*, to imitate what they experience at the hands of others: they imitate the violence of others by in turn responding with violence. This reaction is similar to the triggering behavior; it creates responsive violence that is indistinguishable from the initiating violence and possesses as much or as little reason as the latter. Girard casts this in the mythological image of the hostile twins who fight each other from the same mirror-image motives.

Yet every religion has a ritual that is able to put an end—at least temporarily—to the endless and, in the final analysis, groundless cycle of violence: the *sacrifice*. In the act of sacrifice, social aggression is directed at a specific object chosen for this very purpose. This object must meet certain conditions; for example, it must be socially so marginal that its killing will not trigger the cycle of revenge once again. Originally, Girard believes, the victims were always humans; later they were often replaced by suitable substitutes. However, one must be very clear about the precise nature of this sacrificial substitution:

> The victim is not a substitute for some particularly endangered individual, nor is it offered up to some individual of particularly bloodthirsty temperament. Rather, it is a substitute for all the members of the community, offered up by the members themselves. The sacrifice serves to protect the entire community from *its own violence*; it prompts the entire community to choose victims outside itself. The elements of dissension scattered throughout the community are drawn to the person of the sacrificial victim and eliminated, at least temporarily, by its sacrifice.[1]

What effect, then, does the ritual of sacrifice have? It responds to the threatening dissolution of the social order by assigning all responsibility for the community's ills to the victim. The victim is turned into a *scapegoat*. Once the scapegoat has been eliminated, the social order has been cleansed of evil. All violence is directed against the victim, which has been declared the incarnation of evil. For the sacrificial mechanism to work, it is necessary for those involved to *misunderstand* its nature: first, by the fact that they project the evil—in reality an evil of their own society—onto the scapegoat as outsider; second, by the fact that they regard the violence carried out in the ritual of sacrifice as emanating not from humans themselves but from God. And therein, according to Girard, lies the origin of religion. "To think religiously," Girard maintains, "is to see violence as something superhuman, to be kept always at a distance and ultimately renounced."[2]

At first glance, the story of Jesus' crucifixion looks exactly like the religion-generating collective murder that Girard talks about. It contains the same elements: a violent lynch mob; a single persecuted person onto whom all guilt is displaced; Jesus in the role of the "scapegoat" or, to use Christian imagery, the sacrificial lamb. This act of collective purification allegedly takes place in accordance with God's will and plan, as a result of which not only the guilt but also the violence is externalized and transferred to an outside power.

This would mean that the Passion story is merely one of many similar sacrificial episodes that keep the cycle of violence in motion: victim—pacification—renewed growth of violence—another discharge in a sacrificial ritual. Girard, however, vehemently rejects this interpretation, revealing a basic tenor of Christian belief, especially in his later works.[3] To be sure, Christian theology certainly operated by means of the sacrificial model. But, according to Girard, this happened only because it did not understand the real message of the Gospels. The church fathers transformed the Christian message of redemption into the mere repetition of the mechanism of violence.

For Girard, there is a crucial difference between the mythical stories of sacrifice and the Gospels. The mythical accounts were composed from the perspective of the persecutors and enshrine their misunderstanding of the sacrificial act. They impose on the victims themselves the responsibility for their persecution, attribute all kinds of evil deeds to them, and in this way exculpate the crowd that carries out the sacrifice. These stories do exactly what the persecutors did by making the victim into a scapegoat. By contrast, Girard emphasizes the *antimythological* nature of the Gospels: they put an end to the unending self-reproduction of violence not by mystifying the sacrificial murder from the per-

spective of the persecutors (by blaming the victim, which is supposedly receiv-
ing its just punishment) but by unmasking the *victim's guiltlessness*.

The Gospels leave no doubt that Jesus went to his death innocent and that his
murderers are the guilty ones. In this way, they counteract the misunderstanding of the mechanism of sacrifice and elucidate its blindness, thereby rendering
it ineffective. Jesus takes the guilt upon himself without being guilty. Not even
his enemies can effectively declare him guilty, as the presentation of Jesus before
Pontius Pilate demonstrates. They can no longer charge a figure outside the collective with their own violence; rather, they are confronted with the fact that the
violence, the evil, they seek to expel from the world springs from themselves.

While the New Testament tells the same story as the myths of collective violence, it tells it in a different way. According to Girard, it *ends* the regime of violence. The God of Christianity—unlike the wrathful God of the Hebrew
Bible—is no longer a violent God demanding revenge and retribution. Rather,
he is a God who leads humanity out of the mythical cycle of constantly renewed
violence; a God of love for one's enemy, as his followers attest; a God who demands gentleness and forgiveness from his followers; and, finally, a God whose
worship no longer involves the conventional ritual of sacrifice still common in
the ancient world. In fact, early Christianity is not a religion of *inflicted* violence
(the cult of sacrifice) but of *suffered* violence, *martyrdom* in imitation of Christ's
Passion. Girard writes:

> Let us turn to the gospel themes that are on the surface most mythical in charac-
> ter, like the virgin birth of Jesus as it appears in Matthew and Luke. We notice at
> once that behind a superficial appearance of recounting fabulous events, the
> Gospels are always giving us a message exactly opposite the one conveyed by
> mythology: the message of a non-violent deity, who has nothing in common with
> the ephiphanies of the sacred.
>
> Everything that is born of the world and of the "flesh," as the prologue to
> John's Gospel puts it, is tainted by violence and ends up by reverting to violence.
> Every man is the brother of Cain, who was the first to bear the mark of this orig-
> inal violence.
>
> In innumerable episodes of mythical birth, the god copulates with a mortal
> woman in order to give birth to a hero. Stories of this kind always involve more
> than a hint of violence. Zeus bears down on Semele, the mother of Dionysus, like
> a beast of prey upon its victim, and in effect strikes her with lightning. The birth
> of the gods is always a kind of rape. . . .

To put its message across, no doubt the virgin birth of Jesus still resorts to the same "code" as do the monstrous births of mythology. But precisely because the codes are parallel, we should be able to understand the message and appreciate what is unique to it—what makes it radically different from the messages of mythology.

No relationship of violence exists between those who take part in the virgin birth: the Angel, the Virgin and the Almighty. . . . The complete absence of any sexual element has nothing to do with repression—an explanation thought up at the end of the nineteenth century and worthy of the degraded puritanism that produced it. The fact that sexuality is not part of the picture corresponds to the absence of the violent memesis with which myth acquaints us in the form of rape by the gods.[4]

In Praise of Virginity

Girard's theory—and the decidedly Christian coloration he gives it in its later elaborations—is certainly debatable. But it does have the advantage of at least getting closer to the *self*-conception of early Christianity and its high regard for virginity (derived from Mary's Immaculate Conception) than does Freud and his model of sexual repression/sublimation. Sexual abstinence was not a value in and of itself for the church fathers, who sought to digest theologically the legacy of the New Testament during the first few centuries of the common era. Nor did they isolate sexuality, as was later done, from all the other sins, passions, or merely necessary considerations of secular life.

Sexual desire does not even appear separately in the catalog of the eight Christian deadly sins; it shows up under the rubric *luxuria* (lust, dissipation). In this scheme, sexuality is not thought of as a separate, autonomous drive. Instead, it is inseparably linked to procreation, reproduction, and inclusion within the expansive system of biological dependencies. It is what links the body to the world. It is what keeps this world in motion—an evil, cruel, wicked world ruled by desire, violence, destruction, and death. Although the early Christian church theologians do not speak of the collective violence that Girard had in mind, they do see creaturely life as such as a cycle of violence.

Sexuality means procreation, procreation means birth, and birth means continually sending new human beings into this transitory world in the grip of death. Fertility, not pleasure, is the real problem. Some currents within Christianity take less offense at extramarital pleasure—as long as it has no consequences—than they do at the marital procreation of children and the continuation of the evil of the world.

Unlike the psychoanalytic doctrine of the instincts, in the ancient environment that gave birth to Christianity, procreation and death, birth and dying flow seamlessly into each other. They link up in an eternal dance from which there is no escape. For ancient people, historian Peter Brown reminds us, "sexual intercourse had always carried with it a tinge of sadness."[5] When they think of the female womb, it is always also associated with the grave. Procreation and death represent for them the two boundary posts of transitoriness.

One can turn this around and use it to draw some inferences about the goals of Christian asceticism. Against this backdrop, sexual abstinence is not merely a question of individual restraint or reserve. It is intended to put an end to the ceaseless re-creation/continuation of the misfortune of biological existence, the vicious cycle of worldly things. "Virginity is stronger than the rule of death," writes Gregory of Nyssa,[6] and goes on to elaborate:

After accompanying all the generations and going along with those who were always coming into life, death found in virginity a limit to its own activity which it was powerless to overcome. Just as at the time of Mary, the Mother of God, death who had been king from the time of Adam until then, when she was born, was shattered, being dashed against the fruit of virginity as if against a stone, so in every soul which through virginity rejects life in the flesh, the power of death is somehow shattered and destroyed, since it cannot apply its goad to them.[7]

It [virginity] does not bewail orphanhood, nor does it lament widowhood; it is always accompanied by an incorruptible Bridegroom; it always takes pride in the begetting of reverence; it continuously sees the house as truly its own, abounding in the fairest things, because the Master of the house is always present and at home, so that death effects, not a separation, but a union with what is longed for.[8]

One must recall the social reality during the first few centuries of Christianity to appreciate statements such as these. At the height of the Roman Empire in the second century, the average life expectancy was less than twenty-five years. Only four out of every hundred men—and even fewer women—lived beyond the age of fifty. Given these mortality rates, every woman had to bear five children just to keep the population constant. To fulfill this task, writes Brown, "the median age of Roman girls at marriage may have been as low as fourteen."[9]

Emperor Augustus enacted penalties for male bachelors who were avoiding their duty of keeping the birth rate equal to the mortality rate; a catalog of penalties remained in force until the Tolerance Edict of Milan in 313.

Death was a constant guest in the home. Women died in childbed, which is why serial marriages were common for men, as were considerable age differences between spouses. Most children died in early childhood. There is no question that unrestricted procreation offered the only means of maintaining a minimum degree of social stability. The ancient clan simply had to direct all its energies at ensuring its line of descent.

At the same time, there already existed in Palestine at the time of Jesus strange holy figures who dwelled in the desert or on the outskirts of settlements, and who from time to time appeared in villages and towns to preach the coming of the Kingdom of God, repentance, and sexual abstinence. Asia Minor experienced waves of millenarianism. The book of Acts and the letters of the apostles provide a glimpse of this: again and again, the Holy Spirit comes upon the faithful, throwing them into ecstasy, impelling them to speak in strange tongues and to dance, transporting them to far places, and bringing about miracles and wondrous conversions.

In the emerging Christian communities, young men left their parents and their homes, joined radical ascetic groups, and wandered the land as itinerant beggars and preachers. But an increasing number of girls also refused to enter into marriage; henceforth they lived chastely, either within the framework of the family or in small, mostly informal, groups that were not yet—as they would later be—under the authority of spiritual leaders. In addition, more and more female offspring were consigned by their parents to the virginal life. The third century saw a virtual surplus of virgins in the Christian communities—"virgins of God" as they called themselves.[10] Word of all this spread among the pagan neighbors and led to repeated assaults and attacks.

The fourth century saw the appearance of monastic communities in the Egyptian desert—the model for the later monasteries. In North Africa, the leaders of the church opposed the wandering lifestyle of pious outlaws and visionaries. Saint Augustine finally initiated a radical theological departure from the ascetic, sectarian origins of Christianity in order to satisfy the reproductive necessities of society, which he had to heed as the bishop of what was now the powerful institution of the church.

All these things were, one might say, consequences of the Holy Family. As we know, they would reach their high point only later, in the institution of priestly celibacy and the monastic movement of the Middle Ages. To put it in schematic form, on the one side one finds the social majority, which lives "in the flesh" and is solely concerned about physical continuation. On the other side is a growing minority consisting of believers who repudiate this society and intend to dedicate their future life to spiritual union with God: ascetics and ecstatics who swear oaths of abstinence, alienate themselves from civilized norms, and live exceedingly simple and hard lives; individuals who speak with glowing eyes of a love that has nothing in common with sexuality, who place the spirit above flesh and blood, and who free themselves in scandalous ways from caring for their closest family members; beggars, asocial elements, troublemakers, crazies, dissidents. Exposed to attacks and political repression, they even accept martyrdom for their religious convictions. Their martyrs, suffering excruciating deaths in a hail of rocks or in Roman prisons and arenas, are able to forgive their murderers, to answer violence not with hate but with the commandment to love one's enemies.

Against this backdrop, it seems plausible when Girard contrasts the liberating doctrine of reconciliation of the Gospels with the myths of social violence. It would seem that no path leads from the dissolution of the bonds of blood by Jesus, from the spiritual community of the apostles, from Jesus' repudiation of tradition and the laws of the Pharisees and the high priest, and from his doctrine of love and the acceptance of his Passion to the compulsions and violence of social normality; no path from *love* to *law*; no path from the Holy Family to power.

Nevertheless, one must ask oneself how Christianity was able to become the first official religion of a European state—the Roman Empire—a mere three centuries after its birth. How could it consolidate itself into a church that, for its part, became a persecuting organization? As far as the Holy Family is concerned, one must inquire not only about the status of women within the patriarchal system of this religion but also about the relationship between *family policy* and *political order*. One is thus faced with a classic problem—that of power.

14

THE QUESTION OF POWER

Weber: Early Christianity as a Charismatic Movement

Power is a question that sociology deals with. Max Weber, one of the great thinkers in this field, devised a typology of forms of authority within which Christianity assumed exemplary importance. He distinguished three types of "legitimate domination": the rational, "resting on the belief in the legality of enacted rules"; the traditional, "resting on an established belief in the sanctity of immemorial traditions"; and the charismatic, "resting on devotion to the exceptional sanctity, heroism or exemplary character of an individual person."[1]

Of these three forms of domination or legitimation, charismatic authority is the least stable. It cannot draw support from the sanctity of immemorial institutions, as is the case with traditional/patriarchal authority, nor does it possess a thoroughly organized, regulated, bureaucratic apparatus like the type of authority Weber labels rational. Charismatic authority lives by virtue of the exceptionality of the ruler himself, the suggestive power of his mission, his belief in himself, and, by extension, the faith that his followers place in him. It breaks with tradition and thwarts the regulated administrative processes that are legal or technical in nature.

When Weber comes to characterizing charismatic authority in detail, the figure of Jesus and his successors in the church provide him with a model. This applies not only to the reciprocal support of charismatic leadership and believing followers but also to the noneconomic nature of charisma, which lives "in, not off, this world" and rejects "as undignified all methodical rational acquisition, in fact, all rational economic conduct."[2] As a consequence of this stance, it also rejects property, marriage, and other institutional obligations:

> In order to live up to their mission the master as well as his disciples and immediate following must be free of the ordinary worldly attachments and duties of occupation and family life. Those who have a share (κλῆρος) in charisma must inevitably turn away from the world: witness the statute of the Jesuit order forbidding members to hold ecclesiastic offices; the prohibitions for members of

other orders to own property, or for the order itself, as in the original rule of Saint Francis; the celibacy of priests and knights of an order; the actual adherence to the rule of celibacy on the part of numerous holders of prophetic or artistic charisma.[3]

Weber characterizes charismatic authority as an *exceptional phenomenon*. Its noneconomic nature, its avoidance of traditional social routines and institutions condemn it to a short-lived existence. This agrees well with the basically explosive and revolutionary tenor of this type of authority, which Weber emphasized in a different passage when he says that charisma, "in its most potent forms, disrupts rational rule as well as tradition altogether and overturns all notions of sanctity. Instead of reverence for customs that are ancient and hence sacred, it enforces the inner subjection to the unprecedented and absolutely unique and therefore Divine. In this purely empirical and value-free sense, charisma is indeed the specifically creative revolutionary force of history."[4]

One sign of charisma's creative stance *outside everyday life* is the preference for a celibate way of life. According to Weber's typological perspective, sexual abstinence is not unique to Christianity. It lifts all charismatic figures out of the mass of the conventional, from the prophet to the military leader all the way to the artist. (The connection between—usually male—charisma and—usually male—celibacy virtually assumes the status of a universal cultural element. At any rate, it is still impossible to overlook even in the everyday mythology of our own time—for example, in the persona of the unmarried film star.)

In a sketch entitled "World-rejecting Early Christianity," Weber explicitly interpreted early Christianity as a charismatic mass movement.[5] Using this approach permits one to illuminate central elements of the Gospel account. Charismatic authority rests on a circle of recognition—the charismatic mission sweeps people up and creates groups of faithful followers; conversely, the faith of the followers inspires the charismatic individual in his mission—that can quickly collapse again. Jesus' despairing sense of loneliness at the Mount of Olives, his sentencing, his abandonment by God and humanity on the cross, and the flight and denial of the apostles represent such a collapse of charisma for Weber:

Charismatic authority is naturally unstable. The holder may lose his charisma, he may feel "forsaken by his God," as Jesus did on the cross . . . ; it may appear to his followers that "his powers have left him." Then his mission comes to an end, and hope expects and searches for a new bearer; his followers abandon him, for pure charisma does not recognize any legitimacy other than one which flows from personal strength proven time and again. The charismatic hero derives his authority not from an established order and enactments, as if it were an official competence, and not from custom or feudal fealty, as under patrimonialism. He gains and retains it solely by proving his powers in practice. He must work miracles, if he wants to be a prophet. He must perform heroic deeds, if he wants to be a warlord. Most of all, his divine mission must prove itself by *bringing well-being* to his faithful followers; if they do not fare well, he obviously is not the god-sent master.[6]

Weber's schematic of types of authority permits one to place at least one salient quality of the Christian Messiah and his family background into sociological contexts: the imputed renunciation of sexuality, which was espoused in the early Christian celibacy movements and eventually led to the formulation of priestly celibacy. A doctrine that teaches apostleship instead of familial commitment, love instead of law, and spirit instead of flesh embodies the typical prerequisites of charismatic leadership. The unprecedented movement of religious and social *dissidence* triggered by the idea of overcoming sex/gender can be read as the subsequent story of this original charisma.

Yet there is one difficulty that arises in all of this: Weber considers charismatic authority to be an unstable sociological formation. According to the logic of his arguments, Christ's rule should have come to an end with his pathetic execution as a criminal. To be sure, Weber's theory was subsequently modified—in part as a result of studies on twentieth-century millenarian sects, whose group cohesion was strengthened rather than weakened by the failure of prophesied events.[7] According to these analyses, disappointed expectations and the incomprehension of outsiders promote the conviction of belonging to a chosen circle of believers who will not be swayed by appearances.

In the end, nothing changes Weber's insight that charismatic movements are not sustainable over the long run. They are subject to early dissolution by their very organization. The personal effect of their leaders dissipate; as a result, the internal cohesion of the followers soon weakens again, and an inevitable process of the "transformation of charisma"[8] is set in motion: the young authority hardens and is transformed into either traditionalistic or bureaucratic forms; the heroes of the early days become the petty successors of the succeeding generations, who seek to consolidate the privileges they have acquired; finally, the ideal of poverty degenerates into defending the privileges that come with being functionaries. Although the charismatic period serves to replace the old authorities with younger ones, in the end it merely leads to a new version of the traditionalism of power: "Every charisma is on the road from a turbulently emotional life that knows no economic rationality to a slow death by suffocation under the weight of material interests: every hour of its existence brings it nearer to this end."[9]

Is it possible to summarize the story of Christianity as originally a dissident movement in distant Palestine, over the course of centuries collaborating ever more closely with the old authorities, becoming ossified in its doctrine and church bureaucracy, and losing more and more of its initially liberating, redeeming, violence-transcending features, a religion whose transcendental urge is forced back into the coordinates of earthly power? Are we dealing with what one might call an originally innocent *liberation movement* that was perverted *after the fact* and diverted from its goals? Would this, then, also make the history of the impact of the Holy Family into a story of usurpation, of ideological integration that gradually transformed a constellation outside everyday life into an *instrument of normalization* in the hands of state–church authority?

The counterthesis would maintain that the relationship between early Christian millenarianism and the later emergence of the church's power is not merely that of a misappropriation, a reinterpretation and misinterpretation, a *corruption* in the final analysis. Formulated in positive terms: there is a direct link between ascetic awakening and the reordering of society, between transcendence and power—which also means that there is a link between the Holy Family, on the one hand, and the body politic, on the other.

Fox: State, Individual, Kinship

The work of the British anthropologist Robin Fox is devoted to the history of kinship systems.[10] One essay of particular interest appeared in 1993 under the title "The Virgin and the Godfather."[11] Despite the title, Fox does not deal with the familial circumstances in Christianity, leaving it to the reader to draw the relevant connections. The starting point of his discussion is the play *Antigone* by Sophocles, which revolves around an unresolvable conflict between familial customs and the perceived needs of the state. Fox probes into the fundamental question of how well the state and the family get along. At first blush, the reader might think this a strange question, given the many state measures aimed at ensuring the viability of the family. The spontaneous answer to the question would no doubt be: the state "likes" the family because it recruits subjects or citizens, but it does not like the individual, with whom it is locked in constant conflict and whose expressions it must suppress because the individual has a tendency to be undisciplined and to seek freedom from the constraints imposed by the state. The "individual versus the state" was for decades the favorite antagonistic pairing of social psychologists.

Fox, however, considers this notion a popular misconception of the modern world, with its individualistic orientation. The long and conflict-ridden history of the emergence of the state essentially revolved around two goals: the centralization of power and the state monopoly of power. These goals were obstructed less by the right of individual liberty—which did not become historically important until fairly late—than by the social doctrines of the modern era, especially those of the eighteenth century. During its long emergence, the centralized state was locked in conflict with another opponent: the kinship group or clan.

Clans and extended families are communities of loyalty based on kinship ties. The loyalty that kinship groups demand of the individual at some point becomes irreconcilable with loyalty toward the state as a rational, impersonal, abstract space of political order. A state official must enforce regulations according to general and inflexible rules. This does not allow him to favor his own kinship group at the expense of others. The history of the state in Europe consists of a series of battles about the priority of the state over the particular concerns of kinship groups. That is true of the struggle over the monarchy and the quest for power on the part of feudal noble families. It also shaped, for example, the political quarrels of rival families in the northern Italian city-states, which had only their mutual hatred in common. The principle of the state as a theoretically impartial polity clashed with the principle of the dynasty. Long before recalcitrant individuals became a problem for the state *as individuals*, it had to contend with powerful and quarrelsome "houses," or lineage groups.

Anyone who wishes to erect a more or less functioning state administration in the modern sense must sever the connective tissue of kinship. He must exclude favoritism; eliminate the heritability of offices and privileges; replace the criterion of *birth*, as much as possible, with that of *merit*, with no regard for a person's social standing; and, finally, see to it that everything is governed by a system of independent, reciprocal controls. Even today, entire polities in the Third World can implode if they prove incapable of withstanding the pressure and counterpressure from tribal and clan rivalries. But even states that are formally functional have to struggle with the countervailing forces of kinship. From the perspective of the state, kinship's tangled web of loyalties is referred to derogatorily as nepotism. And the obligation of unbreachable loyalty toward one's own family—a loyalty that is seen as standing above the laws of the state and that no one can violate without making himself liable to the family's own justice—has an Italian name in everyday parlance: the Mafia.

In the face of *this* antagonism, the state and the individual are naturally allies; even more, the two give rise to each other:

> What was happening throughout Europe, in varying degrees, was the growth of a now triangular struggle. Volumes have been written on the Rise of Individualism, . . . and kinship has been seen as the enemy of the individual as much as of the state. But very little has been written on the struggle of kinship with both these institutions. For the state, despite its persecution of the individual from time to time, is much happier with individuals as units than with kinship groups for the simple reason that they are easier to control. If it wants to reduce kinship to the nuclear family (or less), then it wants to reduce its legal units to the individual voter of the eighteenth-century formula: the creature of the social contract . . . kinless, sexless, ageless, and devoid of anything but a sense of personal survival. . . . I think the real paradox here is that the state, at least in the bourgeois democracies, does not so much oppose individuals as promote them.[12]

This finding seems to run counter to the fact that today clear state support and preferences for families exist in all Western democracies. Why does the state offer constitutional guarantees to an institution that historically has always resisted the process of state formation? Fox continues:

> And there is a paradox here too. It is often put to me that the state in fact does a lot to promote the family rather than to destroy it. This is true. But it does not affect my argument, which is that the state abhors kinship—not the family. In promoting the self-sufficiency of the nuclear family unit, the state is in effect attacking the essence of kinship, which lies in the extension of consanguineal (or pseudo-consanguineal) ties beyond the family into strong and effective kinship groups. To put it another way, from the state's point of view, the highest level of kinship group it likes to see is the nuclear family, which is in fact the lowest level of operative kinship group possible that is compatible with effective reproduction and socialization of the young. To be exact, this could be done by the mother–child unit with the state as provider. But this is not the state's aim and in fact causes it a great deal of trouble—for example, the welfare system.[13]

This, according to Fox, is the reason why all states oppose polygamy; conversely, it is also the reason why they are not happy that the nuclear family is now dissolving and fathers are dropping out as providers and must be replaced by a welfare system. "The state," writes Fox, "prefers males to act as providers to the mother–child units and gets annoyed when this doesn't happen."[14] In the advanced industrial countries of the West, the dissolution of the bonds of kinship has thus reached a point where it would be disadvantageous for the state to go any further. As a result, the state tries to preserve the nuclear family by ideological means and through social benefits: "The paradox then is that in promoting the nuclear family, the state (or church) is paring kinship down to its lowest common denominator while appearing to support basic 'kinship values.'"[15]

The Holy Family and the Process of State Formation

Despite the allusion in the title of his essay, Fox says nothing about the Christian Holy Family. (On occasion, though, he at least discusses the organizational forms and political interests of the church by analogy to measures by the state.) Still, one gets the impression that his intent is also to lay bare the meaning, structure, and function of this religious figure. For is it not the case that what happens on the road from Jesus' biological Jewish family to the iconography of the Holy Family is nothing other than what Fox has described for the West as a whole: that the kinship group is reduced to the minimal familial entity? What does Mary's virginal conception symbolize if not the fact that the laws of reproduction of the kinship group have been suspended for *this* family, which was pointing the way to the future? When Jesus instructs, "Let the dead bury the dead," is he not declaring elementary, sacred kinship obligations null and void? (Precisely this is the conflict in Sophocles's drama *Antigone*, which prompted Fox's reflections.)

If one applies Fox's ideas to the Holy Family, one discovers remarkable parallels. His sweeping historical overview—which does, however, threaten to become a grand allegory—leads the British anthropologist to the argument that the state's need for control compels it to individualize its citizens to the greatest possible degree. However, the family has so far proved indispensable when it comes to sexual and social reproduction. Consequently, the state cuts down kinship groups through repressive measures, to the point where only the smallest unit—the nuclear family—remains, which it then seeks to protect against any further erosion. Nuclear family means: mother–child unit plus a male provider. The male provider has a teetering position. He is almost ready to drop out of the picture, but the state will not let him go because it cannot and does not want to replace him altogether. What Fox has in mind is the contemporary situation of the nuclear family in Western societies. Yet in structural terms, one could likewise be thinking about the two-thousand-year-old Holy Family. After all, it, too, consists of a mother–child dyad and a husband who is only partially fulfilling his role. In this case the husband is sharing his position with *God*. In the modern welfare state, the role of the father has been "split" in a different, though analogous, way between the man and the *state*. In the most modern nuclear family, God's place in the Holy Family is assumed by the state:

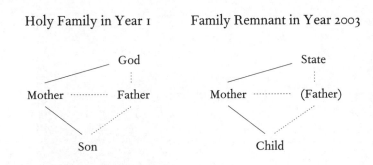

Holy Family in Year 1   Family Remnant in Year 2003

If these speculations are correct, it means that the peculiar construction of the Holy Family relates to the erection of secular power not only in a negative way—negative in the sense that one is, after all, dealing with a family without sexual procreation and with no ties to the kinship structure that undergirds the social body; in other words, a family with negative characteristics. Taking this family as a model of how to live would mean deviating from the prevailing social customs. However, it is now apparent that this same potential for dissidence can be put at the service of a comprehensive and all-pervading polity. The anomalies of the Holy Family take on a different importance if one examines them against the backdrop of the protracted struggle between the regulatory mechanisms of the state and those of the kinship group. If, in retrospect, it appears that inherent in the state is the goal of reducing kinship groups to the level of the nuclear family, the state finds support in its efforts to achieve that goal from religion through the normative effect that emanates from the image of the Holy Family.

The forces working toward a centralization of power can be successful only if they gain control over the reproductive mechanisms of kinship. And the primary locus of this conflict lies in the institution of marriage. For millennia, marriage not only has been indispensable to the biological propagation of the human race, but also has represented the center, the nodal point, so to speak, of the kinship group. Expressed in the language of early Christianity, marriage is the place of the flesh not only because sexual acts take place in the marital bed but also because the chain of bodies, the bloodline, is carried on through marriage. Through marriage, the individual body merges with the social body—assuming that by social body one always means the body of the kinship group.

Cover of *Der Spiegel*, November 17, 1997.

The state, which seeks to prevail as an overarching political formation against the octopus-like organism of the kinship group, must exert influence on marriage. It must shift the biological-social form of reproduction toward a different, more abstract method of reproduction. It must ensure the cohesion of society on a *spiritual* level and, to that end, break through the overbearing nature of the kinship principle. To put it differently, the stuff of which state power is made is less the flesh than the spirit. In contradistinction to the intimate sphere of the kinship system, the state establishes itself as a level of transcendence; and it must build into social reproduction a "switch" that directs the orientation of that reproduction at least partially toward this transcendence.

The Holy Family evidently provides the ideal model to achieve that goal. It abolishes the primacy of biological reproduction. In its dual conditioning, it contains a *switching mechanism between inner-worldly–familial and transcendental linkage*—that is, between the father as the figure of authority empowered by kinship and that other, more distant, higher father authority. One can worship this latter father figure or allow it to be embodied in an institution such as the state, an institution that, not coincidentally, is based on metaphors of fatherhood.

On the one hand, the state must preserve marriage as the foundation of social reproduction because it is biologically dependent on it. Without citizens, there is no state—a simple fact that the population policy of the ancient Roman emperors already took into account, especially by discouraging celibacy and providing legal sanctions against it. On the other hand, the state must strip marriage of its purely biological aspect in order to weaken its role as the hinge of the reproductive system of the kinship group. There are several possible ways for the state to exert what is fundamentally a dual influence on the institution of marriage: first, by making marriage and reproduction a *moral* issue; second, by intervening in the *legal* form of the marriage act, which for a long time was the exclusive preserve of the kinship group; and, third, by seeking to exert influence on the pattern according to which goods are distributed and on charitable assistance in order to undermine the *material* basis for the segmentation of the population into kinship groups.

PART III consequences

15

CHRISTIANITY: ON THE ROAD TO BECOMING THE RELIGION OF THE EMPIRE

The rise of Christianity was the result of numerous factors. The young religion benefited from the peace that Augustus had imposed on the Roman world and from the Roman Empire's permissiveness in matters of religion. It was the beneficiary of the crisis within Judaism following the destruction of the Temple in Jerusalem. In seeking to expand, it was able to draw on the extensive infrastructure of Hellenistic Diaspora Judaism, with which it initially shared both sacred texts and methods of interpretation.[1] Yet the decisive reason behind Christianity's success most likely rests on neither favorable external circumstances nor its intense missionary activity but on its *social character*, its "sense of community."[2] The strict demands that Christianity, as a closed and exclusive community of faith, imposed on its adherents created a group identity that was enormously attractive to members of very diverse social milieus—from the have-nots of the early years to the urban elites of the fourth century.

In the early period, the intolerance of the early Christians, which was unusual in the ancient world, made them the target of cruel persecution. Later, however, in the era of Constantine, the exclusive claim of Christian monotheism offered itself as an instrument of religious policy that could be used to strengthen the central power of the emperor. Peter Brown has described the Roman Empire as a "commonwealth of cities"—wealthy provincial metropolises that controlled the hinterland. The decentralized structure of power corresponded to the diversity and relative autonomy of local cultic traditions.[3] These cults were put under pressure by a growing Christianity, which essentially became the advocate of the state's push toward centralization. According to Brown,

> Constantine's condemnation of sacrifice and the closing and spoliation of many temples further undermined the cultural autonomy of the cities. The local notables found themselves denied the right to resort to precisely those religious ceremonials that had once enabled each city to give public expression to its own sense of identity. It was no longer considered advisable to sacrifice, to visit temples, or to celebrate one's city as the dwelling-place of particular gods bound to the civic community by particular, local rites. Instead, the Christian court offered a new,

empire-wide patriotism. This was centered on the person and mission of a God-given, universal ruler, whose vast and profoundly abstract care for the empire as a whole made the older loyalties to individual cities, that had been wholeheartedly expressed in the old, polytheistic system, seem parochial and trivial."[4]

The strengthening of the imperial administration became especially palpable in the area of tax policy. Whereas it had once been the task of local notables to secure the cohesion of the *demos* with charitable acts and festivals, the growing tax burden in the late empire eroded the significance of local rituals of magnanimity, which were gradually replaced by a fiscal cycle of obligatory payments and return distributions. In addition, the influx of poor country folk reinforced the trend toward the disintegration of the cooperative structure in the cities. The number of poor, who did not enjoy citizens' rights and were therefore not entitled to food doles from the wealthy class of notables, seems to have increased dramatically in the fourth century.[5]

The crisis in the traditional patronage system accorded the Christian bishops a pivotal role in the area of charitable activities. Up to a certain point, bishops operated outside the traditional division of urban society. To the graded system of privileges of the polis they held up a universalist idea. According to Brown,

> The poor stood for the width of the bishop's range of concerns. On the social map of the city, they marked the outermost boundary of the "universal way" associated with the Christian church. . . . A mystical link was held to bind the bishop to the poor of his city. This link passed through every rank of society, "bracketing," as it were, the whole urban community from the very top to the very bottom, as an all-embracing "people of God." Rich man and beggar alike went down into the baptismal pool and crowded around the altar to receive the Eucharist. Even if it were still a minority, in the face of polytheists and Jews, a church that was seen to reach out to the distant fringe of society, as dramatically represented by the poor, had already established a prospective moral right to stand for the community as a whole.[6]

In this way, the Christian idea that all humans are sons of God and the image of the Messiah who stepped down into the misery of the world had exceedingly practical consequences for social policy. The Christian community was not divided up in terms of class membership and thus not according to the principle of descent; instead, it formed a mystical body in which—at least from a theological perspective—all members were equal. That is also why a tendency toward a *communalization of wealth* was inherent in the community. The church established itself as a mechanism of redistribution: "It was essential that the increased wealth of the Christian church, made up as it was of innumerable private benefactions, should be presented as the wealth of the Christian community as a whole. And this wealth could not be more effectively disjoined from its family-oriented connotations than when distributed to the nonpersons who huddled on the edge of the community."[7]

This gave rise to a conception of *public wealth* beyond the segmented differentiation of ancient society, one that pointed in a completely new direction. Brown continues:

> However it might show itself in practice, the bishop's claim to act as "lover of the poor" had edged to the fore a new imaginative model of society. It was a model that ignored the ancient distinctions between citizen and noncitizen and between city and countryside. It pointedly brushed aside the ceremonious dialogue of the civic notables with the urban population, gathered as the traditional *démos* in theaters and hippodromes. The care of the poor emphasized, instead, a very different, more basic bond of solidarity. The poor were nourished not because they were the fellow citizens of a specific city, but because they shared with great men the common bond of human flesh.[8]

With the end of antiquity there appeared a vision of *humanitas* that went beyond distinctions of birth. The "mystical bond" that bound together the bishop as the vicar of God and his community transcended the boundary between rich and poor, the *demos* and the *plebs*, indeed, between the free and the unfree, and put all Christians into a direct relationship to God. This *equalization* of the religious relationships between humans and the transcendence of God corresponded to a movement toward a standardization of the dependencies within the state. There was a large-scale shift in the legitimate exercise of power from small, locally circumscribed units—from the paterfamilias, who in the year 374 was deprived of his nominal power of life and death over family members,[9] up to the provincial elites—to the imperial apparatus of administrators, judges, and tax collectors. Before the emperor, "as before God, all subjects were poor."[10]

This is not to say that once Christianity had been declared the sole religion in 380, secular centralization would have been able to keep up with the now established state religion focused on a single, divine–human ruler. Conversely, Christian piety, for its part, was sucked into the counterforce of a quasi-polytheistic reelaboration—caused by the growing number of saints and the feasts and cults linked with them, which often carried on pagan traditions. Here the province proved its strength of persistence against the centrism of the imperial power. Still, even when it had merged with the empire, Christianity preserved its egalitarian character, which in the long run promoted the dissolution of small-scale dependency relationships in favor of large forms of rulership.

To put it more precisely, Christianity infused the social sphere with a *dual conditioning* that was self-contradictory and had to be continually renegotiated. On the one hand, the steplike social structure of largely impermeable, self-contained kinship groups and estates continued despite all historical changes. On the other hand, however, the believers before God and the subjects before the emperor were "essentially" equal. This essentiality "works"; that is, it entails a potent rhetoric about poverty—poverty in both the material and the symbolic sense, as the abolition of the traditional social markings, as a way of devaluing the structure of more or less subtle social distinctions.

Christians belong with only one part of their existence to the kinship network, which assigns everyone a social place. With the other part, they are members of the community, or, in Christian parlance, children of the virginal church. As such, they originate not from a line of descent that can be traced back in time but from the Virgin's nuptial bond with the sole and almighty God. While the bodily genealogy and corporeal gender of Christians binds them to an earthly existence, which is assigned to them by fate, their spiritual descent abolishes this bond and sets them free. Because they are brothers and sisters of Christ and, as such, spring in some mystical way from the Holy Family itself, their social assignation is not absolute. The mystical society of the believers creates a *displaced* system of coordinates with respect to the visible social world. It makes the order of the flesh appear contingent—that is, fluid and open to question—and places above it an overarching order of a more general kind, one derived from the Holy Ghost, from God's steady and omnipresent love.

16

THE CHURCH'S MARRIAGE POLICY IN THE MIDDLE AGES

Goody: The Struggle Against the Kinship System

From Sigmund Freud to Claude Lévi-Strauss, the grand cultural theories of the twentieth century operated with a universal constant: the incest taboo. In a manner of speaking, Freud went "against the grain" of this taboo by inferring from the power of the prohibition the power of an underlying, unconscious wish—with the consequence that in the final analysis incest disappears within the Oedipal desire. Lévi-Strauss, conversely, offered structural reasons why incest is usually threatened with sanctions: it prevents the necessary social intertwinement of kinship groups, the reciprocal exchange of women and goods.[1]

Jack Goody, in his book *The Development of the Family and Marriage in Europe*, paints a different picture. According to Goody, endogamous marriage customs are widespread outside the Christian cultural sphere: "Today close marriages continue to distinguish the Asiatic and African shores of the Mediterranean, running from the Bosphorus to the Maghreb, from the European one running from Turkey to Spain."[2] The same appears to have been true for Greece, the Roman Empire, and western Europe prior to their Christianization. Marriage between cousins, half-siblings, and in-laws to the widow of one's father or brother was not only tolerated but openly encouraged. Endogamy was considered a legitimate practice for the purpose of keeping together the property of the kinship group—which did not rule out the possibility of "out-marriage to establish or maintain a political alliance."[3]

Only Christianity opposed these customs. It substantially expanded the biblical marriage prohibitions laid down in the book of Leviticus. Not only did this lead to continual uncertainties and problems of justification, both theological and moral,[4] but it called forth resistance on the part of those affected by it. Yet Christianity did not waver in its restrictive marriage policy. During the Middle Ages, the church was able, for a time, to extend the incest taboo to kinship in the seventh degree—which, in purely mathematical terms, meant that for each marriage candidate thousands of potential partners were off-limits;[5] in practical terms, it meant that in order to get married one had to leave one's village or town or violate church law. The church, however, had the power to offer dispensation from the prohibitions—an important means of exerting influence on the marriage policy of a specific kinship group and, not coincidentally, a considerable source of revenue.

In essence, therefore, marriage practice oscillates between two contradictory goals. In terms of their social dynamic, marriages are subjected to a strong tendency toward endogamy—as far as membership in a class, in a group with shared traditions, and especially in the life-shaping kinship groups is concerned. According to Robert Fossier, this tendency manifests itself in an imperative of *purity*, the defense against the "entry into the group of alien and potentially impure blood . . . hence all sexual unions must be consanguineous. On the other hand, such unions could not occur between close relatives—members of the same immediate family or first cousins—because that would violate the incest taboo."[6]

This second aspect is the one that the church adopted. Yet its measures show that the demarcation of the incest threshold is not given by nature but is historically changeable. The question as to whether this demarcation should be applied in a restrained manner or very broadly is decided less by theological than by sociopolitical notions. Moreover, concrete power interests are also always part of the equation. If the church in the Middle Ages expanded the incest prohibition to the limit of what was practicable, it did so, according to Fossier, "perhaps also to forbid the narrow endogamic marriages which contributed to the power of its rival, the warrior aristocracy. Only the lowering of the incest threshold to the fourth degree of kinship in 1215 once again 'licensed' the endogamy to which the nobility was still strongly attached."[7]

Still, it is hardly possible to attribute such a long-term undertaking as the church's policy of marriage prohibitions merely to discrete historical constellations. The purpose of these prohibitions becomes completely clear only when one considers the full extent of the economic significance of marriage alliances. The system of degrees of kinship played an organizing role not only with respect to the incest problem but also in inheritance law. Far-reaching marriage prohibitions made the transfer of property within kinship groups impossible. "In effect," writes Goody, "one could no longer marry anyone from whom one could have formerly inherited, i.e., kinsfolk."[8] Marriage law was thus aimed not only at exerting moral influence but also—and most particularly—at weakening the kinship group materially. It was an instrument of the church's policy against kinship.

Goody lists a whole series of similar rules that concern the institution of marriage as the material basis of reproduction in a segmented society—that is to say, one based on kinship differentiations. The primary aim behind these measures was the strengthening of monogamy. For example, in opposition to the old customs in most countries subject to Christian missionary efforts, the church made divorce vastly more difficult; in this case, at least, it could invoke the words of Christ.[9] The same purpose was behind the devaluation of concubinage—an institution very much accepted in ancient Israel and in the Roman Empire "to provide an heir when the full, legitimate wife, married with dowry, had failed to produce one"[10]—and the exclusion of illegitimate children from succession: "And so, under Christianity, the concubine became the mistress and her children bastards."[11]

Even more far-reaching were the consequences resulting from the abolition of adoption. While under Roman law every paternity, even the natural one, had to be confirmed by a formal act of adoption, Christianity limited paternity to consanguineous offspring;[12] it changed the code of paternity from *legal* to *natural* relationships. Here, too, the effect is clear: "A man could not adopt a son and heir when he had none of his own."[13]

The church everywhere resisted the inheritance interests of the kinship group. "Marriage between kin," writes Goody, "serves to reinforce 'family' ties. These particular forms also prevent female heiresses from removing property from the 'family,' and thus combat the problem of the absence of sons." In a society that had to reckon with infertility and in which high child mortality was the norm, this problem assumed existential importance; society therefore had to devise ways and means of ensuring the continuation of the line and the passing of the inheritance: "These forms of close marriage would take care of the absence of sons; other strategies, adoption, polygyny, divorce and remarriage can be used to provide a solution to childlessness. But prohibit close marriage, discourage adoption, condemn polygyny, concubinage, divorce and remarriage, and 40 per cent of families will be left with no immediate male heirs."[14]

The church benefited, to a considerable degree, from property that could not be passed on within the family but flowed to the church in the form of gifts and testamentary bequests, the legal basis for which was created during this same period. Goody sees a clear "connection between the Church's modification of the accepted strategies of heirship and its wish to encourage bequests from the faithful"[15]— encouragement that appealed to Christians' concern for the salvation of their souls and not infrequently involved coercive pressure. If "one of the most profound changes that accompanied the introduction of Christianity was the enormous shift of property from private ownership to the hands of the Church," if in the early

Middle Ages the church had already acquired immense landholdings and material wealth, then the political suppression of the kinship group through restrictions on marriage and inheritance law played a crucial role in all this.[16]

However, one need not view this redistribution of wealth in favor of the church in a conspiratorial fashion as a pure strategy of enrichment. As Goody has noted, "The accumulation of property by priests and monks was not simply a way of lining their own pockets. For the Church needed revenue not only to support the clergy and maintain the buildings but to provide charity for the poor."[17] The early Christian period was already characterized by a highly developed system of relief for the poor; in addition to charitable work, monasteries also took on economic and educational tasks in the Middle Ages. In other words, the shift of power from the kinship group to the church promoted a new relationship to property and care for the needy; in the final analysis, in so doing it also promoted a new model of *community*.

The restructuring of the old European kinship system, which extended over centuries and was critically influenced by the church's measures to control marital reproduction, went hand in hand with a rebuilding of the community as a whole.[18] Functions were withdrawn from the kinship groups and transferred to the *ecclesia* as the communality of all Christians. The accumulation of property by the church increased *public* property—at least in theory.

In pursuing these goals, the church de facto entered into an alliance with the forces that were working on a long-term basis toward state centralization, on the one hand, and toward the *individualization* of familial structures, on the other. Caught between this twofold movement, the large kinship group was crushed. The target formation of church policy is the nuclear family, which, according to Goody, entailed "eroding the rights of collaterals and of wider kin groups."[19] As Goody has reformulated the program of the church: "If wealth was to be passed on between kin, then it should be kept within the restricted elementary family."[20] Moreover, by coming out in favor of consensual marriages, canon law was placing itself in clear opposition to traditional kinship rights, in which a marriage arrangement was a matter to be decided by families, not individuals. Medieval church law favored the personal choice of a partner over parental authority—an emancipatory trait that the Reformation would nevertheless largely revoke.[21]

At the end, writes Goody, stands the ideal of a "child-oriented" family, a "family which was bound by affective ties and created by mutual consent."[22] In other words, a conjugal nuclear family that conceived of itself as an autonomous unit and removed itself from the web of kinship ties. The church

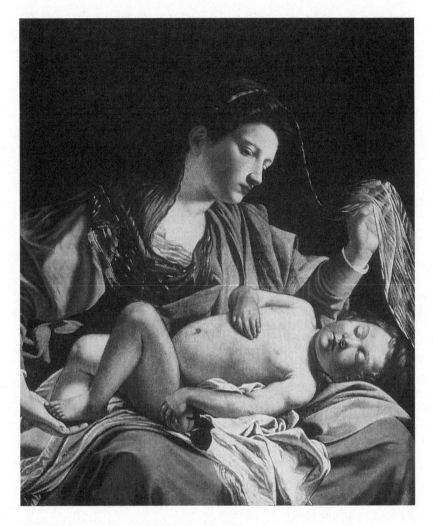

Orazio Gentileschi, *Mary with Child*, before 1610. Florence.

teachers did not have to search long to find a source of imagery to visualize this ideal: it was intrinsic to the Christian religion from the outset in the figure of the Holy Family. Reflecting on all the pictures of the loving Madonna and Child, Goody concludes: "Such paintings do not provide much by way of evidence about the nature of family life, except to remind us that positive sentiments of attachment between mother and child were not an invention of modern man, that Christ was suckled at the breast of a Virgin mother and that the Child was the most important member of the Holy Family, indeed its *raison d'être*. There could hardly be a more child-oriented model than the journey and adoration of the Magi, with its annual re-enactment at Christmas."[23]

The Development of Priestly Celibacy

Under the influence of the strengthening monastic movement, the demand to impose sexual abstinence on ecclesiastical officers spread in the fourth century. A papal decree in 385 C.E. established priestly celibacy as an absolute rule.[24] Yet this was not merely a measure "from above"; among the members of the church themselves there was a desire to see that the sacred cultic act of the Eucharist be performed by sexually unsullied priests. According to August Franzen, "The Eucharistic meal, as a community of love and Christ's sacrifice, suggested the notion that the leader himself in his state of celibacy give expression to the symbolic representation of Christ, his priesthood, and his nuptial love for the church." If he wished to exercise his office with dignity, the priest should be filled only by the Holy Spirit and enter into "a nuptial relationship to the divine logos."[25]

Christianity appropriated the ritual and temporary commandments of celibacy, which were already found in the Mosaic religion as well as in most pagan cults, and expanded them into a maxim of lifelong abstinence. The development of the dogma of Mary's *eternal* virginity has, in a sense, its male counterpart in this priestly celibacy. In 531 C.E., Emperor Justinian decreed the following: "We demand that no one may be elected bishop who is not also in other respects honorable and tested. He should neither live with a woman nor be the father of children; instead, he should be committed with all faith not to a woman but to the most holy church."[26]

In the early years, the leaders of the Christian communities were married men; their qualification for the apostolic office was evident from the orderly governance of their households.[27] This tradition clashed with the growing importance of the demand for celibacy. One possible compromise was the model of the chaste marriage. If priests could not yet be compelled to separate from their wives and families, they were put under double pressure by the ecclesiastical leadership and the laity—which was concerned about the purity of the sacred observances at mass—to observe chastity *in* marriage. Moreover, chaste marriage offered itself as an option not only to the large number of clerics who had married prior to the introduction of obligatory priestly celibacy. In late antiquity and the early Middle Ages, one frequently finds that pious spouses maintained their conjugal relationship but refrained from sexual intercourse. They chose a monastic community in miniature, so to speak, long before the full institutional elaboration of monasticism.

Anyone who chose lifelong abstinence within a marriage could claim to be following directly in the footsteps of the holy parents. In the case of a man, he was leading a "Joseph's marriage," as the popular expression went, and while he deviated from the secular norms by doing so, he was encouraged by the church fathers, especially Saint Augustine, who maintained that such a life was the highest perfection attainable on earth.[28] Still, despite the esteem in which the chaste marriage was held, it remained merely a transitional phenomenon. As the church began to move away from the charismatic chastity movements of the early years, from the life of the radically ascetic desert fathers in Egypt and North Africa, from the still largely unformed communities of men and women living in chastity—and as it began to assume more and more state tasks, which meant that its prescriptions became relevant beyond a small circle of the chosen for the entire population—it became increasingly problematic for the church to elevate the unmarried state and asceticism to universally valid ideals of conduct.

As far as marriage was concerned, Christian believers found themselves in a dilemma. On the one hand, Jesus pointed the way for them in a saying recorded in Matthew: "For while some are incapable of marriage because they were born so, or were made so by men, there are others who have themselves renounced marriage for the sake of the kingdom of Heaven. Let those accept it who can!" (19:12). On the other hand, there was the commandment in Genesis to "be fruitful and multiply," the desire for offspring and heirs, and the sexual desire of all those human beings who are not meant for a holy way of life.

The model of the chaste marriage was the compromise formula in a period when the clergy and the laity had not become clearly differentiated. It was only after centuries of resistance that priestly celibacy finally prevailed. In 1123, the First Lateran Council annulled all priestly marriages. Yet the increasingly hard line when it came to the clergy was only one side of the coin. For at the same time, a chaste way of life became more and more a *privilege* reserved for the clerical estate. One not insignificant reason for this was the fact that the high esteem that conjugal chastity enjoyed gave women who had been married against their will and inclination an opportunity to evade their duty of producing offspring. The religious ideal of chastity not merely was imposed on women, but could be used by them as an instrument to free themselves from the otherwise inescapable power of sexual availability wielded by men.[29]

In other words, the church was working toward not only making priestly celibacy obligatory, but also creating a normative "sexualization" of marriage. It condemned deviation from the norm *by both parties*—to the same degree in which the boundary between the laity, on the one side, and the clerical and monastic existence, on the other, solidified. "If the clerics were to claim that the spiritual was superior to the temporal," writes Georges Duby, "if they were to preserve the hierarchy that subordinated the laity to the clergy, they had to establish a sexual distinction between men, with some of them consigned to perpetual chastity."[30] While one group of men maintained the link between humanity and God, the other group was left to performing the lower acts of the flesh.

Priestly celibacy was a welcome device for medieval noble houses to exclude younger sons from the succession—a step that took on immense importance in the social transformation to feudalism and primogeniture. As part of its sweeping reforms in the eleventh and twelfth centuries, the church used priestly celibacy as a tool in its fight "against the preponderance of familial and proprietary, of dynastic and political interests," writes Goody, and to "establish the priesthood as a hierarchical autocracy. To this end, the priest had to be a man set apart, superior to human frailties."[31]

The institution of priestly celibacy—which became a formal obligation for clergy at all levels of the hierarchy, from the simple country priest to the pope, that is, for all officials of the huge Pan-European enterprise that was the church—was thus a place where a number of powerful political interests intersected. Priestly celibacy constrained the profuse elaborations of the kinship body even as it remained threatened by that body's efforts at recuperating lost ground. "By instituting celibacy," Robin Fox has noted about this development, "the Church outlawed kinship from its own ranks (theoretically) and promoted a system of meritocracy, even if the term *nepotism* had to be invented later to cover the reproductive proclivities of various ecclesiastical dignitaries: kinship fights back."[32]

The obligation of celibacy is the basis for an administrative apparatus that promotes (clerical) merit, not membership in a kinship group—a career system that, in some of its traits, adumbrates the civil-service system of modern times. Time and again, secular rulers took advantage of the qualities of incorruptibility and efficiency that were part of the Catholic Church's celibate conception of office.[33] In this way, sexual abstinence paved the way for the modern bureaucracy.

Duby: Marriage as Sacrament

Yet the attention of the doctors of the church was not focused solely on priestly celibacy. The eleventh and twelfth centuries, in particular, witnessed strenuous efforts at establishing, alongside the theology of asceticism, a theology of marriage that was pleasing to God, efforts that culminated in the elevation of marriage to a sacrament.

This sacramental elevation was supposed to resolve the dilemma inherent in the church's teachings on marriage. Despite its opposition to all matters of the flesh, the church had to take an interest in establishing its influence over marriage as the nodal point of social reproduction. That was possible only by way of Christianizing marriage. In spite of its impure and sullied nature, marriage thus had to be declared a Christian act of grace, and the conjugal ceremony was made into a solemn as well as an obligatory ecclesiastical affair—a development that brought with it a flood of regulations and constraints.

Georges Duby has described the precarious character of this operation:

> As the only one of the seven sacraments not instituted but only "restored" by Christ, marriage existed already in Paradise before the Fall. But the first sin plunged it into a state of corruption, and whatever effort was made to purify and elevate it, a trace still remained to remind us of its descent. Perhaps to make it fall again. Placed at the intersection of the spiritual and the physical, it was the sacrament which most manifestly symbolized the mystery of the incarnation; it was trembling on the brink, in the middle ground, dangerous. But the main thing is that by the middle of the twelfth century marriage had come to be sacralized without being disincarnated. [34]

Carnality, however, was encircled with rigorous conditions. The act of conjugal union was to take place without passion, if possible without pleasure; countless directives limited the time during which it was permissible; ritual commandments of purity—most of which were Christianity's Hebrew Bible legacy, that is, its Jewish legacy—placed a ring of taboos around the woman's menstruation, around pregnancy and birth, around the high church holidays, and around the first three connubial nights, the so-called Tobias nights, which were reserved for joint prayer.

Although the church was not able to and did not wish to put a stop to sexual reproduction, it could inject into it a discordant note, a note of guilt—and then turn around and offer its spiritual help in assuaging that guilt. Many of these acts of help were connected with the dogmatic history and iconography of the Holy Family. Duby speaks of the "notable attempt to spiritualize marriage. Its various aspects are well known, from the development of the Marian cult which led to the Virgin mother becoming the symbol of the Church, that is to say the Bride; to the development of the nuptial theme in mystical literature; and to the relentless examination of texts and their glosses, in order to establish marriage as one of the seven sacraments."[35]

Thus it was not only the celibate lifestyle that linked itself to the model of Jesus and his chaste parents. Normal sexual reproduction also became subject to regulation on the basis of the model provided by the Holy Family. The rise of the Marian cult is connected to *both* the solidification of priestly celibacy *and* the sacramentalization of marriage. Duby writes that "Mary offered an image of a woman who was a partner in a true marriage yet who gave birth to a son without being touched by evil. She was the model of the good wife."[36] A thirteenth-century Franciscan sermon prepared young girls for their future calling as wives and mothers by urging them to place themselves entirely in Christ's hands, "under whom thou shalt, in thy maidenhood, bring forth sons and daughters of spiritual teamings."[37] In late medieval wedding ceremonies, the priest blessed the nuptial bed by recalling the angel's visitation to Mary. If the marriage produced no children, the conjugal chamber was decorated with votive tablets depicting the Annunciation.[38]

Here the virginal relationship between the holy parents and the marriage of normal mortals is no longer antithetical and irreconcilable. Rather, Mary and Joseph now realized the sacrament of marriage in its highest perfection and called on their human counterparts to follow their example in natural parenthood. This is a *paradox* with a pedagogical impulse, which accorded the priests influence over the most intimate area of the lives of the faithful through instruction and confession. By means of its spiritual measures, the church had access to the wild and unrestrained sphere of sexual reproduction to a degree that would never have been possible for a controlling apparatus that merely applied itself externally.

Once sexuality and religious salvation are barely reconcilable, it is possible for the church, as the custodian of this salvation, to penetrate ever more deeply into the mental state and the conduct of the faithful tormented by a fear of guilt. It can leave the business of reproduction to the never completely missionized laity, subordinating it to a privileged caste of celibates who ensure that the transcendental connection of social reproduction is maintained. Let the people be fruitful and multiply—yet they still fear the fires of purgatory because of their sins of the flesh; they pray to the Virgin Mary and plead for her intercession before God. From their lower carnality, the people must constantly look up to the higher sphere of the generative, power-instituting spirit.

Duby recounts the case of the comtesse du Perche, who sought advice from an abbot on the duties of a married woman:

> The abbot endeavoured to enlighten her troubled spirit. The soul and the body, he said, reside in the human being. God is the owner of both. In accordance with the law of marriage which he himself had established, he granted to the husband (in the same way as a feudal tenure was granted, that is to say, by handing over the use of the property while retaining ultimate ownership) the right which he held over the body of the wife. Only the soul was not part of the feudal tenure: "God does not allow the soul to pass into the possession of another."

Duby comments:

> The countess should not forget this: in reality, she had two husbands whom she must serve fairly—one who was invested with the right to use her body, and the other who was the absolute master of her soul. . . . Dissociation, splitting themselves in two—that was their fate: on the one hand (that side which was earthly, carnal and inferior) there was passive obedience; on the other, there was a leap to the heights, to passion—in short, love. Thus the self was divided in two in marriage, but only for the female partner.[39]

A woman who submits to this economy resigns herself to accepting what is imposed on her as her marital duty. But she makes sure that her soul remains pure and unsullied by the intercourse of the body. She can thus become a mother and yet remain immaculate in a deeper sense. Sacramental marriage becomes a ménage à trois, a triangle of the spouses and God. And not only with God, for he allows himself to be represented by the priest, who in turn maintains an intimate relationship of trust with the woman as counselor and confessor. Consequently, while the legal husband is left with the bodily possession of his wife, he finds no pleasure in it. The wife's striving for the Marian ideal condemns him to an absurd, inverted existence as another Joseph. Even in the constellation

"Knight, Lady, Priest" that Duby has examined, the triangular pattern of the Holy Family reappears:

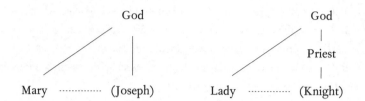

Duby concludes: "Is it far-fetched to imagine that husbands were sometimes exasperated at feeling that between themselves and their wives there was the presence not of the heavenly husband, but of the priest? How many men—such as the one whom Guibert of Nogent wanted to convince his readers was mad—went about shouting, referring to their wives who were stubbornly impassive: 'The priests have planted a cross in this woman's loins'?"[40]

17

THE PROTESTANT HOLY FAMILY

The Abolition of Priestly Celibacy

If there is a legacy of the Holy Family, it is that of having created a *rift* in the world: between natural procreation, sinful and subject to death, and the community of all humans in Christ; between the earthly continuation and the spiritual overcoming of the world; between those who married and raised children and those who arranged their lives in such a way that they embraced only God. Even the dual coding of medieval society into a secular and an ecclesiastical realm can still be understood as an "epilogue" of the New Testament family story.

At the beginning of the modern era, an event took place that seemed to invalidate the structure of this rift—the Reformation. Martin Luther's appearance entailed two profound changes for the history of the family: first, the desacramentalization of marriage, over which the church relinquished the authority it had won in the Middle Ages in a protracted and difficult struggle; and, second, the discrediting and abolition of priestly celibacy.

In a study entitled *The Holy Household*, Lyndal Roper examined the repercussions of the Reformation in the city of Augsburg. One important component of the urban order was the monasteries. They imposed on an important segment of both the male and the female population a life of spatial seclusion and sexual abstinence that spiritually benefited the city as a whole. The abolition of clerical celibacy and the dissolution of the monasteries threatened this economy of collective salvation.

In addition, it created problems that were quite concrete in nature. In particular, the hordes of former nuns eager for marriage caused alarm. People feared that their virginity, now unleashed from its nuptial bond with Christ, might become the source of an easily inflamed sexual lust. Ironically, this made the convents comparable to the public brothels, which were also a place where femaleness could be controlled only through enclosure. "Nuns who left their convents," writes Roper, "were consequently viewed as being in intense sexual danger, both from their own lusts and those of others. In the early years of the Reformation, as the first nuns left convents, Luther's immediate preoccupation was to find husbands for them—a concern he did not have when monks began to leave monasteries."[1]

But the situation was changed not only by the dissolution of monasteries and convents and their transformation into convalescent homes and educational institutions. Even more striking was the abolition of clerical celibacy. The type of the celibate servant of God who renounced the world disappeared—along with its mocking caricature, the lecherous and thoroughly unholy cleric. This also eliminated the deplorable practices that had long aroused the ire of the public and could be successfully pilloried by the Reformers: the toleration of concubinage and offspring in return for monetary fines. All this gave way to the new image of the country or city pastor, who headed a normal household, was usually very prolific in producing offspring, and was surrounded by a wife and a large band of children. This gave rise to a social milieu that would come to carry considerable cultural weight: the Protestant parsonage.

Henceforth—at least in the Protestant realm—closeness to God and sexuality were no longer regarded as irreconcilable. The Reformation dissolved the old union of holiness and abstinence that had played such a prominent role in the history of religion. "In the *imitatio Christi*," writes the Catholic theologian August Franzen, "the priest renounced the intimate sphere of love that is marriage and family in order to give himself to his congregation in a devotional act of universal love."[2] Luther's conception of faith as a personal and direct relationship of every Christian to God removed the ground from under this preferred mediating role of the priestly office: "This more or less eliminated all the ideational presuppositions toward which priestly education had been oriented for centuries. . . . The special place of the priest in the mass and in life vanished. His celibate status was viewed as meaningless and was widely mocked and derided. Indeed, against the backdrop of the Christian conception of marriage he even appeared as a foreign body who was un-Christian and therefore had to be eliminated."[3]

While the Reformation proclaimed the priesthood of all believers, who could establish a direct spiritual relationship to God, it conversely placed the official priest into the ranks of common humanity. Given humanity's state of original sin, marriage was for Luther an unavoidable concession to sexual desire. And he also made this "remedy" applicable to the clergy. In a sense, he accorded the maleness of priests a right to exist, provided it was directed into proper and well-ordered channels.

One could say that in this regard the Reformation destroyed the legacy of the Holy Family as a system of relationships free of sexuality. It abolished the conflict—characteristic of Catholic marriage policy—between, on the one hand, a life of carnal lust and, on the other, the model of the Holy Family, as impossible as it was imperative. This rendered obsolete—for *both* genders—all the theological constructions following in the wake of the Holy Family. The marriage between the monk Martin Luther and the nun Katharina von Bora—the sexual union between a man whose life had been dedicated to the *imitatio Christi* and a woman who had consecrated herself to the *imitatio Mariae*—sealed this break with the great tradition of ascetic spirituality. It is no wonder that many expected that the child born of this sacrilegious union would be a monster.[4]

The secularization of the priesthood was accompanied by the secularization of marriage. Luther stripped marriage of its sacramental status and classified it soberly as a "worldly creation."[5] To be sure, this did not change the fact that even for Luther marriage remained a sacred state and required special pastoral care—an ambiguous, contradictory conception of marriage that would result in a long chain of theological and legal uncertainties.[6] Still, this set the stage for a development that, at least over the long term, would exert a profound influence on the social structure of modern Europe. While the *inner* life of the family attracted the attention and missionary zeal of Protestant theologians and pedagogues, *external* marriage affairs were removed from the sphere of ecclesiastical prescriptions. The regulation of marriage—at least in principle—passed into the hands of secular authorities.[7]

The programmatic secularization of the family that Luther initiated represents only one aspect of the Reformation's innovations. The other, complementary, aspect lay in a *spiritualization* of worldly conditions, in the redirecting of sacred energies into secular institutions.[8] The Reformation has been accused of "making the priesthood worldly," writes Wilhelm Baur, a chronicler of the German parsonage at the end of the nineteenth century. "In truth, the Reformation once again showed to service in the church the healthy foundation of the priesthood of all believers. . . . And if one wants to call this a secularization of the priesthood, one may conversely laud the spiritualization of marriage and secular authority."[9]

To be sure, the Reformational writings on marriage and house fathers, which reached their zenith in the sixteenth and seventeenth centuries, remained within the main tradition of the Aristotelian *oeconomia*, the teachings on the domestic economy, which would be supplanted only by enlightened cameralism and the national economy.[10] Yet it did reaccentuate the classical model in the sense of a specifically Protestant interiorization and "worldly piety." All daily chores within the house, a community of production and a shared life, were now given a reference to God. Diligence, accommodation to the domestic hierarchy, and virtue were no longer regarded as the demands of practical reason but as commandments from God. "On obedience toward these commandments," writes Julius Hoffmann, "depended not only the domestic well-being of the house father and his family but also their entire earthly welfare and eternal salvation."[11] For that reason, religious instruction in particular—that is, the spiritual framing of everyday activities through devotion, Bible readings, and prayer—acquired profound importance within domestic life.

Protestant writings proclaimed the active and productive domestic life as a whole to be a service to God. Families were nothing less than "little churches."[12] According to social historian Lawrence Stone, domestic piety "filled the vacuum left by the decline of the Church and its priests," along with the public ritual acts they performed.[13] Referring to developments in England, Stone speaks of a "general tendency to substitute the household for the church." He concludes: "Thus the Word of God was to some degree removed from the parish church and transferred to the private home: the Holy Spirit was partly domesticated."[14]

This domestication of the Holy Spirit also affected the emotional life of members of the household. It was not only the obedience of children toward their parents, of domestics toward their masters, and of the woman toward the man that was regarded as a divine commandment, with the result that a violation of this duty to obey placed the Christian world order as such in doubt.[15] The love that the superiors bestowed on their charges in return for their obedience[16] also derived from God and was therefore by its nature spiritual. Because of this, Christian and non-Christian marriages were fundamentally different despite external similarities:

> For love is greatly different among the godless and the God-fearing. A godless man loves his wife in such a way that he seeks in her never God's will but only his own. Wherefore such a love is not a pure love, but a filthy and swinish love, in which there can be neither faithfulness nor constancy. . . .
>
> A God-fearing pious husband, by contrast, sees in his wife nothing other than God's commandment and will, and for His will's sake alone . . . he loves and cherishes her as a gift from God and for the sake of his Lord's will, and he thus takes her as good, even though there may something about her that might repel him, such as disfigurement, poverty, or other such faults and ailments.[17]

The wife as a gift from God and marital love as a love for God reflecting back on the partner: such notions turned the Protestant family into an arena for sweeping reform of the emotional life of individuals, one that would radiate far beyond the confessional boundaries and lay the foundation for the bourgeois culture of emotions that established itself in the eighteenth century. This is especially true with regard to the parsonage, which was understood as the Protestant model family and undoubtedly became, by virtue of its key role in the secularization process, the most important nexus of intellectual history, at least for the German educated bourgeoisie.[18] The contribution of the Protestant parsonage to the history of the emotions lies in the fact that because of its historical origins, it was destined to impart an aura of holiness to the relationships among the family members. And that included even sexual relationships. The parsonage, as a model, succeeded in spiritualizing sexuality and natural procreation *as such*. As Bauer wrote in the nineteenth century: "The clerical estate must descend to the same level as the world of the laity; lordship and the house father must lift themselves to the same height as the clerical estate. This was preached most vociferously by the new parsonage, in which the priestly estate became marital and marriage became spiritual."[19]

The House Father

The bearer of domestic spirituality was the man. John Calvin concluded from the fact that Christians called their God "Father" that there was "something divine in every father."[20] One could interpret the position of the Protestant house father in two ways. Depending on one's perspective, it appeared as either a position of strength or one of dependence. Dependence insofar as the head of the family occupies the lowest rung on the ladder of fatherly authority. His fatherhood is not autonomous but derives from a transcendental power. "The house father is nothing without God," writes Hoffmann. "He can do nothing 'on his own,' 'by himself,' 'alone,' because God gives everything. The fear of God is therefore the primary virtue of the house father and the members of his household."[21] In this respect, the paterfamilias can see himself only as the executive organ, as the mouthpiece of the absent Father in heaven.

Yet it is precisely through his role as the mediator of God's Word that the house father acquires a new kind of power. Ever since the Reformation, his right to demand obedience in secular matters was linked to something like a metaphysical privilege of truth. The father was supposed to reveal anew to his charges the path to divine truth. After all, he had been empowered to assume the role of the preacher in the domestic sphere. Any resistance to his superior position was a sin not only against patriarchal authority but—even worse—against the authority of God. The new immediacy of the faith, which Luther asserted against the church's monopoly of interpreting Scripture, did not mean that the same kind of access to faith was available to both genders. On the contrary, the man, in his threefold function as husband, head of household, and domestic priest, newly attained a preeminent and incontestable position.

Luther's notion of the common priesthood of all believers obeyed the same gender logic as did, centuries later, the ideal of equality proclaimed by the French Revolution, which Schiller encapsulated in the famous phrase "All humans will be brothers."[22] Women were excluded from the common priesthood and from the Republic. The authoritative proclamation of God's Word was the duty of the man. The Protestant *father* retained the privilege that was taken from the Catholic *priest*. Luther in a sense democratized the priesthood, but it remained a democracy confined to the male members of the community. The reduction in ecclesiastical authority accrued to the benefit of the family father's position of power.

On the one hand, the Reformation was indubitably a revolutionary movement. It overthrew long-standing components of faith that had been dogmatically solidified by the church, delegitimized the entire ecclesiastical hierarchy with the pope at its head, stripped of its status much of what had been proclaimed good and holy for centuries, and broke with central institutions like priestly celibacy. Not least, it brought in its wake anarchic unrest in the form of peasant wars and iconoclasm, which posed a serious threat to the survival of the ruling authorities and of the civic order.

On the other hand, the religious revolution triggered by Luther itself bore highly authoritarian traits. This had less to do with Martin Luther's personality than it did with the interests in social order pursued by this dissenting movement. After all, this movement arose in large measure from a revulsion—widespread in the sixteenth century—toward the desolate state of both ecclesiastical and secular government.

The house-father literature—which prospered in Scripture-friendly Protestant soil, along with countless other pedagogical tracts and sermons, from the pens of the great Reformers down to the simplest country pastors who rebuked and edified their congregations every Sunday—was aimed not merely at improving the way domestic life was managed, and thereby also improving domestic morals. Its purpose was also to integrate the "house," or *oikos*, the basic unit of the premodern economy, into a stricter overall social architecture. The

Copper-engraved title page of a Protestant house-father book, 1528. The Holy Family, arranged between the Lutheran rose and the tau cross with the snake, is portrayed as the model for the Christian marriage. A vertical line connects it to the Trinity.

house father, his "natural" authority now strengthened, was given the task of preventing disorder and immorality in all spheres of daily life, and by doing so to show his obedience toward the secular lordship as well as toward God. Patriarchal (familial), paternalistic (secular), and ecclesiastical supervision were to go hand in hand, corresponding to the three orders of the Christian society as Luther defined them: *ecclesia*, *politica*, and *oeconomia*.[23]

A rich metaphorical imagery of the caring, nurturing, controlling but also punishing father, which became very popular in the early modern period, linked the three levels of authority. Not only was God given the title "highest house father," who loves the good children and punishes the wicked, but the house father also shared in the sacred authority, which descended on him from God. Anyone who rebelled against the father or the territorial ruler violated the divine order as such; since there was a kind of metonymic relationship among the various manifestations of fatherhood, such a person was virtually guilty of sacrilege.

In his *Great Catechism*, Luther interpreted the commandment to honor one's mother and father so broadly as to include all (male) authorities established by God:

[It] is in place to mention the various instances in which obedience is required by those in authority over us, whose duty it is to command and govern. All authority has its root and warrant in parental authority. Where a father is unable alone to rear his child, he employs a teacher to instruct it; if he is too feeble, he obtains the help of his friends or neighbors; if the parent departs this life, he commits and delegates his authority and responsibility to others often appointed for the purpose.[24]

If "parental authority" is the source from which all other obligations of obedience are derived, if the secular government as well is "embraced in the estate of fatherhood,"[25] then the domestic order takes on a dignity that is virtually constitutive of the state. The eyes and hands of the father are multiplied and become omnipresent. All these father figures confront the individual as a gradation of power that is bound in solidarity and whose diverse spheres of authority are complementary and mutually supportive. While the premodern world was a patchwork quilt of powers that competed with one another and all too often clashed openly, the seamless transferability of fatherly attributes through all social gradations prepared the way for a *standardization of the body politic*, whose immanent goal would become, in the words of Stone, "the authoritarian, all-embracing, inquisitorial, all-demanding nation state."[26]

Protestantism rebuilt the family into the socialization agency of the modern polity. In so doing, it promoted, on an ideological level, a long-term sociostructural development that occurred in discontinuous thrusts during the sixteenth and seventeenth centuries and did not reach its temporary conclusion until the threshold era around 1800. The development I am talking about was the breakup of the kinship group into smaller, autonomous family units. At its conclusion one finds, on the one hand, the bourgeois nuclear family that still exists, though as a historical model that is winding down: a community of parents and children, insular toward the outside world and intimate on the inside. On the other hand, there is a state monopoly of power, one that reaches deeply into matters whose management had previously been reserved for the family in the broadest sense. The widely cast net of kinship relationships thus dissolved in two directions: toward closer ties to the nuclear family and toward the growing demands of loyalty on the part of the state.[27]

One indication of the declining importance of the kinship system could be the fact that during the same period the extensive marriage prohibitions on the grounds of incest, as laid down by canon law, were rescinded step by step, first in the Protestant areas. Invoking the Bible, Luther had already called for a drastic reduction in the number of possible impediments to marriage,[28] though that did not rule out fluctuations and variations in legal practice during the succeeding centuries. In any case, the large European law codes around 1800 liberalized marriage laws to the point where only consanguinity of the first and second degree were named as impediments—for example, in the Code Napoléon and the Territorial Law of Prussia.[29] One can infer from this that the tendency toward endogamy, which was especially widespread among noble families, had ceased to pose a threat to the central power. In this respect, the long period of restrictive ecclesiastical marriage policy, from the end of antiquity into the modern period, had born fruit.

The definition of incest in general followed the long-term trend toward reducing the size of family units and making the choice of a partner an individual matter. Today the topic of incest hardly plays any role at all legally or morally, with the exception of a continuing core sphere of the incest taboo chiefly among relatives of the first degree.[30] The last remnants—such as the prohibition against marriage among people related by marriage or limitations on the choice of a partner in a second marriage—were purged from the law books as late as the final years of the twentieth century. The family group is no longer an organism whose expansion is watched with suspicion and needs to be repressed. It has lost its role as a third power: the state and the individual now stand face to face.

Until it reached that point, the position of the father constituted the hinge, so to speak, between the family and the state. From the Roman paterfamilias and his absolute powers[31] to the bourgeois head of the household in modern times and beyond, fatherly authority has suffered a continual erosion of power. Throughout this process, it repeatedly found itself at odds with the centralization of state power and the establishment of the state's monopoly over law and force. The Reformation settled this conflict by placing all levels of the social order in agreement. House father, territorial father, and Father-God worked in a mutually supportive manner, exchanged attributes and powers, and backed up one another, so to speak.[32] Like God, the monarch in Puritan political doctrine also takes on familial traits: he demands obedience but loves his subjects like children. Conversely, within the circle of his loving family, the house father can regard himself as regent through the grace of God.

To be sure, such notions go back to older images of lordship and are derived from the medieval doctrine of the orders; in this regard, the post-Reformation house-father literature did not fundamentally invent anything that was new. However, it could draw on a *division of labor* among authorities that pervaded all social strata and was previously unthinkable on this scale. There had been profound clashes of interests between kinship loyalty and the principle of the state, between clan and church, between church and state. The father as the leader of a "house" in the feudal sense, as the empowered representative of a kinship group, would never have allowed himself to be transformed into a lower agency, so to speak, of the state apparatus. He was the opponent rather than the placeholder of higher organs of power. That a strict chain of authority from the family father to the territorial father to God the Father could establish itself in the sixteenth century has to do with the fact that the antagonism between kinship and the state was generally diminishing. This development resulted from the successful centralization of state power in the transition from the feudal system to absolutism, as well as from the related trend of making the family increasingly conform to the state.[33] If the paterfamilias in the classic sense could still defend the threshold of his house as the entrance to an autonomous legal sphere, the modern house father was installed in the family as an agent, as it were, of the prince in order to extend the latter's complete power into the penumbral private realm as well.

The Natural Mother

In the sixteenth century, the legal position of the wife deteriorated dramatically, especially in the Protestant regions. One can identify a number of reasons for this. "One obvious cause," according to Stone, "was the decline of kinship, which left wives exposed to exploitation by their husbands, since they lost the continuing protection of their own kin."[34] The dissolution of the support network of the kinship group came at the expense of women, who were now no longer able to invoke the help of counterweights to oppose the advance of the domestic, patriarchal concentration of power. "Secondly, the end of Catholicism involved the elimination of the female religious cult of the Virgin Mary, the disappearance of celibate priests, who through the confession box had hitherto been so very supportive of women in their domestic difficulties, and the closing off of the career option of life in a nunnery."[35]

As a result, the woman was imprisoned in the household both socially and spiritually.[36] To be sure, medieval society had also been dominated by men, but at least it had granted female spirituality its own rituals and methods of articulation. The universe of the saints, whose religious and iconographic diversity counteracted the establishment of a strict official hierarchy within the church, preserved for female believers countless lines of connection to the heavenly realm.

The organizing center of female hagiolatry was the cult of the Virgin Mary. Convents and Beguine houses, which saw themselves as places where lives were lived in imitation of Mary, offered women a real—and by no means always disagreeable—alternative to subjection to the patriarchal coercion of family. The high esteem in which virginity was held played a role in allowing a specifically female religiosity to develop. Moreover, the popular cult of the Madonna tended to elevate Mary herself to the rank of a divinity. The figure of Mary mediatrix, who with maternal love looked after those who prayed and interceded for them at Christ's throne, found itself in growing competition with the official and purely male hierarchy of the Catholic Church.

Perhaps the devaluation of the cult of Mary at the hands of the Reformation should be understood as a counterblow against the feminization of Christianity in the late Middle Ages. At any rate, with the dissolution of the convents, the independent spiritual experience of female believers lost its accustomed locale. A passionate and openly erotic ecstasy of fusion with God—the kind the great medieval female mystics described—was rather suspect in the Protestant world. In general, a woman's unmarried state was henceforth looked on with suspicion and socially stigmatized. It was associated with the profuse fantasies of women's creation-denying insubordination within marriage, fantasies that were played out in the so-called devil's books, the negative counterpart to the house father-literature.[37]

One might expect that against this backdrop the conventional visual repertoire of the Holy Family would be thrown into question. It is well known that the Reformation was hostile toward the Marian cult. The sixteenth century witnessed iconoclastic outbursts in many cities, during which images of saints were removed from churches and destroyed. But Protestantism was also bound to have a difficult time with the Catholic iconographic tradition for reasons of "family policy." After all, the Madonna with Child is the very symbol of woman's privileged closeness to the Christian God.[38] The figure of Joseph, who must watch this intimate mother–God dyad like an outsider, seems incompatible with the role that was defined for the Protestant house father.

In fact, in terms of its program, Protestant fatherhood drew not on Joseph's fatherliness but on that of God. The sanctification of the family in the wake of the Reformation went hand in hand with a deification of fatherly authority. This made it possible to curtail the spiritual importance of the mother's position. Still, Joseph did retain his place in Protestant pictorial art, and over time this place increasingly conformed to the image of the house father.

The first artist one must name in this context is Rembrandt. His oeuvre, writes the art historian Wolfgang Kemp, is characterized by the paradox that he "was also and primarily a painter of biblical stories in a society that denied— indeed, actively opposed—the substantial functions of the religious image."[39] This forced Rembrandt to devise new pictorial strategies. Although he made numerous sketches depicting the life of the Holy Family, he did know how to impart to these family scenes a high degree of everyday realism as a form of "camouflage," so to speak. Even the insignia of holiness blend with the empirical design of the pictorial space. This can clearly be seen in the sketch *The Holy Family with Cat and Snake*, where Mary's nimbus simultaneously becomes a realistic motif—that of the window oval. Kemp speaks of Rembrandt's "iconographic style," of using a "religious attribute" in such a way "that it simultaneously appears entirely grounded in reality."[40]

And yet this naturalization of the holy points in two opposite directions. On the surface of the picture it causes the explicit iconography of sainthood, with all its anecdotal and allegorical markers, to disappear. In return, it suffuses the daily life of the family with an "implicit" holiness, thereby multiplying the elements that become the successor to the sacral. The result, therefore, is a dual effect: the pictorialness of the holy is absorbed by a certain kind of everyday realism and at the same time finds refuge in it. Henceforth one need no longer worship the Christ Child and the Madonna to place oneself in relationship to the model of the Holy Family. Instead, sacral energies are already flowing into the genre sketches of everyday, demonstratively secular family life. Artists like

Rembrandt, *The Holy Family with Cat and Snake*, etching, 1654.

Rembrandt drew the visual consequences from Luther's dialectic of secularization and spiritualization.

In this context, Joseph, too, is increasingly depicted at quotidian activities—in situations that would have been expected from a father who was a craftsman at that time. He goes through a process of iconographic *normalization*. Although he did retain a certain distance to the intimate and, to a certain degree, exclusive relationship between mother and child, he overcame his inferior and marginal position to the same degree to which the Holy Family transformed itself into a natural family. The Reformation saw to it theologically that this transformation could take place.

Although the Reformation endowed the role of the father with a greater degree of consistency, it did split it into two variants. As God's placeholder in the family, the father is the absolute figure of authority, both practically and spiritually. The link to God is clearly focused on the fatherly authority; the figure of the mother, as the successor of the Madonna, is disempowered. Mary, once the queen of the world, has thus been demoted in this scenario; she is merely left with the role of the handmaid. Once again, the model of the pastor's family is relevant, for it shows a clear functional division: under the terms of the rules of the

Abraham Bach the Younger, *The Four Times of the Day*, ca. 1670. Augsburg. House father Joseph is heading off to work.

office, the pastor is exclusively concerned with higher affairs; the pastor's wife, with affairs of daily life.[41]

And yet the Protestant mother did preserve something of the mystery that had once surrounded Mary, the virginal Mother and Bride of God. However, the coordinates shifted compared with the Marian cult. Like all other attributes of the Holy Family, this mystery was secularized: it transformed itself into the mystery of *natural motherhood*. Woman can redefine herself in Protestantism as a natural mother placed under the care of a man who is close to God. In this role, she takes on an almost religious solemnity. That is why the same man who has secured his spiritual primacy can take a step back, with a certain awe, in the face of his wife's motherhood. In a sense, he changes the frames of reference and temporarily returns to the role of Joseph. And not only because sexuality and birth have always been enigmatic matters whose meaning could never be fully plumbed "in the flesh," or because the theories of procreation, well into the modern age, postulated God's involvement in every soul's act of coming-into-the-world, thus limiting the procreative authority of the biological father.[42] The primary reason was because natural motherhood took on a new meaning in the institutional association of family and state. If Enlightenment pedagogy, which grew in the soil of Protestantism, declared the mother to be the key figure in the socialization of the child; if the national state—right down to the period of National Socialism[43]—mythically elevated the figure of the natural mother, then what is at work here is still the dialectic set in motion by the Reformation between secularization and resacralization, between the politicization of God, on the one hand, and the deification of the polity, on the other.

The Professional Civil Service

The Reformation reduced the schism between the holy and the unholy family, between the spiritual connection to God and the physical connection of marriage. What prevailed instead was the tendency to reconcile the two sides. One can conclude from this that the celibate ideal, pertinent declarations from the reformers notwithstanding, did not simply come to an end but henceforth unfolded its moral and power-forming force *inside the worldly existence*.

Protestant familialism had a long-term historical mission, so to speak: it found fulfillment in the bourgeois marriage model of the eighteenth century. The German Enlightenment, in particular, received—by way of the parsonage—important impulses from the social reformist and pedagogical élan of the Reformation. This is especially true of the areas in which the Enlightenment thinkers carried the work of secularization beyond its original religious breeding ground.

For the enlightened marriage can be described by a paradoxical formula precisely as the *inclusion of the exclusion of sexuality*. In the form of a union that was ideally entered into solely out of love, it not only represented the opposite of the compulsory alliance driven by class politics but also set itself programmatically against the sphere of sexual desire. The countless marriage guides that appeared in the decades around 1800 positioned marriage in the direction of a consistently ethical Platonism. In this emphatic understanding of marriage, it ceased to be a place of sexual encounter, of sexual reproduction, which meant it was also no longer the stage for masculinity realized in the traditional sense. The reproductive aspect takes a backseat to the importance of a partnership of mutual affection and its emotional demands. At any rate, in the idealized depictions, the procreative function of marriage—its chief purpose in traditional church dogma—played only a subordinate and increasingly dispensable role.[44]

Within this context, the Holy Family could take on new importance, no longer through its sacral irreconcilability with human marital behavior but as *the* exemplar for the bourgeois family. Many literary texts worked at overlaying natural parenthood with motives drawn from the Mary–Joseph constellation. In the process, they also reproduced its ambiguities. Mary's holiness changes into the holiness of the bourgeois mother's chaste and devoted love for her child. The man, for his part, splits himself into the two roles provided by iconography: when it comes to the holy dyad between mother and infant, he behaves like an outside third party, though he does protect and provide for them. But he supervises the development and path of the growing child as one who not only represents but seeks to *incorporate* the divine and state paternal power.[45]

And what about the child? One could hardly claim that all male Protestant children were treated like infant Jesuses. Still, there are indications that also point to a sanctification of the position of the child. This has to do with the emotionalism that grew out of Protestant religiosity. It played a significant role in what social historians have called the "discovery of childhood."[46] By this they mean not only the development of a stable emotional climate between parents and children but also the fact that people were beginning to concede that children had something like an individual personality to begin with. And this, in turn, had repercussions for the nature of the love for children, which ceased to be merely an animal instinct—in the form of the "doting love" that pedagogues wanted to cure parents of—and, at least in theory, changed into a *reasoned affection*. In the new family—in which sympathy was to take the place of passion, affection the place of instinctual behavior; whose members, in other words, were to recognize and appreciate one another as *soul-beings*—the child's soul was also accorded a previously unknown attention.

Child rearing changed its tone in the course of the Enlightenment. No longer was its goal to instill absolute obedience in children or drive out original sin.[47] Instead, it applied to the child's soul the old metaphor of the tabula rasa.[48] Contrary to the teachings of Saint Augustine, the child became a creature that was a priori innocent. Consequently, the important thing is to preserve it in its state of natural innocence by carefully shielding it from the corruption of culture. This development produced a radical change in the semantics of the childlike. The child was now suitable for attributes that can be derived from the rhetoric of Christ: it is sweet, angelic, heavenly, innocent, sent among humans by God as a supernatural being.

This is documented not only by Romantic and Nazarene paintings of children, which in many respects assimilated the Christian pictorial tradition, but also in many literary works of the time. One striking example is a short tale by the theologian Friedrich Schleiermacher entitled "The Christmas Celebration: A Conversation," published in 1806. In this conversation, all positions within the family are in turn transfigured and elevated into a state of holiness. That is especially true of the children. When it comes to a mother's true love for her children, one of the female conversationalists explains that this "love is directed toward what we believe to be lovely and divine in him already, what any mother looks for in every movement of her child, as soon as its soul begins to find expression. . . . You see . . . in this sense every mother is another Mary. Every mother has a child divine and eternal, and devoutly looks for the stirrings of the higher spirit within it."[49] A little later in the conversation we are told:

> Thus it is that every mother who, profoundly feeling what she has done in bearing a human being, knows as it were by an annunciation from heaven that the Spirit of the church, the Holy Spirit, dwells within her. As a result, she forthwith presents her child to the church with all her heart, and claims this as her right. Such a woman also sees Christ in her child—and this is that inexpressible feeling a mother has which compensates for all else.[50]

While these statements may be unorthodox from a strictly theological point of view, their thrust is very much in agreement with many other testimonies from the Protestant sphere that document the striving to sanctify the familial world. The child, as embodied innocence, as an allegory for the childlike trust of the true Christian believer in God, is, in the words of Andreas Gestrich, surrounded by "a virtually sacral aura."[51]

Yet this is not the only motif reflecting a special, religiously motivated devotion to children in Protestantism. There is a second reason, one that can be traced back to Luther's writings. It lies in a historically modified attention to the *future path* of young boys. From the very beginning, Protestant pedagogy placed schooling alongside the father's role as educator. Luther admonished parents and princes to educate their offspring. This concern was driven by a simple institutional calculation. According to social historian Barbara Beuys,

> The new Protestant church needed people—as pastors, to build up a hierarchy, as servants to the state who were favorably disposed to this very church. Luther did not ignore this; instead, he made a virtue of necessity. He couldn't possibly know the ramifications of what he was doing. Henceforth a second, all-powerful authority sat invisibly at the family table next to the father, one to which all had

to submit: the state. The family was no longer merely a group in which human beings could grow up sheltered for a few years. It was given a higher purpose: that of raising subjects who were obedient to authority. The family as the germ cell of the state was born with this Protestant doctrine of marriage. [52]

To put it into anachronistic terms: Luther's reformation of church, state, and family paved the way for the idea of the *career*, a path of work that did not conform to a person's social status but was determined by individual ability and education. But even this preparation for advancement in the world had a spiritual background. First, Luther ultimately wanted to recruit the next generation not only for spiritual but also for secular governance. Second, through this setup sons were to find their place in a world order dominated by the regulatory idea of the father: they were to rise up the ladder of authorities, whose legitimacy was guaranteed by the highest authority of the Father in heaven.

Thus a son's plans for an occupation were also given a spiritual component in the Protestant family. His destination, wishes, and options were never merely secular and selfish in nature. His life's path was aimed at fulfilling higher tasks; in the home, the son was equipped with a narcissism that disposed him to a certain sense of mission. That was especially true of the sons of clergymen, who, if they did not follow their fathers into the preacher's calling, did put the energies of secularization to productive literary and philosophical use.[53]

In institutional terms, the Protestant upbringing benefited a certain professional group. On the one hand, it provided fertile soil for the rise of the educated bourgeoisie. On the other hand, it spawned the tradition of a closeness to the state—a closeness, one might say, imbued with messianism. Both currents merge in the type of the German civil servant. What Luther had demanded came to pass: the sons of Protestantism became recruits of the modern state in Prussian Germany. The two qualities of the Lutheran Christian—first, unconditional loyalty toward authority; and, second, the preservation of individual freedom of religion and conscience—made their way into the professional profile of the modern civil servant. Although this imbued this professional class with its fixation on authority, it also gave it a certain measure of inner independence.

If there is such a thing as a "Protestant mission," it produced surprising results far removed from the realm of the church. The Reformation constitutes an important stage in a long-term process, at the end of which the family's orientation toward God was transformed into its *orientation toward the state*; the position of the father, in any case, was co-occupied by the state. As part of this process,

the Virgin Mary transformed herself into the *natural mother* of the bourgeois
family ideology. The child, finally, found its destiny in the very polity that had
already invaded the micro-universe of the family. In other words, it became—
ideally—a civil servant:

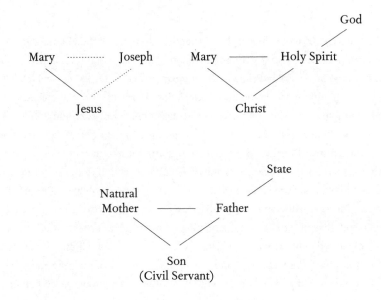

18

THE RETURN OF JOSEPH

Joseph led a shadowy iconographic existence right through the Middle Ages. He remained a colorless saint without any contours. Even when he is added to the image of the Madonna and child as the companion and foster father—which happens almost without exception only in depictions of the birth and in scenes of the flight to Egypt—he is an old man and can attract much less attention to himself.

All that undergoes a striking change beginning in the fifteenth century. Despite the awkward position from which he started in the narrative of the Holy Family, Joseph experienced a considerable cultic elevation in the early-modern period. The initial impulse came from the late medieval theologians Bernhard of Sienna, Pierre d'Ailly, and, especially, Jean Gerson. In a work dated 1413, Gerson makes Joseph into a young, strapping man who did not take on his important role in redemptive history reluctantly, but actively and willingly.[1] He highlights Joseph's dignity as "head and master of the mother of the head and master of the whole world."[2] The Parisian church reformer Gerson succeeded in founding an independent cult of Joseph, which the Counter-Reformation later adopted and intensified.

According to Hildegard Erlemann, Joseph's "growing importance for the piety of the seventeenth and eighteenth centuries"[3] bestowed on him the status of a deeply venerated saint in Bohemia, Bavaria, Austria, and Mexico. He is usually presented to the faithful as a simple, hardworking artisan content with his lowly status: a thoroughly human father, yet one to whom the divine Christ child accords the proper respect. In this regard, Joseph represents the unassuming side of Christian piety.

Yet it is his chaste connection to the Virgin Mary that makes it possible to elevate him above the domestic realm and to include him in the system of theological allegory. Baroque writers in particular were noted for doing this. The Viennese preacher Abraham a Santa Clara makes Joseph into the pilot of the ark of Mary, the librarian of the sealed book, the steward of the Heavenly Queen, and the guardian of the paradise won back by her locked garden.[4] If Mary, in her nuptial bond with Christ, symbolizes the church as a whole, Joseph is also in this mystical context her God-appointed protector. Eventually, during a festive ceremony in 1870, the pope solemnly declared Joseph the patron saint of the Catholic Church.

In the meantime, family depictions in which Joseph plays the part of head of household and ersatz father increasingly approximated the reality of everyday life. The Counter-Reformation already highlighted him in this role as a way of countering the Protestant house-father literature with a Catholic saint of equal visual power. In the nineteenth century, the figure of the honorable craftsman Joseph accommodated itself not only to the bourgeois-tinged family ideology but also to the church's propaganda against industrialization and the proletari-anization of the workers. Genre scenes, for which the members of the Holy Family assemble in demonstrative harmony, are marshaled in sentimental fashion to contrast with the disintegration of the familial world through industrial work outside the family. In this context, the veneration of Saint Joseph, whose intention was to save fatherly authority and the sense of family, was imbued with an openly anticommunist accent.[5] "What our time needs," one reads in one among countless appeals on this topic, "is the man of work, of diligent, serious work; the man of the selfless performance of one's duties, the man of submission to God and all legitimate authority, the man with a fear of God and true love for his neighbor and for God; the man, quiet, simple, even if overlooked by the world, yet tall before God by virtue of his justice. Such an exemplary man . . . we possess in Joseph."[6]

This kind of monopolization reduced the *religious* significance of the reference to the biblical story. "If the point during the Baroque was to follow in the Holy Family's footsteps, in the sense of an *imitatio*, in order to enter heaven," writes Erlemann, the authors of the late eighteenth and nineteenth centuries suggested that "the Holy Family could be *embodied* in a Christian family."[7] An appeal penned in 1893 declared: "Oh that every *Christian* family should strive to become a *holy family!* And why should we not be able to do so? What is so special about the *worker's family from Nazareth* that elevates it above others?"[8]

The difference between the sacred and the profane vanishes in the light of everyday piety. The awkward exceptional phenomenon of Christ's birth family is smoothed out and placed at the service of a sentimental, ecclesiastical–restorative family idyll. In a sense, the Holy Family and the bourgeois family exchange attributes: while the image of the Holy Family loses its spiritual significance and becomes increasingly secularized—at the cost of an unavoidable flattening out of the pictorial motifs—the genre scenes taken from everyday family life are bathed in the glow of borrowed holiness.[9]

Johann Carl Loth, *Saint Joseph and the Child Jesus, God in His Glory, and Mary*, 1681.
San Silvestro, Venice.

As a result of all of this, Jesus, Mary, and Joseph appear as normal individuals singled out merely by their outstanding virtue: Jesus, a well-mannered model child; Mary, an exemplar of love and chasteness; Joseph, a "shining example of fatherly watchfulness and solicitude."[10] In this way, the anomaly in Joseph's relationship to mother and child was largely erased; the wound resulting from his role as witness without being part of the procreation,[11] his truncated fatherhood, finally appears to have been healed.

How could that happen? How is it possible that Joseph, a figure cut off from his wife and child and thereby deprived of his manliness, could end up—after a long historical detour—as the figure that (petit-)bourgeois heads of families identified with? Why is it that Jesus' foster father had restored to him some of the powers he lost when he had to share his role with God?

The precarious position of the man Joseph provides the key, as it were, for determining the sociohistorical function of the Holy Family. Far from being merely a pictorial exemplar, the model of the Christian ur-family becomes enmeshed in basic conflicts between social forces and principles in Europe. As we have seen, these conflicts were about, on the one hand, the kinship group, with its allocation of social place through *seed* and *blood*—or, in Roman law, through a corresponding legal act of recognizing a child[12]—and, on the other, the agencies of a more far-reaching, more spiritual social process aimed at creating a centralized power independent of kinship considerations. One of these agencies—and for a long time the most powerful—was the church.

Whether openly expressed or not, the family policy of the medieval church had a simple goal: to destroy the web of kinship loyalties and replace them with the more easily controlled social form of the nuclear family. In pursuit of this goal, the church took advantage of the popular model of the Holy Family. All in all, its campaign was successful, especially since it was carried on by secular powers in the modern age. In this altered constellation as well, the conflict revolved around the rivalry between central power and family power. The growth in the power of the centralistic polity went hand in hand with the progressive disempowerment of the male head of household in the old sense. While the real father lost influence, the central power arrogated to itself more and more comprehensive symbolic fatherly qualities.

Only after the struggle between the absolutist state and segmentary kinship groups had been decided in favor of political centralization was it possible for the paterfamilias, a figure of authority rich in tradition, to be imbued with new meaning. The disempowerment was followed by the *reinstatement*, so to speak, of the father—although now with an altered function: the adversary who had opposed the advance of the centralized power became its *representative* within the family. The Reformation devised the model of a hierarchical filiation stretching from God the Father to the territorial father to the house father. With some delay, the Catholic Church pursued a similar path by declaring itself to be the advocate of a family that is internally consolidated by fatherly authority but acts externally in conformity with the state. This is precisely what is reflected in the renewed efforts to strengthen the figure of Joseph ideologically and to rehabilitate it iconographically.

Joseph's importance rises and falls, depending on the extent to which the position of the man at any given time fits into the overall plan of social order. The figure of Jesus' marginalized foster father demonstrates that the authority of the natural father had to be weakened to allow a different, supernatural power—one that transcended the biological frame of reference both spiritually and politically—to prevail. It was only after that operation had been completed that Joseph could take on a new task: supporting and passing on the transcendentalized authority through his humble human means. At that point, however, Josephean piety could also be used once again by the retreating church to *oppose* the state's secular claim of universal jurisdiction.

In any event, from all of this one must conclude that patriarchal society by no means rests on the glorified power of natural fathers. On the contrary, it demands considerable sacrifices from these fathers. Historically, the arbitrary tyrant over the family is forced to step down to make way for a type of the "father-deputy" who exists only by virtue of borrowed powers granted him by a higher authority and subject to recall, as it were. Paradoxically, what is commonly referred to as patriarchy is based on the outright *weakening of the patriarch*.

Against this backdrop, perhaps it is possible to provide one of Jacques Lacan's conceptual pairs with something like a sociohistorical foundation. One can follow Lacan in differentiating between a *real* and a *symbolic* father figure. The real father is the father as visible, acting, individual person. The symbolic father is the embodiment of symbolic order—the *law*—which precedes and guides the creation of any subject.[13] The two can never be made congruent without at the same time being entirely separable. In a commentary on Lacan, Lena Lindhoff notes that the authority of the symbolic father, "while actually being anonymous, apersonal, and thus gender neutral, can only be represented by a male figure, according to Lacan, since the symbolic order of the Western world is structured by patriarchy."[14]

If one applies this distinction—perhaps somewhat daringly—to the two fathers of Christ, God would be equated with the symbolic father, in whose name the symbolic order issues forth, while the figure of Joseph would reflect the vacillating and changeable part of the real father. On the one hand, this division of tasks makes it plausible why the symbolic order is inseparable from the person of the real father; after all, it (re)enthroned him, endowing him with the magnificence of a "small" symbolic father, a lawgiver, ruler, preacher, and patron in miniature. On the other hand, it becomes clear that the real father as an empirical person can never completely take the place of the symbolic father, can never merge with this authority free of contradictions. He always stands "beside himself," since he is, for his part, subject to the ineffable and, in the final analysis, incomprehensible authority of the law; he is constantly being undermined in his efforts at identification and put in his place—he is, psychologically speaking, castrated.

19

JOSEPH, ABELARD, SAINT-PREUX

The Love Marriage

The eighteenth century saw the spread of the custom of the love marriage. This is not to say that love—even love between spouses—did not exist prior to that time. But love, an emotion that is changeable and transitory by its nature, was not regarded as a suitable *foundation* for such a momentous step as marriage. In premodern times, marriages were entered into chiefly for economic reasons or out of convenience; personal affection played a subordinate role. The social order based on estates, which predominated into the age of industrialization, could show only limited regard for individual preferences.

This changed during the process that led to the individualization of the social structure. Young, marriageable men and women began to emancipate themselves from parental dispositions. Little by little, they asserted the right to choose one's partner freely. Consensus between partners, not the anticipatory arrangements by parents, became the crucial criterion for marriage. Ironically, this development, though late and interrupted by the Reformation, fulfilled an old demand by the medieval church, which had always tried to strengthen the right of the individual vis-à-vis the kinship group.[1] The champions of the Enlightenment, most of whom were anticlerical, unwittingly became the executors of the old ecclesiastical marriage policy.

However, as for the emotional elaboration of the concept of the love marriage, which established itself in the eighteenth century with profound literary ramifications, one must place greater emphasis on the cultural contribution of Protestantism, especially the movement of internal cultivation embodied in Pietism. In simplified schematic form, one can say that this concept of the love marriage went hand in hand with three innovations. First, marriage became an intimate relationship between two people that was grounded in love, or at least affection. Professional and poetic advice books had to adjust to this. No longer were they primarily concerned with managing the conflicts that arose from the natural differences between the spouses. Instead, they were now supposed to accompany the difficult process of finding a partner, making a sensible free choice, aiding the emergence of lasting mutual affection, and, if need be, balancing out any estrangement. This led to a far-reaching *psychologization* of the marital and familial system of relationships that has persisted to this very day.

Second, marriage was freed from social obligations[2] to the extent that the definition of the purpose of marriage was increasingly limited to the happiness of the spouses themselves; old-style kinship concerns and reasons of state took a backseat to this happiness. Moreover, marriage was now understood less as the continuation of the family line, and was instead given the status of an individual new beginning of two people who loved each other—a process that has been described as the *romanticization of marriage*.[3]

Third, this kind of marriage most certainly must not be based solely on sexual attraction. As everyone knows, this kind of attraction wanes quickly, is easily redirected to other people, and is difficult to reconcile with lifelong monogamy. That is why enlightened marriage instruction worked at disseminating a relationship ideal that disempowered sexual desire and was grounded in "love" as a rational and virtuous *soul union*. In so doing, it brought to completion a process that had begun much earlier and consisted of *moderating* the conjugal bond as such—to make it immune to the fluctuations of intense passions. From this perspective, modern rituals of finding a partner—whether we admit it or not—still adhere to the eighteenth-century tradition of the psychological "stabilization" of the individual.

In connection with the enlightened reform of marriage, the Holy Family could also take on new significance, now no longer by virtue of its sacral irreconcilability with human mating behavior but as the model case of the bourgeois family par excellence. This does not mean that bourgeois spouses were being exhorted to practice sexual abstinence but that they were sworn to a concept of love that transcended mere sexual attraction. Even sexual love could now be joined to such notions as spirit, reason, virtue, or good nature. It took on order-establishing characteristics. What was once animalistic and chaotic sexuality proved to be amenable to reform; it could be refined into a feeling of sympathy for all human beings and thus became a social binding agent of the highest order—indeed, a kind of civic virtue. The ideal republic that was imagined in the eighteenth century consisted of *loving individuals*. This is the only way to explain the enormous propagandistic exertions with which the infusion of emotional warmth into the family, on the one hand, and its cleansing of crude, unsublimated sexuality, on the other, were pursued and elevated into a model of social policy. If one takes the period around 1800 as the end point, the Holy

Family finds its destiny here in its successful contribution to the *rationalization of love*.

Yet all these affective transformations were not simple or linear. Efforts to articulate them utilizing the tools of poetry reveal their complexity and the labyrinthine channels in which desire unfolds. The process that established the modern family, and the transformation of love it entailed, gave rise to an endless literary output; conversely, in that period more than ever before love became a matter of the written word, of eloquence captured on paper. The transition from *passion*—the intense ardor that finds satisfaction only in possession—to linguistically refined and differentiated *sentiment* took place in novels and letters.[4]

Heloise and the New Heloise

One of the key figures in this literary as well as affective process is Jean-Jacques Rousseau. In 1761 he published a novel of marriage that was pathbreaking for the age of sentiment; its full title is *Julie, or The New Heloise: Letters of Two Lovers Who Live in a Small Town at the Foot of the Alps*. The chief plot of the book is based on a triangular relationship. For social reasons, Julie d'Etanges is not permitted to marry her bourgeois tutor, to whom she has given herself. Instead, she marries the older Monsieur de Wolmar, her father's choice. She polishes herself in this marriage of convenience and turns herself into a model housewife and mother who carries out her duties in a rural world marked by virtue, love, and harmony. Despite this ideal backdrop, her earlier passion continues to consume her below the surface and eventually leads to her untimely death. While rescuing her drowning son, Julie contracts an illness and dies. Her death is tantamount to an apotheosis. In death, she confesses to Saint-Preux her unbroken love. She thus fulfilled the duties of her marriage in exemplary fashion and yet never betrayed the great passion of her youth.

Rousseau takes the reader into a world that is as far removed from the dilemmas of Catholicism as can be imagined. The "good nature" he idealizes in Julie's world, both aesthetically and morally, forms a programmatic countercreation to nature after the Fall, to the fallen creatureliness in the older Christian thinking. In the ambiguity of marriage as outlined in the theological debates of early Christianity and the Middle Ages, virtue/spirit/morality, on the one hand, and nature/animalism/carnal instinct, on the other, formed a more or less rigid contradiction. Rousseau, however, lets his—fallen—heroine Julie elevate marriage itself into a state of virtue and innocence. In so doing, he situates his novel at the center of the enlightened discourse about love and marriage, though without agreeing completely with that discourse.

Traditionally, the Christian Holy Family presented the faithful with the model of a sinless marriage that was directed toward God. Inevitably, human beings who mated and produced offspring fell short of such an ideal. This was the original dilemma from which there was only one way out: asceticism. Luther already did a great deal to relieve orderly marital life from this pressure of sin. The novelists of the Enlightenment continued along that path. Rousseau, in any case, depicts the familial world in Clarens, where most of the story is set, as a *healed* and restored nature once more in harmony with the demands of virtue. A second, idyllic nature appears, one that has overcome the Fall and done so precisely through the institution of the procreative marriage and the parenthood that was part of it.

One must ask oneself what sort of narrative maneuvers permit this kind of process of turning marriage into something *positive*, a process that formed the core of the new bourgeois family ideology. How could sexual intercourse and innocence be joined—indeed, rendered all but indistinguishable in the image of the good marriage? How could the celibate and ascetic element disappear and yet live on in the notion of virtue? To rephrase the question: What place does the bourgeois model of marriage assign to *God* without putting the spouses under the obligation to observe abstinence?

The title of Rousseau's novel offers a first clue. *Julie, or The New Heloise* alludes to a subtext and transposes it into a contemporary setting. That subtext is the great medieval love story between Abelard (who eventually became a monk) and Heloise (who eventually became a nun), preserved in a correspondence that attracted renewed attention in the eighteenth century.

By means of this title, Rousseau laid out an intertextual trail that in a strange way connects his main character, Julie, with the medieval form of the chaste marriage. In medieval times, the chaste marriage seemed to be the only possibility in approximating the model of the holy parents. Abstinence *in* marriage offered a compromise formula between martial life and celibacy. In that respect, the practice of connubial chastity fit into the high tradition of early Christian asceticism, even if only transitionally.

One of the founders of this ascetic tradition and also a theoretician of the Holy Family was the church father Origen, who was said to have gone so far as to emasculate himself. Another (unwilling) practitioner of martial chastity in the twelfth century was the philosopher Abelard (1079–1142), who would later become famous and whose correspondence with his wife, Heloise, is one of the great examples of medieval love literature. Already a prominent theologian in his younger years, Abelard was hired as a tutor for Heloise and began a passionate, erotic affair with her. Although the two entered into a formal marriage, Abelard was emasculated by some of Heloise's relatives in an act of revenge. Thereafter, he lived as a monk, and Heloise as a nun. Only years after their separation did the two reestablish contact.[5]

At the beginning of the famous correspondence (whose authenticity, to be sure, is disputed) stands Heloise's rebellion against the demands of renunciation and self-denial imposed by her status as a nun. She does not wish to forswear her longing for Abelard even after he has been mutilated. The correspondence ends with Heloise's successful spiritual education at the hands of Abelard. As Christ's ecclesiastical deputy, Abelard transforms her once again— this time from the heart—into Christ's bride. It is therefore not solely the model of the chaste marriage that connects the story of Abelard and Heloise to the history of the Gospel's cultural ramifications. According to Catholic dogma, Heloise, as a nun, is the immediate spiritual successor to Mary—an honor Abelard repeatedly instructs her about.

In his fifth letter to the convent, now headed by his former lover, he writes: "[B]ut you who have been led by the King of heaven himself into his chamber and rest in his embrace, and with the door always shut are wholly given up to him."[6] And in a sermon that Abelard sent to Heloise and her nuns on the occasion of the Feast of the Annunciation, he wrote: "Hear now, Virgins, you who have chosen not a man but God as your bride and have agreed to follow the example of her—Mary's—holy confession! Betrothed to a human being, Joseph, she does not openly seek this man but quietly seeks God. She did not turn her eyes back upon the world but lifted them up to heaven. Her ears did not ask for wedding songs; instead, she nourished her soul with the food of divine readings."[7]

Abelard says much the same in his personal letters to Heloise; he steps back entirely into the role of the spiritual adviser and the *servant of Mary*:

> It was a happy transfer of your married state, for you were previously the wife of a poor mortal and now are raised to the bed of the King of kings. By the privilege of your position you are set not only over your former husband but over every servant of that King.[8]

Nor would you have been more than a woman, whereas now you rise even above men, and have turned the curse of Eve into the blessing of Mary. How unseemly for those holy hands which now turn the pages of sacred books to have to perform degrading services in women's concerns![9]

When Abelard in this way proclaims his civil wife, Heloise, to be the Bride of God—in accord with the confusing circumstance that God himself exists in two male generations—he implicitly moves into a position that is already occupied in the Christian family myth. This is the position of Joseph, Mary's lawful husband, who is nevertheless excluded from physical union by God. Although Abelard does not state so explicitly, his marriage to the nun Heloise, who is committed to God, mirrors the holy marriage; this means that his imposed chastity repeats Joseph's chastity.[10] The famous theologian drew a higher meaning from his misfortune, for he thought of his emasculation less as a human intervention than a divine one, accepting it in a spirit of penance: "that this member should justly be punished for all its wrongdoing in us, expiate in suffering the sins committed for its amusement, and cut me off from the slough of filth in which I had been wholly immersed in mind as in body."[11]

Like Joseph, Abelard is married but incapable of consummating the marriage; married to a woman who devoted herself to the monastic life and "transformed Eve's curse into Mary's blessing"; married to a woman who was living in mystical union with God. Like Joseph, he acquiesced in this separation and recognized its redemptive quality. In this way, the fate of the Parisian theologian and philosopher is—through a literal enactment, so to speak—a commentary on the circumstances of the role played by the figure of Joseph.

The Two Bodies of Man

The correspondence between Abelard and Heloise is an important link in the intertextual web that connects the bourgeois marriage stories of the eighteenth and nineteenth centuries—either as a whole or in individual traits—to the Christian perspective on the family. The critical bridge text comes to us in Rousseau's novel *Julie, or The New Heloise*. There is a whole series of parallels between the medieval precursor text and its sensitive revival by Rousseau.

In both cases, the medium of the letter plays a crucial role. The starting point is also the same in the two stories: a tutor seduces his student. In Abelard's case, the erotic relationship gives rise to a chain of events consisting of his flight, his successful effort to procure the consent of Heloise's family to the marriage, and, finally, his treacherous emasculation.

Rousseau arranges the positions in a new way. In his novel, the conflict no longer takes place between the lovers and God as the third authority; rather, it moves exclusively within the setting of the family. The tutor Saint-Preux is not robbed of his masculinity but merely prevented from marrying his student. Julie—who, by virtue of the title, is already most closely associated with the medieval reference text—does not withdraw into a monastery but into the bastion of virtue that is marriage. Her bridegroom, moreover, is not Christ but an older, paternal figure. The place of God is occupied by the legitimate husband chosen by her father, while the position of the emasculated lover is transformed into that of the distant soul mate.

In this way, Christian asceticism is turned toward the familial sphere and made intimate. Rousseau renders implicit what was manifest in the precursor text: castration is mitigated into loving renunciation. Monastic seclusion and love of God are fused in the tableau of an exemplary domestic marriage. The sensitive lovers behave *as if* an act of castration had taken place, though technically it no longer occurs within the narrative.

If one were to trace this interpretation of the tutor Saint-Preux, who has committed himself to renunciation, back to the New Testament figure of Joseph via Abelard, it would surely result in some contradictions. After all, Rousseau's "Joseph" has a passionate affair with his "Mary" before he has to relinquish her to a paternal man who outranks him in social status. Thus considerable deviations occur on the way from the biblical ur-text, via the medieval story of monasticism and castration, to Rousseau's sentimental novel. Still, the *structural* agreements are impossible to overlook. Julie's fate is likewise touched by a religious dimension. Virtually forced by her father into a marriage with a man she does not love, the *sacred mystery of marriage* reveals itself to her at the moment the marital bond is formalized:

> When I reached the Church, I felt as I entered a sort of emotion I had never before experienced. I know not what terror seized hold of my soul in that simple and august place, filled through with the majesty of the one who is served therein. A sudden dread made me shiver. . . . I thought I saw the instrument of providence and heard the voice of God in the minister's grave recitation of the holy liturgy. The purity, the dignity, the holiness of marriage, so vividly set forth in the words

of Scripture, those chaste and sublime duties so important to happiness, to order, to peace, to the survival of mankind, so sweet to fulfill for their own sake; all this made such an impression on me that I seemed to experience within me a sudden revolution. It was as if an unknown power repaired all at once the disorder of my affections and re-established them in accordance with the law of duty and nature. The eternal eye that sees all, I said to myself, is now reading the depths of my heart; it compares my hidden will with the reply from my lips: Heaven and earth are witness to the sacred engagement into which I enter, as they will be as well to my faithfulness in observing it.[12]

Entrance into marriage for Julie means solemn submission to the law of her father, which is a divine, social, and moral law. As she utters the marriage vow, she is seized by the Word of God. She is entering into a union not so much with the man at her side as with God. Julie goes through a conversion crisis in the full religious sense. After the wedding, she withdraws into prayer and seals her union with the Father in heaven. Rousseau places something like the credo of bourgeois wives into her mouth:

At once, acutely sensing the danger from which I was delivered and the state of honor and safety to which I felt restored, I prostrated myself on the ground, I lifted toward heaven my supplicating hands, I invoked the Being whose throne it is and who when it pleases him sustains or destroys by means of our own strength the freedom he grants us. I will, said I, the good that thou willest, and of which thou alone art the source. I will love the husband thou has given me. I will be faithful, because that is the first duty which binds the family and all of society. I will be chaste, because that is the first virtue which nurtures all the others. I will everything that belongs to the order of nature thou hast established, and to the rules of reason thou gavest me. I place my heart under thy protection and my desires in thy hand.[13]

Saint-Preux's youthful love cannot prevail against the alliance of paternal authorities—Monsieur de Wolmar, the paternal husband chosen for Julie; Julie's father herself; and, finally, God, who reveals himself to her at the wedding in a way that bears a distinct motivic resemblance to Mary's Annunciation. For Julie, who now yields to a veritable intoxication of virtue, the affair with the tutor becomes no more than "the error of a moment."[14] Although Rousseau is so precise and great a writer as to be able to carefully record even the moments that resist this virtuous decision, this does not alter the fact that the novel, in the manifest course of its narrative, offers a *model of discipline* and can be read and emulated as such. The teaching he imparts can be summarized, more or less, as follows: a marriage that is truly filled with virtue must leave behind every residue of passion; the inclination of love that makes marital life harmonious and virtually paradisiacal is grounded rather in *reason*, and this reason is in league with the patriarchal authorities.

Rousseau's novel is mutable; it changes color, so to speak, depending on how one looks at it. From the perspective of the separation of the youthful lovers, it can be read as the story of an unfulfilled love forced into renunciation—indeed, a tragic love. But this kind of interpretation—which is also reflected in the statements and lives of the protagonists—merely mirrors an "immature" perception of things, one that has not yet attained real understanding. Rousseau presents the happiness of a partnership at the level of a higher understanding, one that brings inclination and reason into harmony. His novel strives to attain the same goal preached by the marriage guidebooks of the Enlightenment: to make renunciation and happiness, asceticism and the fulfillment of love *indistinguishable*.

The claim to be offering a model of womanly morality is another feature that Rousseau's adaptation shares with the medieval love story. Both sets of correspondence provide instruction for a higher understanding of female virtue. A crucial difference lies in the fact that the civilizing initiative in the sensitive novel is shifted to the woman. Abelard drafted for Heloise the first female monastic rule complete with a wealth of behavioral rules; the new Heloise makes herself the exemplar of the domestically cloistered woman and loving mother; whereas the men in both cases are traveling scholars, inhabitants of marginal spaces, assailants who are put back in their place.

On the surface it would appear that in Rousseau's triangular story inclusion and exclusion, virile power and renunciation, are simply distributed between two mutually independent male roles within and outside marriage, respectively. As such, the *New Heloise* appears to describe the much-lamented circumstance that love and marriage rarely overlap: Julie does not marry Saint-Preux, whom she loves, but Wolmar, whom she is obliged to love and who gains possession of the connubial privileges by virtue of paternal and divine dispensation. However, one can also see in this triangle—and this perception goes much deeper—an explication of the dilemma of the marital partnership of love, which became a prime topic and problem in the eighteenth century. From this perspective, the novelistic dual tale—of a passion that is not permitted to prevail and an inclination to duty that makes Julie seem like an exemplary wife—would appear to be nothing more than a complex description of the dramaturgy of the bourgeois marriage. That description does not contradict the concept of a love marriage. Instead, it relates the price that must be paid to render this concept feasible as well as morally tolerable.

Within the context of such a marital dramaturgy, the woman has to deal not with various male characters but with a *discursively split masculinity*: on the one hand, with the husband as the guarantor of the patriarchal order, and, on the other, with the husband as a desirous being who must pay a liminal price to enter into this order and identify with it. Wolmar would be the name for one side and Saint-Preux the name for the other side of a masculinity that is performing with divided roles, so to speak. To direct a marriage in the sense of bourgeois moralism, the woman must transform the lover of the courtship phase into the paternal husband who is certified by God and who, in his wisdom and omniscience, occupies God's place. She must understand and shape her marriage as the emanation of divine reason. Above all, she must learn *to deify her husband*. That does not necessarily rule out a certain wistfulness as she looks back on her encounter with that other, passionate masculinity, which had to be abandoned on the road to marriage.

One would be hard-pressed to imagine Mary's Joseph as a passionate, premarital lover. But he is a man of flesh and blood who must yield to a higher paternal authority. To that extent, therefore, there are parallels between the marriage of the holy parents and the bourgeois model of a union of affection. For the latter model also revolves around the replacement of physical love with spiritual love. All positions of the Holy Family reappear in slightly disguised form in the countless programmatic writings on the bourgeois marriage partnership. The mother devotes herself chastely and virtuously to the child she has conceived by her husband, who outranks her and reaches higher into the heaven of patriarchy. The man filling the father role disappears as an individual human being in the chain of authority of all the paternal powers that extend beyond the circle of the nuclear family. Finally, there is also the nontranscendental side of masculinity, which is occupied by figures whose most important task lies in orderly retreat—Joseph figures.

20

HOLY FAMILY, BOURGEOIS FAMILY

Beneath the *motivic history* of the Holy Family—expressed in a series of theological, pictorial, and literary assimilations—there emerges a *structural history* in which two ways of creating society compete with each other. One way obeys the order of procreation, of descent and kinship ties. The other addresses the collective as a spiritual entity transcending the visible individual bodies—in the process propelling, on whatever convoluted historical pathways, the formation of a large, abstract, uniform aggregate of power: first the church and later the state.

In the model of the Holy Family—as a nuclear family that is broken open, fragmented, and *in the thrall of the transcendent*—the state found something like an ideological ally. To that extent it could pick up the thread of the church's "preparatory work": centuries of effort to gain control over the center of society's biological reproduction through the legal and moral regulation of marriage; and all those sociogenetic and psychogenetic processes that allowed the social ordering power of *love* to arise from lower, wilder, animalistic *sexuality*. Love is reconceptualized as a *higher* feeling and a feeling *inclined toward the higher*—a feeling whose *haute école* in the West was the Christian religion.

If, against this background, one tries to draw a flowchart of the application of the Holy Family, the result is a progressive *naturalization* of the model. In the beginning, holiness and family were thought of as clear opposites. But after marriage had been declared a sacrament in the High Middle Ages and, at the very latest, since the Reformation, more and more traits of the divine migrated into the normal human family itself. Lower and higher love, sexual desire and desire for God formed psychodynamic amalgams. More precisely, the original religious impulse of elevation and spiritualization pervaded increasingly larger spheres of "lower" everyday reality: in the end, as the example of the various marital reform movements demonstrates, even sexual love could become virtuous and "godly."

Christianity formulated its creed in a metaphysically divided world, and it processed this split on the level of theology as well as the level of emotional dynamics. Yet its goal was always to reunite the two parts—a goal that had already existed in exemplary fashion in the unity of the person of Christ.

"Spirit" and "flesh" were thus no longer two utterly alien realms; the alternative to the inseparable unity of fleshliness, lust, and death—which is how early Christian writings conceptualized marriage—was no longer the renunciation of marriage. Instead, abstinence and marriage became intertwined; they blended and reinforced each other. In the process of the interior colonization of the human being, the "spirit" sinks ever more deeply into creaturely bodies and their reproductive ways. In this manner, the old dilemma of the Christian theology of marriage seems to have been resolved. Yet the price for this *dis-ambiguitization* is new complications. Now, more than ever, the problem of what a *holy sexual relationship* is supposed to look like emerges in pronounced form and in all its weightiness. Comprehensive semantics are required to render the model of the Holy Family translatable into the sphere of the human family.

Semantics of Sanctification

The possibilities for a narrative "sanctification" of the family can be sorted out according to the three members of the classic nuclear family: father, mother, child.

As far as the male position is concerned, "sanctification" is possible only at the price of a split that is already prefigured in the Holy Family itself. In literary terms, this split can be played out in a variety of ways. First, it can take the form of triangular stories as a split between physical-sexual masculinity here, and higher, paternal-divine masculinity there, between the husband as the authority of bourgeois order and the man as a sexual being physically desired, who must be forced out of the game by means of symbolic or real castration.

Second, it can take the form of a subtle conflict between the often unimpressive empirical appearance of the man, on the one hand, and his status as God's deputy and his resemblance to God, accorded him by his role, on the other.

Third, it can appear through the exchange of position by several of the men involved, through the unclear affiliation of children, and through paternity by way of adoption. Here one is dealing with the topos of displaced, *nonprocreative fatherhood*, which appears in many stories dating from around 1800. Time and again, these literary fantasies deal with children who enter the world in mysterious ways, whose origins remain obscure, and who are exchanged for a natural child and are thus not natural children themselves—part of the family yet removed from the bonds of blood kinship.

As for the woman, Christian culture pursued her "sanctification" with special vigor. Traditionally, the key to these efforts was virginity. By preserving her virginity, a woman not only was removed from the desires of men, but also offered her inviolate body to God as a holy vessel. Her sexual closure forms only the prerequisite condition for the other, principal, aspect—the opening up toward the side of transcendence. The inviolate female body serves as the symbolic stage for the passage from this world into the other world—a "bridge," as Mariologists term it.

Now, bourgeois wives and mothers were not virgins in the sense of the asceticism of the early church. To that extent they had to endure the paradox of Mary, who was able to be both, in their own bodies, except that they had to do so with natural means. This was achieved with the help of a semantics that translated the notion of virginity into that of virtue, and, even more far-reaching, into that of female *innocence*. Femininity was fundamentally redefined in the course of the eighteenth century, roughly speaking, through a change from the baroque to the sensitive womanly type. The baroque woman, understood as a topos, still had much of the creaturely addiction to the passions about her; she was wild, untamed, pagan-hetaeran. The sensitive woman left behind this kind of dramatic physicality; her body was the ephebic envelope of her psychic being. Virtue not only served as external armor against the temptations of the other sex but had now descended to the profoundest depth of her soul. This *virginity of the soul* could certainly be reconciled with biological motherhood—provided that the woman kept herself *inwardly* free of all sexual pollution.

If the bourgeois woman as mother wanted to preserve the honorable badge of innocence, it was possible only through spiritual virginity, in distant imitation of medieval notions of a fulfillment of the sexual duties of marriage that ideally was devoid of passion. But what remained in the Middle Ages the exception of a holy way of life, the middle-class discourse on marriage proclaimed to be the everyday norm. While the woman had to fulfill the duties of her sex—after all, that was the only way to attain the female ideal of motherhood—in her innermost being she must not participate in it. Ideally she is not present during the act of consummation, neither actively (a woman is expressly prohibited from showing sexual initiative) nor consciously (which would tarnish the immaculateness of her soul).

The sexual anthropology and ethics of the Age of Reason found various approaches to resolving this paradoxical demand placed on the virtuous woman and mother. On the medical level, while intercourse without a female orgasm was considered infertile during the previous centuries—a notion that accorded the woman's pleasure a certain justification—the medical profession in the age of sensibility arrived at the opposite conclusion, a view that remained normative even for the nineteenth century. A woman no longer required arousal to become pregnant; she could conceive a child without participating in the act through her physical sensations. During the Victorian era, this postulate became an empirical fact. Leading British doctors active around the middle of the nineteenth century even believed that women were constitutionally incapable of experiencing orgasm.[1]

On the psycho-economic level, this attitude meshed well with a cultural technique that became a veritable emblem of female decency in the bourgeois era. Enlightenment moralists never tired of assuring their readers that innocence meant not merely the avoidance of indecent acts; more than that, it was *ignorance*, unawareness of sin. On this point, the bourgeois ideology of innocence differed from the older notion of virtue, with its courtly imprint; the latter was conceived as *defensive* and to that extent incorporated experiential knowledge about the possibilities of temptation. How, then, was it possible for the bourgeois woman to fulfill her biological task, on the one hand, and, on the other, to remain "ignorant" from the perspective of moral understanding? There was one behavioral option to resolve this performative contradiction, one that was liberally used not solely by female fictional heroines of the eighteenth and nineteenth centuries. As soon as circumstances demanded it, these women literally put themselves into a state of mental absence: they fainted. Whereas an angel appeared to Mary, bourgeois women—to the extent that they were obeying the prescriptions of innocence imposed on them—let their spirit depart their bodies. The villain of the novel of manners à la Richardson as well as the groom of a perfectly pure girl embraced a woman who was, according to the ideal, mentally absent, unconscious.[2]

This physiological regulating mechanism could be supplemented by narrative measures. On the level of narration, one is, after all, confronted by the problem of how the pure *bride* becomes the pure *mother* without allowing female sexuality to break forth as an active, threatening power in the uncoded interval *between* the two manifestations of the female ideal. One can call this the narrative problem of the wedding night. The usual solution was to render the interval between marriage and motherhood imperceptible by leaping ahead in the narrative or using some other literary devices of narrational interruption. These kinds of literary maneuvers of silence and concealment are analogous to female fainting as a psychological technique of the unconscious.

Holy mothers conceive holy children. In a certain sense, all bourgeois children—or at least boys—are successors to Jesus: surrounded by a soft halo that reflects the afterglow of the mystery of their origins; objects of a supernatural maternal happiness. In the intimate nuclear families of the age of sensibility and the era of Romanticism, the child is accorded the role of the bearer of grace. If— according to the pedagogical doctrines of the seventeenth century and in the patriarchal familial tyrannies well into the middle years of the Enlightenment— children had still been little devils from whom original sin had to be driven out with the rod, children and angels now entered into an iconographic liaison. One of the pivotal writers who reflected this change was Rousseau. The stain of original sin seemed to have been expunged; Enlightenment pedagogues delighted in the tabula rasa condition of the child's mind, which, they believed, could be completely trained and educated in accordance with their own ideas.

Split paternities; innocent and sexless mothers; salvific children of mysterious origin: if one is correct in regarding these three designations as partial postfigurations of the Christian typology of the family—often distorted and also seized on by other contexts—then one can say that the embourgeoisement of the family brought with it a veritable proliferation of religious motifs. That has led to a strangely distorted picture since the second half of the eighteenth century. The official, middle-class propaganda of virtue developed the new norm of the complete, loving, and happy nuclear family as a refuge for the work-harried family father and the place where children were socialized on the path to a entirely new life's goal: giving expression to their own *individuality*. At the same time, literature dealt almost exclusively with families that were fragmented, thwarted by outside forces, and whose individual positions were coded in multiple and contradictory ways. Both the official texts and the literary narratives make use of Christian topoi, but they do so with apparently contrary tendencies. Once again, the Holy Family supplied norms and, it would seem, constellations contrary to the norms. However, it is not enough simply to identify the contradiction. One must probe into the functional division between normality and deviance.

Kleist and Krug: Philosophy of the Sexes

Although the writer Heinrich von Kleist (1777–1811) never married, he was, like Kafka, briefly engaged. His fiancée was Wilhelmine von Zenge. In another parallel to Kafka, a voluminous correspondence between the betrothed has survived. Unlike Kafka, however, Kleist embarked on the purposeful endeavor of educating the woman he had chosen in accordance with his own ideas. At the time, this was the usual way of preparing for the wedding. To achieve his end, Kleist chose

a proven device still widely used today: the reflective essay. Kleist was thus acting as the teacher selecting the topics. Wilhelmine figured as his obedient pupil,
who was given her assignments and had them corrected in the form of letters.

On one occasion Kleist posed the question: "Which of two spouses, each of
whom fulfills his duties toward the other, loses more in case of the untimely
death of the other?"[3] Along with the question, he provided Wilhelmine with the
answer: the husband loses more than the wife. Why? Because the relationship of
the sexes to each other and to the state is not symmetrical but unequally bal-
anced. Kleist maintained that

> the man is not merely the husband to his wife but also a citizen of the state, where-
> as the woman is nothing other than the wife to her husband; that the man has ob-
> ligations not only towards his wife but also toward his fatherland, whereas the
> woman has no obligations other than those toward her husband; that, conse-
> quently, the happiness of the wife, while an important and indispensable concern
> of the man, is not his *only* concern, whereas the happiness of the husband is the
> *sole* concern of the wife; . . . that, lastly, the husband is not always happy if his
> wife is, whereas the wife is always happy if the husband is happy, and that the
> happiness of the husband is therefore actually the chief object of the efforts of
> both spouses. From a comparison of these statements, the power of judgment
> now determines that the husband receives far more—indeed, immeasurably
> more—from his wife than the wife receives from her husband.[4]

The nature of woman is love. Her husband, who is compelled to pull back from
his wife because he also has civic tasks to fulfill, is the sole content of her life.
Kleist is not alone in this attitude; one could describe it as the commonsense notion of the philosophy of the sexes around 1800. The asymmetry in the roles of
men and women is closely linked to the unequal relationship they have to their
respective sexual constitutions. For the woman is not only all love but also all
gender. The man *has* a gender; the woman *is* her gender. A man is conceivable
independent of his gender; a woman is not, for without gender she would miss
her entire destiny.

A prizewinning pedagogical essay of 1791 had this to say about the topic:

> The stirrings aroused by the feeling of lust express themselves in the male sex pri-
> marily and almost exclusively in areas that are, by their location and nature, not es-
> sential and indispensable for life. Thus, they also do not indicate an essential need

indispensable for living; consequently they are not as urgent as the need that can be satisfied by nothing other than the immediate attainment of the desired object. [5]

However, the sex that is something incidental in man must be regarded as something essential in woman. Sex—remarked *Rousseau*, if memory serves me right—does not exist for the sake of the woman but woman for the sake of sex. [6]

In short, you can amputate a man's sex, but you cannot do the same in a woman. Something is left over in a man—his citizenship in the state. The woman would be obliterated anatomically and in her sexual nature by such a procedure. That is why a man can have sexual desire without putting himself at stake; his existence comprises more than merely his sexual lust. A woman, however, must have no sexual desire, for she would allow herself to be devoured by her carnal impulses. A man can split himself; he exists in two dimensions. A woman is one with herself and for that very reason is in constant danger of losing herself completely.

We do not know what Wilhelmine von Zenge actually thought about Kleist's essay topics and the answers he suggested. Their engagement, in any case, was broken off after two years. Wilhelmine later married a certain Wilhelm Traugott Krug, a professor of philosophy and Kant's successor in Königsberg. A long-standing joke among Kleist scholars has it that Kleist, jealous and angry, wrote the comedy *Der zerbrochene Krug* (The Broken Jug). When it came to leading a secure bourgeois life, Wilhelmine was better off with Wilhelm Krug than she would have been with her former fiancé. But as far as ideas about love and marriage were concerned, she went from bad to worse with her new companion.

Krug was the author of a work entitled *Philosophy of Marriage*, which appeared anonymously in 1800, the same year, in fact, in which Kleist posed his essay topic. In it, one reads the following:

At first man merely seeks his pleasure, and woman is at first the part that yields to him for his pleasure; consequently she is the means of the man's pleasure. But when the man's urge is afterward refined through love, he also makes the happiness of his lover his goal. . . . In the woman it is exactly the other way around. Originally she merely seeks to satisfy the man's desire; nature, however, rewards her for this surrender, this voluntary sacrifice, by which she lays claim to her dignity as a creature of reason, with pleasure as well, which is thus not purpose but merely a natural result of her surrender. Only in and through this reflection, of which the (pure and innocent) female heart actually knows nothing—or at most suspects something in dim sensations—does the man become for the woman a means of sensual pleasure, since beyond and without this reflection he is to her merely an object of delight and the most intimate affection.[7]

The woman has no desire, and she does not enjoy pleasure sui generis. If she feels pleasure, she is enjoying the pleasure of the man. And if this enjoyment of that pleasure makes her feel lust, the "pure and innocent" female heart still does not know what that is. She has nothing more than an intimation "in dim sensations." Her conception in a state of unawareness is tantamount to a *conceptio immaculata*.

One is here precisely at the threshold where the religious notion of divine conception becomes Victorian, so to speak, where a virginity that is directed toward the supernatural yields to a not-knowing, an unawareness prompted by decency or, psychoanalytically speaking—and psychoanalysis itself in its innermost nature belongs to the Victorian era—suppression.

Kleist's "Marquise of O——"

In Kleist's writings, one finds many allusions to the motivic complex of the Holy Family. It is clearly apparent in "Earthquake in Chile," a story whose middle section reenacts, almost in a painterly manner, the artistic subject of the "Rest on the Flight." The allusions are less direct in the story "The Foundling," which, like so many of Kleist's works, revolves around the replacement of a natural by an adoptive child, around the relationship of nonbiological parenthood. His dramatic plays as well—at least the complementary plays *Käthchen von Heilbronn* and *Penthesilea*—deal with the issues of the female unconscious and the female desire for God and develop a religious dimension. But Kleist carried the theme to its extreme in a novella that—by its very title and its subject matter borrowed from Montaigne[8]—is at heart a bawdy tale: the story of how the Marquise of O—— became pregnant by Count F——.

Kleist himself provided a commentary on this text. It is a peculiar commentary, laced with irony, and as is so often the case with irony, one cannot be sure exactly how to take it. An epigram he inserted into the journal *Phöbus*, published by him and Adam Müller, reads:

THE MARQUISE OF O——
THIS novel is not for you, my daughter. Unconscious! Shameless farce! For all I know, she merely kept her eyes shut.[9]

The novel, whose possible bawdy deeper meaning Kleist himself brings out, begins—very much in keeping with the classic definition of this literary genre—
with a *novella*, an item of news in the paper:

> In M——, an important town in northern Italy, the widowed Marquise of O——,
> a lady of unblemished reputation and the mother of several well-brought-up chil-
> dren, inserted the following announcement in the newspapers: that she had, with-
> out knowledge of the cause, come to find herself in a certain situation; that she
> would like the father of the child she was expecting to disclose his identity to her;
> and that she was resolved, out of consideration for her family, to marry him.[10]

The entire story revolves around this announcement, "so strange a step," which
exposes the Marquise "to the derision of society." It resembles a crime story in
which a case must be solved. A kind of flashback explains what compelled the
heroine of the title to take this step; only toward the end does the story return to
the time when the announcement was placed in the paper. In fact, the father
makes himself known, and the mystery of how the Marquise could become pregnant unbeknownst to herself finds a rational resolution. Less than a page is
enough for the author to relate the outcome of this strange liaison, which is
sealed with a marriage after the fact.

The Marquise's father, in whose house she has been living since the husband's
death, is commandant of the local citadel. That circumstance drags his family into
the conflicts of war. Her father must defend the citadel, which is attacked and finally captured by Russian soldiers. During the capture of the citadel, an incident
takes place that violates the code of honor of the war, which was still being fought
according to old aristocratic rules of conduct. The Marquise and her children
(though the latter mysteriously disappear from the scene) fall into the hands of a

> troop of riflemen, who as soon as they saw her suddenly fell silent, slung their
> guns over their shoulders and, with obscene gestures, seized her and carried her
> off. . . . Dragging her into the innermost courtyard they began to assault her in
> the most shameful way, and she was just about to sink to the ground when a Russ-
> ian officer, hearing her piercing screams, appeared on the scene and with furious
> blows of his sword drove the dogs back from the prey for which they lusted. To
> the Marquise he seemed an angel sent from heaven. He smashed the hilt of his
> sword into the face of one of the murderous brutes, who still had his arms round
> her slender waist, and the man reeled back with blood pouring from his mouth;

he then addressed the lady politely in French, offered her his arm and led her into the other wing of the palace which the flames had not yet reached and where, having already been stricken speechless by her ordeal, she now collapsed in a dead faint. Then—the officer instructed the Marquise's frightened servants, who presently arrived, to send for a doctor; he assured them that she would soon recover, replaced his hat and returned to the fighting.[11]

"Then—the officer instructed . . . " It is probably no exaggeration to speak—in reference to this small, barely noticeable narrative pause—of the most famous dash in world literature. The very basis of the story lies hidden in this silent expansion of the otherwise breathless pace of the sentences. The entire tale unfolds from this gap. For it is this very Count F—— who, on the third day after the publication of the notice, appears before the Marquise and reveals himself as the man who raped her.

But before coming to that point, Kleist's text spins an exquisitely wrought hermeneutics of corporeal signs and how they are interpreted and misread. In the process it leaves out none of the possible nuances and ambiguities. One is, after all, dealing with *the* classic question of bourgeois sexual morality: the question of whether it is possible to prove a woman's innocence.

Count F—— continues to besiege the family not in a military but in a social sense: he wants to marry the Marquise as quickly as possible, and he pursues his wish with an ardor that breaks all conventional rules: "All were agreed that his behaviour was extraordinary, and that he seemed to be accustomed to taking ladies' hearts, like fortresses, by storm."[12] The Marquise, meanwhile, soon experiences unmistakable signs of pregnancy. She consults a doctor, who confirms her suspicion. To make doubly sure, she calls for a midwife. Kleist relates the scene with his unique brand of humor:

When the latter arrived, the Marquise was still lying with her mother's arms around her and her breast heaving in agitation. The Commandant's wife told the woman of the strange notion by which her daughter was afflicted: that her ladyship swore her behaviour had been entirely virtuous but that nevertheless, deluded by some mysterious sensation or other, she considered it necessary to submit her condition to the scrutiny of a woman with professional knowledge. The midwife, as she carried out her investigation, spoke of warm-blooded youth and the wiles of the world; having finished her task she remarked that she had come across such cases before; young widows who found themselves in her ladyship's situation always believed themselves to have been living on desert islands; but that there was no cause for alarm, and her ladyship could rest assured that the gay corsair who had come ashore in the dark would come to light in due course. On hearing these words, the Marquise fainted. . . .

The Marquise, now nearly swooning again, drew the midwife down in front of her and laid her head against her breast, trembling violently. With a faltering voice she asked her what the ways of nature were, and whether such a thing as an unwitting conception was possible. The woman smiled, loosened her kerchief and said that that would, she was sure, not be the case with her ladyship. "No, no," answered the Marquise, "I conceived knowingly, I am merely curious in a general way whether such a phenomenon exists in the realm of nature." The midwife replied that with the exception of the Blessed Virgin it had never yet happened to any woman on earth.[13]

As a result of the confirmation of her pregnancy, the Marquise, though insisting on her innocence, is repudiated by her parents. She takes up residence at a rural estate and hits upon the idea of placing the announcement with which the story opens. Her forlornness strengthens her resolve. While the comparison of her fate with that of the Virgin Mary from the mouth of the midwife carried elements of a fierce parody, one now finds in the text a growing number of markers that impart a sacral connotation to her mysterious conception. In hindsight, it becomes clear that the story was interlaced—like a leitmotif—with such connotations from the outset. They concern the Count, who seemed to the swooning Marquise in the citadel like "an angel sent from heaven." Later, when he appears at the family's house, he looks "as beautiful as a young god," his arrival totally unexpected because he was believed dead, which is why the commandant's wife refers to him as a "ghost" who "rose again from the grave in which you were laid."[14] They also concern the Marquise: the Count, in a feverish dream, saw her as a pure, white swan who kept washing off every stain—indeed, in general the Marquise is constantly linked to metaphors of purity. Finally, they also concern the unborn child (a boy, as it turns out). "The only thing she found intolerable," we are told of the Marquise, "was the thought that the little creature she had conceived in the utmost innocence and purity and whose origin, precisely because it was more mysterious, also seemed to her more divine than that of other men, was destined to bear a stigma of disgrace in good society."[15]

Donadeo, a gift from God, is what Italians called foundling children left at the portals of churches. Genealogically unmarked and thus belonging to a realm of origin outside society, they laid out a path to their supernatural progenitor.

Kleist's novella, too, plays with the kinship of the unknown to the holy. For example, he transforms the tale of a rape into a different story about the establishment of a holy family. The axis along which the translation between the two narratives can succeed is the woman's ignorance. An angel appears to the heroine, she faints, and then awakens as a mother-to-be. This provides material not only for a short novel of morals with a double meaning that can be read as the very foundation of "The Marquise of O———," but also for a transfigurative reading supported by the text through a wealth of clues. Everything hinges on the woman's unawareness. But this unawareness, which makes the woman *pure*, is itself marked by an ambiguity that pervades Kleist's text. The unawareness that the Marquise claims for herself does not escape the paradox that it *knows* that *it must not know*.

Kleist composed *the* classic scene to express this ambiguity. Count F——— gains access to the country estate where the Marquise is living in seclusion, and he does so in a way that once again calls forth erotic connotations. At first we are told that he entered "by a door which he found unlocked," and a little later the Count elaborates with peculiar—one could almost say perverse—specificity: "I found a back door open and came through it into your garden." The Count comes on strong to the Marquise, telling her that he is "fully convinced" of her "innocence . . . as convinced, Giuletta, as if I were omniscient, as if my own soul were living in your body." The whole thrust of the scene is toward a final revelation, but then comes this response from the Marquise: "'I *do not want to know* anything,' she retorted, violently pushing him back; then she fled up on the terrace and disappeared."[16]

And yet, the Marquise, who did "not want to know anything," places her appeal in the paper. When Count F——— appears on the stipulated day and time, she is beside herself, calling him a "devil." Her family has a difficult time convincing her to honor her promise of marriage. The wedding itself is a cold and formal affair: "During the ceremony the Marquise stared rigidly at the painting behind the altar and did not vouchsafe even a fleeting glance at the man with whom she was exchanging rings." After the birth of the child, the Count is allowed to attend the baptism, and he leaves behind in his son's cradle "a deed of gift of 20,000 roubles to the boy" and a will appointing the Marquise as his heir. "From that day on," we are told, "the commandant's wife saw to it that he was frequently invited." Finally, a second wedding is arranged:

His instinct told him that, in consideration of the imperfection inherent in the order of the world, he had been forgiven by all of them, and he therefore began a second wooing of the Countess, his wife; when a year had passed he won from her a second consent, and they even celebrated a second wedding, happier than the first. . . . A whole series of young Russians now followed the first, and during one happy hour the Count asked his wife why, on that terrible day of the month, when she had seemed willing to receive the most vicious of debauchees, she had fled from him as if from a devil. Throwing her arms round his neck, she answered that she would not have seen a devil in him then if she had not seen an angel in him at their first meeting.[17]

The novel thus has two endings; it contains two stories. One story forms an inner ring, so to speak; the other story an outer ring. The inner ring consists of sexual violence, a formal wedding, and the arrangement of legal claims and matters of inheritance. However, this interior tale is framed by a very different narrative: the story of how a family, which in many traits imitates the Holy Family, is eventually united in love. The inner ring presents the man as rapist and "devil"; male love reveals the core of a violent and brutal desire. In the outer ring, by contrast, the man appears as an "angel"—that is, as God's messenger, the woman's "desire for God."[18] The "interior story" presents a cycle of violence and possession; the "framing story" places this context of violence into the transcendent realm of a higher love that reaches beyond the crude realism of the narrative action. The bridge between the two is established by fainting—that is to say, by innocence— which means (inner) female virginity. Once again, the bridge function of *virginitas*, on which the church fathers had already meditated, comes into play.

If one pieces all of this together, Kleist's novel becomes decipherable as simply a fictional version of the bourgeois phantasm of marriage. That love is conquest, that the woman is like a fortress or is defended by the father in the fortress of her birth family, and that the groom invades this fortress—these are venerable rhetorical topoi. In the love literature of the eighteenth century, one encounters not only the fortress metaphors, but also the man—once admitted into this fortress—described as a more or less violent usurper. Courtly literature even recommended pretending that a desired erotic "attack" was a rape. The seventeenth-century courtesan Ninon de l'Enclos, for example, wrote this about her sex: "We simply want to conceal that we like to be loved. One has to get women to the point where they can convince themselves that they were being raped or overpowered."[19]

How very different bourgeois sexual morality. Unconsciousness—Kleist's meaningful dash—and the subsequent belief in innocence on the part of those who were overpowered, an innocence that stands up to every test, are precise ciphers for the paradox that the virtuous woman must not know what is happening to her. The rape without a woman's mental participation represents the initial act of violence of the marriage; it is compensated for by legal transactions, property transfers, and the appointment of heirs. That would fulfill Kant's definition of marriage as a legal property relationship.

Possession, violence, and law, however, circumscribe only the innermost circle of the phantasm of marriage. The external, all-encompassing ring is *love*—and in love the husband reveals himself not as a rapist but as God. In *Amphytrion*, Kleist plays out this very dual role of the husband in a dramatic play of confusion. In the process, the woman's love must focus not on the body of the rapist, but only on the man's gender-transcending divinity; the man's love, in keeping with the motif of the "Marquise of O——," must focus only on the woman's holiness, her resemblance to Mary. Beyond the realm of the act of taking sexual possession, the establishment of every bourgeois family can be reduced to the establishment of a Holy Family. Such a *foundation story*—precisely in its *unfathomableness*—is what Kleist presents.

21

CHRIST AND OEDIPUS: FREUD'S COUP

The Reinstatement of the Flesh

The Enlightenment in Germany generally tended to leave religion's standing untouched, to the extent and as long as it could be reconciled with the guiding idea of a rational order of the world. By contrast, the nineteenth century—from Marx to David Friedrich Strauss and Nietzsche to Freud— is *the* era of religious criticism, of the materialistic-psychological unmasking of religious illusions.

The philosopher Ludwig Feuerbach set the tone when, in his work *The Essence of Christianity*, he formulated the famous saying that it was not God who created man in his image but man who created God in his.[1] Others continued in the pattern set by this inversion: Marx decoded religion as an ideology in the service of power; Nietzsche declared that God was dead because humankind, his creator, had killed him; even Freud, the inventor of the doctrine of the unconscious, was still operating entirely on the basis of the scientism of his time when he employed the psychological concept of projection—the (mistaken) transfer of subjective psychic contents onto an objective reality that was (in actuality) untouched by it—to explain the effects of religion.

Yet the antispiritualism of the nineteenth century revealed itself not only from this critical angle. Religious criticism in the name of an unprejudiced scientific understanding that was focused on the positive went hand in hand with a concern that Theodor Mundt, a German author of the first half of the nineteenth century, described as the "reinstatement of the flesh."[2]

The broad current of Neoclassicism around 1800 already devalued Christianity aesthetically and in terms of weltanschaung. It placed Christianity into an unfavorable light by comparing it with an idealized Hellenic culture. Christian culture was accused of being stuck in the categories of guilt and sin, while attributes such as sensual enjoyment and a sense of beauty and art were grouped on the side of Classicism. To put it in mythological terms, Venus was gaining ground against Mary. This mythological "catch-up" movement laid the ground for the erotic dispositions in the subsequent period. The emancipation of the *sensual human being* became one of the revolutionary slogans of the pre-1848 period.

Heinrich Heine, in particular, should be mentioned in this context. Paganism, whether in a classical-ancient or a Germanic-nationalistic garb, was given new cultural credit. Nietzsche, whose verdict of the Christian cult of suffering was particularly radical, elevated Dionysus into the countergod of a boundless, destructive lust incapable of being tamed by civilization.

On the whole, the affective and moral order in the Victorian age continued to be dominated by strong sexual guilt imperatives derived from the legacy of Christian thinking. At the same time, however, one witnesses the harbingers of a fundamental shift that still governs sexual consumerism: asceticism, spiritual exertion, and the quest for transcendence lose their power; values and life motifs become restricted to goals in this world; a "common sense" takes shape that reduces all higher stirrings in the religious understanding to purely corporeal-physical reference points. The continuing demand for a renunciation of physical urges is superimposed on this trend toward desublimation, resulting in contradictory and calamitous synergies.

At first glance, this does not seem to provide fruitful conditions for a motivic complex related to the Holy Family. What use does a period have for the sacred when many were striving to transform all the martyrs and saints of the church back into human beings of flesh and blood—indeed, into human beings with abnormal psychic dispositions (madmen and madwomen, hysterics)? To be sure, the nineteenth century saw an unexpected revival of Christian–Catholic forms of devotion.[3] Visions of the Madonna multiplied as the Marian cult experienced a late but intense flowering. At a time of intensifying struggles over church politics—waged under the banner of *Kulturkampf* in Germany—the church held aloft its image of humankind —especially of women—against the new alliance between biologism and the secular polity.[4] Still, a process of *de-Christianization* dominates the overall picture of the nineteenth century.

The remarkable fact is that the Holy Family as a cultural pattern effortlessly survived this extensive *de-Christianization*. Its image was used even where the emancipation from religion was pursued with programmatic urgency. That the Romantic cult of the mother drew on Christian sources is obvious. But even the progress-oriented authors of the pre-1848 era frequently let Christian motifs shine through in their texts like a watermark whenever they are talking about erotic and familial relationships. Even a literary current like Naturalism, totally committed to the new religion of science, remained entirely at home in the Christian–Western tradition in its choice of images. One only needs to read the early family dramas of Gerhart Hautpmann to be persuaded how deeply the naturalistic faithfulness to milieu is rooted in religious patterns, whose center is almost always formed by fragments or—since the dramas always end in catastrophe— *contrasting memory traces* of the Holy Family.

One can point to a variety of reasons why that was so. The pictorial inventory of the Holy Family agrees well with nineteenth-century bourgeois life, tailored as it was to the nuclear family. In fact, during this period the family is transformed into a devotional space pervaded by love—as shown by the history of the observance of Christmas,[5] which developed from a sociable holiday into the key intrafamilial ritual of the church year. Ever since, the happiness of children on Christmas Eve has been a popular, sentimental background stereotype against which the coldness of actual human relationships stands out all the more harshly.

Yet there is more to this reference back to the Christian Holy Family than this nostalgic, Biedermeier period undertone. For stirrings hostile to the family can also draw on biblical themes. They can lay claim to and update the model of Jesus as a family rebel, a son with a missionary claim to renewal, the destroyer of tradition. This particular trail in the Gospel story suited the semantics of individuality and innovation that had been forging ahead since the eighteenth century.

According to the old European social order, the role of the son lay in *continuing* the line of the fathers. The father was to be resurrected in rejuvenated form in the likeness of his son. The son was, in a certain sense, the reincarnation of paternal authority. The generational succession consisted of a chain of *resemblance relationships* whose constancy overarched all temporal vicissitudes and rendered them insignificant. Given the widening gap between the new and the old and the emergence of a genuine historical consciousness in modern times, this genealogical traditionalism revealed deeper and deeper cracks. It was no longer able to cover up the fracture points in the generational change, the increasing irreconcilability of the age differences.

The Revolt of the Sons

The Sturm und Drang period has been called the first youth movement in the history of literature. That description is correct insofar as the period around 1770 saw the creation of a vocabulary about the otherness of young people, their common deviation from the normative world of their parents. This vocabulary proved to be a model for later self-descriptions of the "young"—from "Young Germany" prior to 1848 to Jugendstil in art. The more life is seized by the dynamism of historical *acceleration*, the greater the ideological and individual polarization between those who represent tradition and those who stand for the future and consequently for a break with tradition. While tradition can lay claim to the sacredness of what has been valid since time immemorial, the design of the "future" can invoke the messianic sacredness of what is yet to come.

This generational conflict became radicalized in the literature of modernity around 1900. In these texts—and no doubt in social reality as well—it was carried out essentially among men; in other words, it remained a *homosocial* affair.

The rivalry between fathers and sons was not limited to the realm of the family. It articulated a break with tradition and a historical era that was of general importance—a *crisis of decision* between past and future that culminated in the avant-garde movements and the First World War. In this context, the father appears as the archetype of an order that has become obsolete but all the more repressive in its downfall. He is confronted by the son as the broken and despondent or impassioned and visionary adherent of the new, the unprecedented. Messianic traits collect in the image of the son and his suffering at the hands of the hostile world of the fathers. In this way, fragments of the Christian family story come into play time and again. What gives its motivic world a remarkable persistence even in the largely post-Christian textual milieu at the turn of the century is the fact that it can be read as the prefiguration of a generational struggle among men.

And what about the mother? She increasingly becomes the "prize" in the struggle between the menfolk of both generations. Predominant in the nineteenth century are two connected mother images. First, there is the loving mother of the Romantic cast, who embraces, nurses, teaches, and educates the child[6]—a protector of the intimate domestic realm that was created as a result of the embourgeoisement of the family. This mother haunts the literature like a vanished but life-determining primal image of an earlier bond that arouses a sense of longing.

Second, there is the figure of the Madonna who has descended from heaven and been won back to life in this world. Writers and poets fantasized Mary as a lover and the object of an openly erotic desire of possession. Theodor Mundt's slogan "reinstatement of the flesh" occurs in a travel story dating from 1835 entitled "Madonna," which provoked a vigorous scandal, both literary and with respect to censorship policies.[7] Mundt's journalistic–political chronicle intermixes Marian saintliness, women's emancipation, and physical eroticism, with the final product being a love story that his contemporaries considered deeply offensive. However, in many of these literary fantasies—for example, Heinrich Heine's

"Journey from Munich to Genoa"—Mary as a lover is removed from the man's desire by death or some higher dispensation.

To be sure, the mother-yearning / Mary-yearning of the literary works emulates a Catholic figure of faith: through the Virgin's intercession, the believer seeks access to the transcendent, to God's love. But the works at the dawn of modernity *pervert* this figure. They strip the veneration of Mary of its spiritual character and shift it into a sphere of this-worldly claims to possession. This erotic desire no longer points the path to God's majesty but finds its place within the context of an open father–son rivalry. The thrust of this rivalry is to *steal* the woman at God's side and hand her over to the son—in both the generational and theological sense: the younger, the human being.

The period after 1900 is the era of patricide. The male clash of generations has intensified to the point where it calls for violent solutions. In the history of literature, however, the violent eruptions of the Expressionistic works of patricide—by Walter Hasenclever, Franz Werfel, and Arnolt Bronnen, to name only the best known among German authors—were preceded by a long martyrdom, a *passion* of the sons.

The naturalistic family dramas from August Strindberg to Gerhart Hauptmann present a world in which fathers are sick, stricken, obsessive-compulsive, and lonely figures. Their tyranny bears the paradoxical face of authoritarian helplessness. This paradox continues in the sons, whose desire for liberation is countered by a peculiar longing for the restoration of paternal authority. They are weak characters whose rebellion is thwarted and transformed into hopelessness by their desire to fail.

One such figure, who is destroyed by his own contradictions, appears in Hauptmann's artist drama *Michael Kramer* (1900). Arnold Kramer, the son of the hero of the title, is unable to bear the pressure to succeed exerted by the domineering model of his father, who has been secretly working for years on a masterpiece: a "picture of the Christ."[8] Arnold is homely, deformed, awkward, insincere, and incapable of giving an account of himself to his father, by whom he is forcefully condemned. His weakness of character gets him embroiled in a situation that eventually costs him his life. But precisely at that moment, his father's behavior changes. After Arnold's death, he shows a tenderness and respect he withheld while he was alive. More precisely, he deifies the dead son.

The final scene of the play constitutes an act of communion. In the background the dead son is laid out as though on an altar. The father has the word, but the power of his speech is broken. He wants to "drink," to "pour a libation" in the face of this "great majesty": "All his life long I was his schoolmaster. I had to maltreat him and now he has risen into the divine. . . . I have shriveled into nothingness. I have become a wretched creature beside him. I look up to that boy now as though he were my farthest ancestor."[9]

In this final scene, Arnold Kramer has become one with his father's artistic subject: a messianic figure. His passion is complete. He has sacrificed himself to his father, whose godlike authority appears confirmed by this act. But Hauptmann's hero himself inverts the power relationship: he humbles himself before the Messiah of the next generation. The messianism of the young is thus not their own "achievement" but is virtually imposed on them by their elders. The classic patriarchy has become unhinged. While the sons support their fathers in their effort to maintain their posture of authority, the fathers refashion the suffering of their own sons into religiously grounded ideas of salvation.

A little more than a decade later, this sacrificial relationship was inverted. Walter Hasenclever's Expressionistic drama *The Son* already indicates as much in the typologically recast title role. The play is suffused with the pathetic desire to administer the fatal blow to the morbid tyranny of the fathers, which has now reached its end. And this is to be done in a very violent sense—even though editorial considerations turned the originally intended murder into the father's fatal heart attack. In Hasenclever, too, the son is elevated into a messianic figure. However, the ambivalence toward paternal authority and the self-paralysis it creates now seem to have been overcome. The rebellious sons no longer acquiesce in the sacrificial disposition, instead giving in to their patricidal desires. Hasenclever's play stages the patricide as an explicit *reversal* of Christ's passion: "You don't need a Christ on the cross," says a friend who is egging on the revolt. "Kill what has killed you!"[10] The murderous design is joined by erotic insubordination: the son takes his governess, who for him represents the mother's role, as his lover—with the explicit intent of "defiling" the paternal sphere of authority.[11]

It is readily apparent that in the literary struggle between the generations, the weight has shifted in favor of the sons. The role of the fantasized mother figure also changes: she now takes the side, politically and sexually, of the younger of the two rivals. In this way, the repeatedly invoked *imitatio* of Christ is pervaded by structures of Oedipal desire. But unlike the case of Oedipus, who is excluded from the community and banished after his double crime, the patricide of the Expressionistic Messiah figures is a *collectivizing* deed. It establishes a new, fraternal regime through the seizure of power by the sons. So much for the phantasmal plan of action, which psychoanalysis and literature articulated almost at the same time and, in part, independent of each other.

The antagonism between fathers and sons deals not only with dichotomies of the type "tradition versus revolution" or "law versus mission." There are also two forms of male rule at stake: old-style patriarchy, on the one hand, and the fatherless[12] band of brothers inspired by political expectations of redemption, on the other. Precisely this clash of male forms of rule made it possible for the history of the social repercussions of Christological motifs to be joined to the formulas of pathos articulated by the emerging National Socialist movement. In Joseph Goebbels's novel of conversion entitled *Michael*, Christ is *the* central figure—anti-Semitically appropriated as an allegory for the Germans enslaved by the Jews and awaiting their resurrection.[13]

From Christian Passion to Oedipal Rivalry

Freud has taught us to read the cycle that Jesus goes through—from a child in the crib bathed in the mother's loving gaze to a corpse in her arms, as depicted in the Pietà scenes, and finally to the heavenly nuptial relationship between the two—as the expression of an incestuous bond. In fact, with the rise of the *mater dolorosa* motif and the bridal mysticism of the thirteenth century, the Holy Family acquires a coloring that makes it suitable for such an interpretation. As a result, there has been no shortage of efforts to insert the Oedipus myth as rediscovered by Freud into the myth of the Holy Family.

There are, however, major and unresolvable discrepancies between the two. The most obvious lies in the fact that in the New Testament it is not the father but the son who is killed. And this "filicide" cannot simply be interpreted—as Freud attempted to do in his essay *Moses and Monotheism*—as the equivalent punishment for a primeval desire to kill the father and lay claim to the mother. If one allowed the calamity of Oedipus to remain valid through the Passion of Christ, its theological core, the message of atonement and reconciliation, would be meaningless.

The Gospels do not contain any indication whatsoever that Jesus had a regressive desire to unite with his mother. On the contrary, such fantasies make their appearance in Christian iconography only much later. Chronologically and iconographically, the union of mother and son is not the cause but the *result* of the son's death. Mary lovingly and symbiotically bends over her dead son, whose manhood has been taken from him by death. In fact, it is the son's sacrifice that establishes the closeness to the child she has won back. As great as Mary's pain is, she does not rebel against the redemptive death that God has decreed; too great is her understanding of God's plan of salvation—or, to put it differently, her complicity with the father. She does not yield to the son's posthumous desire, so to speak, but acts in suffering yet willing agreement with the great, invisible and fate-decreeing third party in the mournful triad.

The life of Jesus bequeathed to the artists and writers of the Christian period a dual legacy. First, there is the story of his *detachment* from his family, whose place is taken by his status as the Son of God and by his circle of disciples. Second, there is the story of the Passion, linked with images of the *return home* of the son's body. This story was effective for centuries as a narrative pattern for male biographies. What it means to be a son in European culture cannot be sufficiently grasped without this Christological subtext. It enacts the tension between two goals: substantial unity with the Father in heaven, glorification, and participation in divine rule; the precondition for which, however, is passion, abandonment, and death—though with the despondent–consoling participation of the Mother.

To the extent that the psychoanalysis of this model of the suffering passion imputes to it the pattern of an aggressive, Oedipal competition with the father, it not only reaccentuates the internal dramaturgy of the Christian model family, but also alters in profound ways the operative plan, the reproductive mechanism of patriarchal power as such. According to the psychoanalytic reading, the patriarchal succession of power is no longer regulated through a *merging with the identity of the father* at the price of the son's self-sacrifice, but through the phantasmal *killing and replacement of the father*; not through affiliation, but through substitution. In both schemes, father and son are ultimately identical—except for one decisive difference: while the Christological model leaves the father's sovereignty unchallenged and places the son at his side as a junior partner, so to speak, the generational succession in the Oedipal scheme is a series of *hostile*, belligerent identifications with the respective father figure.

The opposition between Christian passion and Oedipal rivalry reflects a long-term sociohistorical shift in the power relationship between the generations. Instead of describing the Holy Family in Freudian terms, it would therefore make more sense to define more precisely the historical locus of psychoanalysis: the late nineteenth century, a time when the cultural hegemony of Christianity was breaking up for good. Freud's fundamental works on the topic of religion appear during an era rife with political, religious, and literary fantasies of patricide. *Totem and Taboo* offers merely one variation on the theme. In

Throne of Grace, 1450. Saint-Pierre, Louvain.

all these fantasies, the *violence* passes from the father to the son—a genuinely modern attitude that cannot be accommodated within the thought world of Christian theology. The principle of the ancestral line, which accords the son a place at the end of a long succession of paternal authorities, is now considered obsolete and is abolished. Its place is taken by an ethos of a new beginning *beyond authority*—a new beginning for the sake of the future, of youth, of the sons. Psychoanalysis, as a direct contemporary of these developments, deals with the double binds and loves–hates that arise from such a departure from the old-style paternal system of authority.

The blow struck by Freud was the fact that he "overturned" the Christian tradition on three critical points. First, he reversed its fundamental distinction between sensual love (eros) and suprasensual love (agape). In so doing, he pulled the ground from under the edifice of Christian sublimations.

Second, psychoanalytical theory achieved a complete reversal in the polarity of the cultural imagination by making the image of the suffering redeemer-son pale beside the spectacular subject of a patricide desired since primeval times, and the image of the grieving mother pale beside that of the father's desired wife. This repolarization is so pertinent and *irresistible* that it is difficult to even remember the older semantics of the martyrdom submissive to God's will. *In retrospect*, it seems as though the succession of generations was always suffused by Oedipal ambivalence and acts of substitution. One is dealing here with what is surely one of the rare moments in which a theory has been able to intervene, with lasting effect, in the narrative foundation of cultural memory.

This is connected to the third point: Freud overlaid the Christian account (Jesus) with a myth (Oedipus) derived from Greek tragedy—that is, from pagan sources. Structurally, all of Western tradition is bilingual. It has two points of origin: Jerusalem and Athens. The Judeo-Christian line assumes its shape, from the outset, in contrast to the polymorphous, Greco-Roman world of images and thoughts. The monotheistic god, the god who prohibits images, was locked in a quarrel with the image-loving pagan deities. The two worlds of the imagination coexisted side by side in constantly changing relationships of power, exclusion, and exchange.

In this confrontation, the Passion story took on special weight as an obvious *marker of difference*—offering, as it did, an inexhaustible storehouse for Christianity's unique devotional culture, both in its pathetic formulas of pain and in its reminder of the Redemption. Moreover, it articulated most clearly the boundary between the Christian and Jewish faiths. The Jews are excluded from the Passion in two ways. First, the Crucifixion and the lament of Mary finalize the change in the position of the father and consequently Jesus' detachment from his Jewish genealogy. Second, it was supposedly the Jews who rejected their Messiah and demanded Jesus' death. Representations of the Passion incorporated the *structural anti-Judaism of the Christian religion*, which meant that it could be exploited for anti-Semitic purposes as needed.

There is therefore a certain irony in the fact that the recasting of the code of male socialization from Christ to Oedipus, from the Christian "primary language" of the West to its pagan-classical "second language," was the work of a Jewish creator of discourse. In any case, Freud, one of the educated Jewish "philhellenes" during the crisis years of modernity, did his part to invalidate the normatizations of the Christian pictorial language. It is possible that specific Jewish experiences entered into this recoding—less for individual psychological reasons than as the result of conflicts of assimilation, the Jewish apostasy from the religion of the fathers. Yet, in general, such conflicts reflect the transitional dilemma of a society seeking to free itself from religious obligations, thereby transgressing the commandments of a god who is still powerful even though the society no longer believes in him. Freud was not alone in this *abandonment* of religious considerations; rather, he carried on the work of other critics of the Christian religion, chief among them the pastor's son Friedrich Nietzsche. Cultural theory around 1900 revoked the historical victory of Christianity.

22

REMNANT FAMILIES IN THE WELFARE STATE

The familial order is in retreat. Kinship ties, which by their very nature are not freely chosen, are becoming increasingly less important in the developed industrial countries. Moreover, the general decline in the number of children per family makes the genealogical trees much smaller and narrower: they now extend almost exclusively in a vertical direction and no longer produce side branches. The trend within the legal system is to put familial and nonfamilial partnerships on an equal footing. Among the urban middle classes, stable families are by now the exception, not the norm. Marriage is being reduced to a temporary union.[1] Many children are growing up in single-mother households with changing male role models. While the mother–child axis retains a certain stability—whereby, at least in Germany, the model of domestic motherhood is transforming itself into a no less perfectionistic profile of what is expected of the single mother[2]—the crisis of fatherhood is proclaimed everywhere. Often it is done with an undertone of nostalgia, now that the antiauthoritarian and family-critical reformist zeal of the 1970s has dissipated.

Historians of the family describe this process dispassionately as the progressive functional *unburdening* of the family. From the long-term perspective, that process is affecting the man more than the woman. He is gradually losing his position of preeminence in the exercise of the domestic functions of religious practices, protection, legal representation, education, and material support.[3] While the day-to-day upbringing and emotional care of the child was delegated to mothers in the eighteenth century (a fact that is still fundamental to contemporary divorce law), the other patriarchal rights and duties largely passed into the hands of state institutions—to the school, the youth welfare office, and the military. The only obligation from which the biological father has not been released is that of providing material support; he shares that responsibility with the welfare state.

The images are similar. The mother–child dyad persists; in fact, it has grown substantially stronger in the bourgeois age and is considered irreplaceable. The father "on location," conversely, leads a kind of Josephean existence in secularized form. He coexists in a precarious and contradictory way with the modern, transcendental father authority: the state. He has relinquished most of his attributes to the state and is hovering at the margins of the scene, perhaps on the verge of disappearing;[4] yet he must bear a remnant of responsibility as a "foster father."

A peculiar dialectic links the dismantling of patriarchal power and the advance of the state. Even contemporary feminist concerns, such as the struggle against domestic violence, get caught up in this dialectic. As justified as these concerns are, in their legalism they objectively promote an even deeper penetration of state control into the sphere once reserved for the family. Ironically, in the name of women's rights they merely shift the weight from one paternal authority to another: "The family, at first formed and instrumentalized as a 'satellite of the state,' later falls victim to the expansive colonization by the state."[5]

But the state is not the only agency that works toward the dissolution of the familial order. One must add two other life-giving powers: the media and the laboratories. As far as the new media are concerned, in many respects they represent the technical implementation of what appears in religious terminology as that which is *beyond the senses*. In the Middle Ages, media theory was angelology (which included demonology, its negative side). Angels were envoys between the realms, bringers of messages both oral and written. This traffic of communication—which bound every person with everyone else into a large community, linked limited individual knowledge to the All-Knowing, and connected what one saw with what nobody could see—has today, at the close of the era of written culture, passed to other data carriers and informal processes.

No less so than at the time of the Annunciation, such transmissions break into the realm of domestic interaction and decenter it. No less so than at the time of the *ecclesia*, communal aggregates are created that serve in equal measure to integrate and indoctrinate members of the community. These aggregates of a media-created society interrupt the corporeal network of relationships among individuals and focus them on an inaccessible totality that, by its nature, cannot be fully encompassed and for that very reason arouses desire.

The growing discussion about new media that has spread during the past few years has not been very productive analytically. It does, however, attest to a vital need to recast the language of the holy into a rhetoric of virtuality. The Internet is perhaps no less a mystical place than the church was. It creates a realm where everything and everyone is connected, where all the sensory conditions are destructured and restructured—and it does so in a way that is similar to how the great theological texts brought forth such a realm.

In the meantime, biological laboratories are realizing the long-held dream of abolishing the human being: the sexually created, biologically limited—in a word—creaturely human being. Here, too, it would seem that the modern agencies of production are driven by old theological programs of which they are unaware. In retrospect, Christian theology seems like a conceptual avant-garde for *the* great Western movement of transformation: from natural existence to existence created (again) out of the spirit, from creatureliness via the attempt to spiritualize the human being to the dawning technological posthumanism of our day.

Laboratories are wish machines. Their thirst for knowledge acts out desires that remain invisible in the experimental setups. To borrow from Freud, one could speak of an "archaic legacy" of technological processes. One of these archaic desires is aimed at overcoming fleshly reproduction. No longer must this desire generate from within itself an entire semantics of chastity, of the ethical conquest of the flesh. Instead, it travels the path via *virgin machines*; it expresses itself *technologically* instead of theologically,[6] doing so not only through the instrumentally created facts as such (sperm banks, artificial insemination, asexual genetic replication) but also through the diffuse milieu of approval that promotes such developments and—in spite of the occasional expression of uneasiness—seems to make them unstoppable.

The body of the Christian Virgin was for believers proof of an *alternative blueprint* to the sexual procreationism of the world. From this perspective, Mary's conception by the Holy Spirit becomes the starting point for all the nonsexual methods of reproduction and celibate machines that stand in open competition with sexual procreation and testify to cultural instead of natural powers of creation. Western tradition is rife with these kinds of experimental arrangements of artificial production, be they supernatural or technological in nature. In this context, the technological and the supernatural are not in conflict. They are linked by their shared opposition to the world of sex and gender and form countless narrative composites. They recount the always new union of "spirit" and "matrix," the marvelous creation of this union and the falling behind of the merely natural human being.

Memory theory uses the term "crypt"[7] to describe these dungeons where the unspoken and the repressed reside and from where they engage in their baleful ghostly activities. If the laboratories of genetic technology have a crypt, one finds in it a recognizable group of figures. And when they invent stories as a way of articulating their own purposes—real scientific science fiction, which maintains a close exchange with the literary and cinematic fictions of the New Human—these are stories about *liberation from the captivity of the flesh*, whose basic patterns come from a distant time.

23

THEOLOGY AND FAMILY IN GEORGE LUCAS'S STAR WARS

The Use of Religious Symbols

Anyone who has studied the history of religious motifs discovers that they possess a surprising quality—*elasticity*. As long as certain indispensable background conditions are met, these motifs can accommodate themselves to every conceivable adaptation, decontextualization, and reinterpretation without losing their recognizability or symbolic power. Even when used in a distorted or profane manner, they hardly seem to become "exhausted." They are tenacious far beyond the religious milieu in which they were created, able to persist in more or less concealed form under completely different cultural conditions. They provide a highly variable *stock of visual patterns* that the collective imagination can continuously draw on and update. In that sense, they must meet two contradictory requirements: first, they must be memorable enough to serve as commonplaces of cultural memory; second, they must be sufficiently underdetermined so as not to offer too much resistance to the changing perspectives of their use.

The Christian Holy Family is a perfect example of this mutability. It represents an inexhaustible storehouse that, in Western culture, has for over two millennia been used in the most diverse ways by theologians, moralists, social reformers, artists, and, finally, fathers and mothers themselves. And yet one would not be doing justice to the functionality of religious symbols if one looked only at their "user-friendly," pluralistic side—or, to put it differently, if one reduced them to the dimension of pictorial *pragmatism*. For the handling of such symbols is not really without cost; it is not placed at the discretion of sovereign subjects. On the contrary, one could almost say that the symbols *use their users* to process meanings whose reach extends far beyond the specific act of intentional use. There is a hidden, deep structural side to the social use of symbols, a *power of the symbolic* that, in turn, intervenes in a guiding fashion in the productions of the imagination and becomes effective through them.

In other words, religious symbols retain their characteristic of being social guideposts regardless of whether or not those who use them are aware of it. The following excursus into the world of contemporary film-making is intended to substantiate the hypothesis that such symbolic guidance will show its effects even where the connection to the relevant religious contents of faith have been severed or become obscure. These are phantasmagoric effects, but possessing the power to shape reality. One could also say ghostly effects from the afterlife of a tradition declared dead, buried, and seemingly dissolved in the syncretistic sea of images of the pop era.

Star Wars as a Double Trilogy

George Lucas's *Star Wars* trilogy, released between 1977 and 1983 and one of the greatest cinematic successes in the history of film, was seen by 1.2 billion people in movie theaters alone. With its mixture of hypertechnology and primeval fantasies, its fighter pilots, Jedi Knights, princesses, robots, tyrants in medieval garb, human–animal hybrids and monsters of every kind, detailed models of intergalactic means of transportation, space stations, and weapons, *Star Wars* created a completely new inventory of cinematic dream images. This visual upheaval was aided by a revolution in the technology of special effects. Lucas's films are phantasmagorias of digitalization: visual worlds generated by computer programs. Their dissemination worldwide is helped by a highly efficient marketing strategy. Lucas is the director who introduced merchandising on a grand scale to Hollywood, thereby opening up previously unimagined sources of income for the entertainment industry.

All this, taken together, has made *Star Wars* into an event of great commercial importance but also of profound significance to the *politics of memory*. Lucas's cinematic dream universe constituted a generation-shaping experience for young Americans in the 1980s and 1990s. The fact that Ronald Reagan named his plan for a space-based antimissile defense system "Star Wars" not only shows that computerization formed the common foundation for the rise of both the entertainment and the defense industries, but also sheds light on the dimension of the cinematic plot as a national myth.

With his film *Episode I: The Phantom Menace*, which opened in theaters in the summer of 1999, George Lucas was able to continue the box-office success of the original trilogy and, moreover, help in its revival. *Episode II: Attack of the Clones* followed in 2002. Another episode is in production; when it is released, the entire series will comprise six parts. Lucas's additional foresight in terms of marketing strategy is revealed by the fact that he conceived the new episodes not as the continuation of the original trilogy but as their *prehistory*: the new films take place earlier than the action in the *Star Wars* movies of the 1970s and 1980s. Lucas provides the *Star Wars* universe with which the thirty- and forty-year-olds of today grew up with a belated past. The new episodes take place a generation earlier than the original ones. They expand the war of liberation of the star warriors into a generational epic with all the narrative possibilities this entails.

In actuality, *Episode I* was not much more than a remake of the 1977 *Star Wars*. As it is, the developmental construction of the series is pervaded by a repetitive structure that repeats the same constellation in several versions. The elements shared by the new *Episode I* and the original first movie can easily be summarized. In both films, the action revolves around a young hero. In 1977 his name is Luke Skywalker, and he lives with his aunt and uncle on an isolated farm on the desert planet Tatooine. In 1999 his name is Anakin Skywalker, and he is being kept as a slave on Tatooine together with his mother. Although a few years younger—and this is important for the episode-connecting context—Anakin is the future father of Luke, yet the fate that both must endure is similar.

All *Star Wars* episodes take place against an apocalyptic background. The legitimate central authority is in the process of a complete breakdown due to external enemies and internal corruption. The old, shining, godlike authorities, the Jedi Knights, are no longer able to guide the fate of the universe. The last knights go into exile. A sinister imperator—a former Jedi who has gone over to the dark side—is trying to seize power. The only thing still standing in his way is a small band of rebels, against whom he is preparing a crushing blow. This scenario creates room for the law of the strongest, heroic courage, and a personal ethos—indispensable ingredients for that mixture of action and eschatology from which Lucas's *Star Wars* story—like nearly all films of this genre—is constructed.

It is easy to spell out the stereotypes of the story line as American adolescent fantasies. They are rebel dreams of white mainstream America. In these dreams the central authority appears distant and faceless; its representatives are mummified and cynical functionaries; it is in league with the devil or is already in his hands. In the meantime, dark conspiratorial figures are reaching for world power. Only a savior figure, one who will unite the forces of resistance, can still stand up to them, and this savior figure is a child.

Both Luke and Anakin are portrayed as boys who are more imprisoned in than sheltered by their familial milieu. They are unaware of their true origins or their calling. One day a charismatic teacher enters their lives and notices their unusual abilities. This teacher, a Jedi, has a privileged connection with the "Force"—understood here as a beneficial godlike principle that pervades the universe and promises peace. He undertakes the boy's guidance and removes him from his domestic bonds.

This begins an initiation phase, in the course of which the young hero is increasingly drawn into the fighting. The teacher hands him the weapon of a Jedi, a laser sword, and teaches him how to use it. The boy proves to be a space pilot endowed with a supernatural kinetic intelligence. He has a remarkably close personal bond with two nonhuman beings, a robot and an android—lovable childhood relics called R2-D2 and C-3PO, who remain his faithful companions throughout all his adventures. (One could translate these aspects of the plot back into the American rituals of manhood under the catchphrases "bearing arms," "driver's license," and "computer skills.")

Fairy-tale elements are woven into the fighting. In both films, the plot revolves around saving a beautiful princess, her ceremonial court, and her home planet from the destructive intentions of the dark forces. Feelings of affection blossom between the princess and the young hero. Childish, primitive animal beings, who inhabit spheres free of civilization, enter the scene and become helpful allies. Even classic duels are present. No matter how enormous the array of warriors and weapons in the war between the planets, in the end the decision comes down to personal sword-fights between the leaders of the good party and the commander of the evil party. Yet the principal role in the eschatological events in each case is played by the young hero Skywalker, who in daredevil solo maneuvers destroys the command post of the evil party. It all culminates in a jubilant victory parade that unites everyone—princess, heroes, and helpers—in exultation over the salvation of the world.

The Autonomy of Religious Motifs

According to his hagiographers, Lucas collected the ideas for *Star Wars* from science-fiction magazines and comics.[1] In addition, he watched countless movies while he was working on the screenplays. His method corresponds to what Claude Lévi-Strauss once called "bricolage." There is good reason why biotypes of bricolage—junkyards and storehouses of used hypertechnology wares—play an important role in the *Star Wars* series. In the process, there are amusing effects of citation and alienation. The android C-3PO is a harmless male mirror image of the artificial woman in Fritz Lang's *Metropolis*; the "pod race" in *Episode I* quotes the chariot race from *Ben Hur*. Experienced movie buffs will discover many such adoptions and adaptations. The memory of the film consists of—at least for large stretches—echoes of other films.

Yet there is also a deep symbolic dimension to these Hollywood fantasies that reaches back into the prehistory of the technological media. From what has already been said, it should be self-evident that *Star Wars* processes religious motifs and, in the final analysis, tells nothing other than a secularized story of redemption. Luke Skywalker, the hero of the original version from the 1970s, already has messianic traits. This subtexts is even more pronounced in the 1999 version. It is worth subjecting the constellation of figures around Anakin, Luke's predecessor, to a close analysis.

Tatooine, the desert planet, is a lawless place. Criminals and shady creatures run it; the people who live there are kept as slaves. This is true of Anakin Skywalker and Shmi, his mother, who are owned by a shopkeeper named Watto. Shmi plays only a secondary role. When the two Jedi Knights appear and notice Anakin as a result of his remarkable abilities, she lets her child go and remains behind alone. Anakin promises to return to Tatooine to free his mother and all the other oppressed humans. There is a brief separation drama, and then Anakin is off to the great intergalactic world.

Still, the brief scenes in which Shmi appears are sufficiently significant. We come to know her as a simple woman, still beautiful though downtrodden by her fate and completely devoted in her maternal love. She is shown at length in front of her oriental dwelling—a kind of Arabian desert town in shades of sand and ochre. If that is not enough to catch one's attention, the dialogue that Shmi carries on with Qui-Gon, the older of the Jedi envoys, is an eye-opener:

> *Qui-Gon:* The Force is unusually strong with him, that much is clear. Who was his father?
> *Shmi:* There was no father, that I know of . . . I carried him, I gave birth . . . I can't explain what happened.[2]

The allusions to Jesus of Nazareth, the Christian Messiah, are clear. One does not have to be a historian of religion to decipher them. In the film, this messianism is even given a biological basis: Anakin Skywalker's midi-chlorian count—that is, the substance one must picture as the physiological bearer of the all-pervading "Force"—is unnaturally high, higher than in any other being.[3] "It is possible that he was conceived by the midi-chlorian," Jedi master Qui-Gon will mention later.[4] Anakin would thus be a direct offspring of the "Force." Among the Jedis, however, whose highest body is a solemn council of twelve, there is disagreement over whether the young hero is really what they call the "chosen one."[5]

In one way or another, the film establishes a clear parallel between Christ and the future space pilot Skywalker. Nor can there be any doubt about the mother's resemblance to Mary, with her Hebrew name Shmi, possibly derived from the root *schemen*—that is, name (of the Lord). To that extent, the message of the film is explicit and intentional. It banks on a religious preknowledge or, to put it more cautiously, on at least a vague memory of the content of Christian doctrines of faith. That applies to the Jesus and Mary typology as well as to the many oracular statements about the numinousness of the "Force," to which the figure of the child-savior is connected. In the postmodern universe of mythologisms, which Lucas's cinematic imagination seemingly weightlessly navigates at will, the memory trace of the Christian Holy Family also has its place.

Yet this voluntary use of motifs once again demarcates only one side of religious symbolism. There is a second side in which the inherent logic of symbolic traditions makes itself felt—a logic that intersects the visual calculation and infuses it with additional, implicit meanings. This independent power of symbolism produces unforeseeable and, in some instances, highly unwelcome effects.

The Holy Family consists of three people. The role of the solicitous guardian watching over the mother and the holy child is not cast in *Episode I*. But there certainly is a *structurally* similar position—that of the stranger, a man who possesses patriarchal powers without being a father. This is the junk dealer Watto, for whom Shmi Skywalker and her miraculous son work as slaves.

Watto is not a human creature. He is among the many shady characters on Tatooine—a pot-bellied, snout-nosed, unshaven, birdlike creature with a croaking, ugly voice. His outstanding character trait is greed. It is only with great reluctance (and because of a lost bet) that he hands Anakin Skywalker over to the visiting Jedi. One can recognize in his physiognomic disfigurement the type of the possessive and hostile father who, in any case, is not accepted by his own son.

In the United States, *Episode I* triggered a bitter controversy when it was released. The film was accused of reproducing racist clichés. Unlike the thematically related *Star Trek* series, which transposed the ideal of an enlightened multiculturalism into the science-fiction genre—here beings of the most diverse appearance and cultural backgrounds deal with one another in an exceedingly tolerant and politically correct manner—critics claimed that Lucas's *Star Wars* saga was reverting to cinematic discrimination, something that was thought to be a thing of the past.[6] In particular, the bumbling amphibian creature Jar Jar Binks caused offense; it was suspected of reflecting colonial and antihomosexual sentiments. A passionate debate raged on the Internet about Jar Jar Binks.[7] The slaveholder Watto was also a target of criticism. New York City law professor Patricia Williams was reminded of an anti-Semitic caricature published in Vienna at the turn of the twentieth century.[8]

The suspicion voiced by Williams is supported by more than just external indications. Watto's greed, his wiliness, and his passion for haggling all point in
the same direction. Part of this picture is also Watto's unreceptiveness to the
spiritual power exercised by the Jedi apostles: he cannot be won over by the spirit, only by money.[9] Here Lucas's film is using one of the more subtle discrimi-
natory accusations that Christianity leveled against its Jewish religion of origin.
That the Jews—in this respect like the Devil—are incapable of consubstantia-
tion and consequently of community, and that they exclude themselves from
every spiritual bond is something one can read in many anti-Semitic polemics,
from Achim von Arnim, a poet of German Romanticism,[10] to Joseph
Goebbels,[11] the chief propagandist of the Nazi regime.

Of course, Lucasfilm vehemently rejected the charge of racism—using the
rather weak argument that the characters of *Star Wars* were merely creations of
a playful imagination. Indeed, it is not necessary to accuse George Lucas and his
crew of racist *interests*. But that does not in any way change the fact that they are,
in a sense, haunted by the symbolism they employed for the purpose of commercial entertainment. In the case of Watto, this would mean that they permit a
line of conflict that runs through the construction of the Holy Family at the very
outset—the aggressive expropriation of Judaism by Christianity, reflected in the
amputation of the figure of Joseph—to reemerge in the midst of a universe built
from the posthistorical construction set. Obviously one cannot reference the
Christian ur-family without becoming entangled in this religion's foundational
paradoxes and original acts of violence. *Star Wars*, a saga that, its futuristic play-
fulness notwithstanding, in the end revolves around nothing other than the question of the relationship between *power* and *salvation*, an epic that, while superfi-
cially pretending to offer a satisfying solution to such a fundamental problem to
everyone in the audience inclined to the good, quite unintentionally unearths the
costs and complications of the Christian message of redemption—that is, its inherent anti-Judaism.

The Dark Side of Power

In the para-Christological scheme of the *Star Wars* saga there is another difficulty that touches on the symbolic position of the father. As I have already mentioned, Anakin, the hero of *Episode I*, turns out to be Anakin Skywalker, the father of the hero of the classic trilogy. But the relationship between father and son
is by no means harmonious: in the person of his father, Luke will encounter not a

divine figure of light but the incarnation of evil. He bears the suggestive name Darth Vader and has become the right hand of the dark emperor. Luke thus recognizes in his father his antagonist in the battle for salvation. The logical outcome is thus the decisive duel between father and son, from which the son emerges victorious—a classic patricide that cannot be accommodated in any kind of Christian eschatology. In the figure of the evil father-God, George Lucas—in his own way also an evangelist—upsets the otherwise simplistic Manichaean good/evil scheme of his films.

How the likable boy Anakin turned into Lord Vader—always dressed and masked as a black knight—is a mystery that is narratively addressed in *Attack of the Clones, Episode II* of the grand epic. Here Anakin Skywalker is a young man of twenty, with the film unfolding the action over long stretches as a *drama of adolescence*. A variety of explanations are offered for why the young Jedi student, distinguished above all the others, will soon change sides. The first and most obvious one is that he loses his mother. After an absence of ten years from his home planet, Tatooine, he is driven by nightmares to set out in search of her. When he finally finds her and frees her from her captors—desert bandits—she dies in his lap, reversing the Pietà figure. "You liberated me" are her final words. While this scene again plays with messianic overtones, it leaves behind a son who expresses open hatred for her murderers and thus violates the law of spiritual brotherhood to which he should have submitted.

The second explanation offered by the film is that Anakin drifts farther and farther away from the law of the Jedi: a rebellious adolescent who tries to escape the tutelage of his teachers–brothers.

The third and final explanation is that Anakin strays from the path of the Jedi virtues because he loves, and by doing so transgresses the prohibition against passion. In the narrative of the film, this is clearly the strongest motif.

Jedis should not have attachments to father or mother but should practice unconditional obedience within the spiritual brotherhood; in addition, the law of celibacy applies to them—rules familiar from monastic communities. But the drama of adolescence lies not only in the departure from these rules. Rather, it would appear that in the imaginative systems of the *Star Wars* series, any departure from the community of adolescents, and thus *any generational change, any becoming a father*, is punished as a descent into the world of evil.

The images of mothers and women in the cinematic epic are, for the most part, painted in soft, sentimental ways, or they become blurred. Fathers, conversely, are characterized by their nonexistence, or they are highly problematic figures. (That also applies to fatherly secondary figures like the bounty hunter Jango Fett in *Episode II*, who, as the seed donor of the clone warriors, assumes *the* biological father position par excellence. Yet when he is decapitated in the tumult of battle, his only natural son is forced to realize that he is a hybrid mechanical monstrosity.) In the world of the star warriors, it is evidently equally precarious to have a father as not to have a father. All worldly authority figures who take on father imagery gravitate toward the dark side of power. Patriarchal authority itself seems to become a synonym for political corruption.

Based on the fact that the generational change in these films appears as a radical change in character, one might infer—from a psychoanalytic perspective—that the father image is profoundly split in America's collective unconscious. Or, to put it in opposite and perhaps more precise terms, one might infer the *abolition* of the traditional split of the cultural superego, which, under the sovereignty of the traditional Christian doctrine, was able to separate good and evil parts and in this way achieve a lasting victory in moral outlook

To be sure, at the end of the *Star Wars* series the hero's longing for his father supersedes the motif of patricide. Darth Vader, the fallen savior of the world of the first generation, is redeemed. The final scene of the third film in the original trilogy, *The Return of the Jedi*, shows Luke, his back turned to the celebrating crowd and the viewers, in an imagined conversation of reconciliation with the luminously transfigured figures of his father and teachers. Yet these attempts at harmonization are not able to undo the painful insult that was inflicted on the distinction between the two sides of the Force in the course of the story. In a redemptively fatal way, God the Father and his adversary, the Devil, have become interchangeable.

Twice the *Star Wars* saga has to play out a cycle of salvation as a double trilogy. First Pass: Hero I, Christlike, who originally wanted to free his mother and save enslaved humanity, forgets mother and humankind and allows himself to be alienated from the good resolutions of his youth. When he finally remembers the place from which he came, it is too late; hatred, lust for power, and erotic desire turn him into an agent of the dark forces. Second Pass: Hero II, Luke, the son of Anakin as Darth Vader, flees his "false"—that is, his foster—family, follows a spiritual leader, does not allow the dark forces to lead him astray, also resists his father's offer of dominion over the world, and in the end redeems him by killing him. The enmity between the generations—and thus the diabolical—has crept into the trinitarian unity of God the Father and Son (with the "Force" as the Holy Spirit). The son who becomes a father must be led back to the good by his own son. God himself turns out to be in need of salvation.

If this reading is correct, it would also mean that the war the Republic of the Stars must endure is, in the final analysis, something like a familial civil war, one that bears within itself the risk of constantly renewing itself in the chain of male generations. However, the final verdict on this question—or concerning the dispute over republic or dictatorship stirred up by *Attack of the Clones*—will not be in until the appearance of the definitive conclusion of the *Star Wars* chronicle. It will be interesting to watch the direction in which Hollywood will develop the political theology of the American empire during the next few years.

It all could have turned out very differently, looking forward from year 1. There probably were myriad possibilities. A series of coincidences has, in retrospect, made it possible to recount the past two thousand years as the afterhistory of the Holy Family.

NOTES

1. Around the Year Zero

1. Hans Maier, *Die christliche Zeitrechnung* (Freiburg: Herder, 1991), 42.

2. Faith and Code

1. See, among others, Joachim Gnilka, *Jesus of Nazareth: Message and History*, trans. Siegfried S. Schatzmann (Peabody, Mass.: Hendrickson, 1997); Klaus Berger, *Wer war Jesus wirklich?* (Stuttgart: Quell, 1995); John Dominic Crossan, *The Historical Jesus: The Life of a Mediterranean Jewish Peasant* (San Francisco: HarperCollins, 1991), and *Jesus: A Revolutionary Biography* (San Francisco: HarperCollins, 1994); Bart D. Ehrman, *Jesus: Apocalyptic Prophet of the New Millennium* (Oxford: Oxford University Press, 1999); and Paula Fredriksen, *Jesus of Nazareth, King of the Jews* (New York: Vintage, 1999).
2. Marina Warner, *Alone of All Her Sex: The Myth and the Cult of the Virgin Mary* (New York: Knopf, 1976); Ida Magli, *La Madonna* (Milan: Rizzoli, 1987); Klaus Schreiner, *Maria: Jungfrau, Mutter, Herrscherin*, 2d ed. (Munich: Hanser, 1996).
3. Adolf Holl, *The Left Hand of God: A Biography of the Holy Spirit*, trans. John Cullen (New York: Doubleday, 1997).
4. Luther Link, *The Devil: A Mask Without a Face* (London: Reaktion, 1995).

3. Positions I: Jesus and His Fathers

1. Jean-Louis Flandrin, *Families in Former Times*, trans. Richard Southern (Cambridge: Cambridge University Press, 1979).
2. All biblical citations are taken from the New English Bible (Oxford: Oxford University Press, 1972).
3. According to Schalom Ben-Chorin, "This expresses everything the angel has to say. And this, in turn, is in line with an old Hebrew tradition, according to which the messenger (angel) and the message are one and the same. Which is also why, in the talmudic interpretation, an angel can deliver only *one* message, carry out *one* mission. The messenger is also the message—particularly in this case, for evidently Mary becomes pregnant by the Holy Spirit through the annunciation itself" (*Mutter Mirjam: Maria in jüdischer Sicht*, 8th ed. [Munich: List, 1971], 41).

4. Positions II: Mary and the Trinity

1. Caroline Walker Bynum, *Jesus as Mother: Studies in the Spirituality of the High Middle Ages* (Berkeley: University of California Press, 1982).

2. Elisabeth Gössmann, "Reflexionen zur mariologischen Dogmengeschichte," in Hedwig Röckelein, Claudia Opiz, and Dieter R. Bauer, eds., *Maria—Abbild oder Vorbild? Zur Sozialgeschichte mittelalterlicher Marienverehrung* (Tübingen: Diskord, 1990), 23.

5. From the Jewish Birth Family to the Christian Destination Family

1. The New English Bible has: "Your concern, mother, is not mine." However, the literal Greek says "woman" and reflects a more disrespectful tone than "mother," which is why I have changed it here. *Trans.*

6. The Man Joseph and Monotheistic Religion

1. Gabriela Signori, "Die verlorene Ehre des heiligen Joseph oder Männlichkeit im Spannungsfeld spätmittelalterlicher Altersstereotypen: Zur Genese von Urs Grafs 'Heiliger Familie' (1521)," in Klaus Schreiner and Gerd Schwerhoff, eds., *Verletzte Ehre: Ehrenkonflikte in Gesellschaften des Mittelalters und der Frühen Neuzeit* (Cologne: Böhlau, 1995), 213.

2. *New Testament Apocrypha*, rev. ed., ed. Wilhelm Schneemelcher, trans. and ed. R. McL. Wilson, vol. 1, *Gospels and Related Writings* (Louisville, Ky.: Westminster/John Knox, 1991), 429–30.

3. Ibid.

4. H.-M. Guindon, "L'Angoisse de Saint Joseph," *Cahiers de Joséphologie* 24 (1976): 187ff.

5. Christoph Burger, *Jesus als Davidssohn* (Göttingen: Vandenhoeck & Ruprecht, 1970), 91–106.

6. *Jüdisches Lexikon: Ein enzyklopädisches Handbuch des jüdischen Wissens in vier Bänden* (Berlin: Jüdischer Verlag, 1927; reprint, Frankfurt am Main: Jüdischer Verlag, 1987), s.v. "adoption," col. 108. See also Uta Ranke-Heinemann, *Putting Away Childish Things*, trans. Peter Heinegg (San Francisco: Harper San Francisco, 1994).

7. Ida Magli, *La Madonna* (Milan: Rizzoli, 1987), 85.

8. Klaus Schreiner, *Maria: Jungfrau, Mutter, Herrscherin*, 2d ed. (Munich: Hanser, 1996), 423–29.

9. Quoted in Joseph Seitz, *Die Verehrung des hl. Joseph in ihrer geschichtlichen Entwicklung bis zum Konzil von Trient dargestellt* (Freiburg: Herder, 1908), 46. Seitz adds that "Epiphanius elaborates further on this idea when he says: 'The Virgin was given to Joseph . . . as a testament for things to come, so that it should be made clear that the human nature assumed by God did not stem from an act of adultery but should rather be revealed in truth as having been generated without the seed of a man, solely by the power and workings of the Holy Spirit'" (47).

8. Combinatorics I: The Mother–Son Axis

1. According to Caroline Walker Bynum, "The God of early medieval writing and art is a judge and king, to whom propitiation is offered by the hordes of monks presenting correct and beautiful prayers before countless altars; Christ is a prince, reigning from

the throne of the cross after defeating humankind's captor, and Mary is his queen. The fundamental dramas of religion are cosmic—wars between Christ and the devil, saints or angles and demons. . . . In contrast, eleventh- and twelfth-century writers begin to stress Christ's humanity, both in affective and sentimentalized responses to the gospel story . . . and in a new compulsion to build into the Christian life a literal imitation of the details of Jesus' ministry. The fundamental religious drama is now located within the self, and it is less a battle than a journey—a journey toward God" (*Jesus as Mother: Studies in the Spirituality of the High Middle Ages* [Berkeley: University of California Press, 1982], 16–17). On the humanization of the image of Christ in Renaissance painting, see Leo Steinberg, *The Sexuality of Christ in Renaissance Art and in Modern Oblivion*, 2d ed. (Chicago: University of Chicago Press, 1996).

2. To be sure, these reflections represent the application of terminology—specifically psychoanalytic terminology—that arose in a different context. For example, Luisa Accati summarizes feminist research by saying that "the archetypal model of the possessive mother appears to be the Madonna. All those figures of Virgin and child hold their sons with expressions of pride, fulfillment and self-satisfaction. The Madonnas thus sing a eulogy to the mother–woman who finds happiness and self-fulfillment outside the father" ("The Larceny of Desire: The Madonna in Seventeenth-century Catholic Europe," in Jim Obelkevich, Lyndal Roper, and Raphael Samuels, eds., *Disciplines of Faith: Studies in Religion, Politics, and Patriarchy* [London: Routledge & Kegan Paul, 1987], 75).

3. According to Julia Kristeva, "The ordering of the maternal libido reached its apotheosis when centered in the theme of death. The *Mater Dolorosa* knows no masculine body save that of her dead son, and her only pathos (which contrasts with the somewhat vacant, gentle serenity of the nursing Madonnas) is her shedding tears over a corpse" (*Tales of Love*, trans. Leon S. Roudiez [New York: Columbia University Press, 1987], 250).

4. The English translation is literal, with no pretensions to poetic artistry. *Trans.*

5. My view in this regard departs from that of Elisabeth Bronfen, *Over Her Dead Body: Death, Femininity, and the Aesthetic* (Manchester, Eng.: Manchester University Press, 1992).

6. On the National Socialist cult of the mother, see Claudia Koonz, *Mothers in the Fatherland* (New York: St. Martin's, 1987).

7. Viktoria Schmidt-Linsenhoff, "Kohl und Kollwitz. Staats- und Weiblichkeitsdiskurse in der Neuen Wache 1993," in Annette Graczyk, ed., *Das Volk: Abbild, Konstruktion, Phantasma* (Berlin: Akademie, 1996), 185–203.

8. This was theologically elaborated by, among others, Saint Augustine, *De sancta virginitate*, ed. and trans. P. G. Wals (Oxford: Clarendon, 2001).

9. Peter Brown, *The Body and Society: Men, Women, and Sexual Renunciation in Early Christianity* (New York: Columbia University Press, 1988), chap. 13; Susanna Elm, *"Virgins of God": The Making of Asceticism in Late Antiquity* (Oxford: Clarendon, 1994).

10. According to Ida Magli, "The Christian virgin is actually married to Christ. . . . St. Jerome treats the mother of a consecrated woman as 'God's mother-in-law' and applies the laws governing marriage between a man and a woman also to the marriage between a virgin and Christ. The punishments that befall women who betray their real husbands are also

imposed on virgins who violate their vow: they are treated either as bigamists or adulteresses and are punished accordingly. The reality of marriage assumed strange forms. These forms, however, are all the more revealing when the various ceremonies symbolically depict a kind of 'first night' between the bishop and the newly consecrated nun: a wedding chamber is symbolically prepared and the bishop, with great pomp, enters the convent for a night, accompanied by a procession displaying the well-shrouded and festively adorned bed in which he will sleep. But the most striking testament to the surrender of their own women to God on the part of men is the monastic seclusion and the cutting of the hair. These are the two most expressive signs for the loss of virginity in the marriage and the act of taking possession by the man" (*La Madonna* [Milan: Rizzoli, 1987], 24).

11. Dante, *La Divina Commedia: Paradiso* (Florence: Le Monnier, 1968), canto 33.

12. Helga Sciurie, "Maria-Ecclesia als Mitherrscherin Christi: Zur Funktion des Sponsus–Sponsa-Modells in der Bildkunst des 13. Jahrhunderts," in Hedwig Röckelein, Claudia Opiz, and Dieter R. Bauer, eds., *Maria—Abbild oder Vorbild? Zur Sozialgeschichte mittelalterlicher Marienverehrung* (Tübingen: Diskord, 1990), 110–46, esp. 123ff.; Helga Möbius, "Mutter-Bilder: Die Gottesmutter und ihr Sohn," in Renate Möhrmann, ed., *Verklärt, verkitscht, vergessen: Die Mutter als ästhetische Figur* (Stuttgart: Metzler, 1996), 34.

13. Ernst H. Kantorowicz, *The King's Two Bodies. A Study in Mediaeval Political Theology* (Princeton, N.J.: Princeton University Press, 1957), 216.

14. Marina Warner, *Alone of All Her Sex: The Myth and the Cult of the Virgin Mary* (New York: Knopf, 1976), 105.

15. Kantorowicz, *King's Two Bodies.* On the iconographic quarrel between the church and kingship, see Sciurie, "Maria-Ecclesia als Mitherrscherin Christi," 129.

16. Warner, *Alone of All Her Sex,* 95. On the theological background, see Elisabeth Gössmann, "Reflexionen zur mariologischen Dogmengeschichte," in Hedwig Röckelein, Claudia Opiz, and Dieter R. Bauer, eds., *Maria—Abbild oder Vorbild? Zur Sozialgeschichte mittelalterlicher Marienverehrung* (Tübingen: Diskord, 1990), 32.

9. Combinatorics II: The Sacred Marriage

1. Hugo Koch, *Adhuc virgo: Mariens Jungfrauschaft und Ehe in der altkirchlichen Ueberlieferung bis zum Ende des 4. Jahrhunderts* (Tübingen: Mohr, 1929).

2. According to Marina Warner, "The virgin birth of Christ began to redound along the line of the Virgin's ancestors in infinite regression" (*Alone of All Her Sex: The Myth and the Cult of the Virgin Mary* [New York: Knopf, 1976], 243).

3. Ibid., 65–67.

4. Elisabeth Gössmann, "Reflexionen zur mariologischen Dogmengeschichte," in Hedwig Röckelein, Claudia Opiz, and Dieter R. Bauer, eds., *Maria—Abbild oder Vorbild? Zur Sozialgeschichte mittelalterlicher Marienverehrung* (Tübingen: Diskord, 1990), 30.

5. Warner, *Alone of All Her Sex,* 249–50.

6. On the many faces of Mary, see Klaus Schreiner, *Maria: Jungfrau, Mutter, Herrscherin,* 2d ed. (Munich: Hanser, 1996). On the elaboration of the Christian image of Mary in an-

tiquity, see Hans Belting, *Likeness and Presence: A History of the Image Before the Era of Art*, trans. Edmund Jephcott (Chicago: University of Chicago Press, 1994), 30–46.

7. On this and the discussion that follows, see Carol P. Christ's brief, informative essay "Virgin Goddess" in Mircea Eliade, ed., *The Encyclopedia of Religion*, 16 vols. (New York: Macmillan, 1987), 15:276–78.

8. Warner, *Alone of All Her Sex*, 47–48.

9. Christ, "Virgin Goddess," 276–78.

10. Ibid., 276.

11. Schreiner, *Maria*, 197–201.

12. Ibid., 57–60; Warner, *Alone of All Her Sex*, 273–84.

13. M. Ester Harding, *Women's Mysteries*, quoted in Christ, "Virgin Goddess," 278.

14. Christ, "Virgin Goddess," 278.

15. Ida Magli, *La Madonna* (Milan: Rizzoli, 1987), 85ff.

10. Combinatorics III: The Father–Son Axis

1. Bernhard Lang, *Sacred Games: A History of Christian Worship* (New Haven, Conn.: Yale University Press, 1997), 419.

2. Ibid., 422–23. On the semiological dimension of this understanding of faith, see Jochen Hörisch, *Brot und Wein: Die Poesie des Abendmahls* (Frankfurt am Main: Suhrkamp, 1992).

3. Lang, *Sacred Games*, 431.

4. Caroline Walker Bynum, *Jesus as Mother: Studies in the Spirituality of the High Middle Ages* (Berkeley: University of California Press, 1982), 162.

5. Lang, *Sacred Games*, 433.

6. This is the subject of Bynum, *Jesus as Mother*. She wonders "why the use of explicit and elaborate maternal imagery to describe God and Christ, who are usually described as male, is so popular with twelfth-century Cistercian monks" (112). A reform in church governance went hand in hand with the "feminization" of theology: "Cistercian abbots were in fact increasingly called upon to respond with qualities that medieval men considered feminine. Anxious, even guilty about ruling, these religious leaders tried to create a new image of authority (both their own and God's) that would temper that authority with compassion and 'mothering'" (157–58).

7. Peter Brown, *Power and Persuasion: Towards a Christian Empire* (Madison: University of Wisconsin Press, 1992), 155.

8. Ibid., 156.

9. Ibid., 154.

10. In an essay entitled "A Psycho-Analytic Study of the Holy Ghost Concept," Ernest Jones discusses this theme with a somewhat crude use of the instrumentarium of classical psychoanalysis: "In the Christian mythology a startling fact appears. It is the only one in which the original figures are no longer present, in which the Trinity to be worshipped no longer consists of the Father, Mother and Son. The Father and Son still appear, but the Mother, the reason for the whole conflict, has been replaced by the mysterious figure

of the Holy Ghost" (359–60). "Although in the Christian Trinity itself the Holy Ghost is the only figure that replaces the primal Mother, nevertheless there is in Christian theology a female figure, the Virgin Mary, who also plays an important part. It would thus be truer to say that the original Goddess has been 'decomposed'—to use a mythological term—into two, one of which goes to make the Holy Ghost and the other of which becomes the Madonna" (369) (*Essays in Applied Psycho-Analysis*, vol. 2, *Essays in Folklore, Anthropology and Religion* [London: Hogarth, 1951]).

11. The connection between feudal primogeniture and the strengthening of monogamy, on the one hand, and of celibacy, on the other—as well as the rise of the Marian cult—has been frequently examined. See Georges Duby, *The Knight, the Lady, and the Priest: The Making of Modern Marriage in Medieval France*, trans. Barbara Bray (New York: Pantheon, 1983), and David Herlihy, "The Making of the Medieval Family: Symmetry, Structure, and Sentiment," *Journal of Family History* 8 (1983): 116–30.

12. I quote the *sermones* of Isaac of Stella in the available French translation: "Pour moi je déclare, je suis à présent un étranger et un pélerin ici-bas, c'est-à-dire dans le monde entier, comme si j'en étais nullement originaire; je ne suis pas fils de l'homme, mais fils de Dieu caché sous l'apparence et la ressemblance de l'homme; désormais, je ne suis plus le fils de mon père et de ma mère, ni le frère de mes frères, même s'ils disent, affirment et jurent faussement que je suis de leurs. . . . Ensemble nous sommes tous pupilles et orphelins; nous n'avons pas de père sur la terre car notre père est dans les cieux et notre mère est vierge. C'est de là que nous sommes originaires" (*Sermons*, vol. 2, *Sources chrétiennes 207*, ed. A. Horte and G. Galet [Paris: Cerf, 1967–1987], sermon 29, p. 173).

13. Saint Ambrose of Milan, *Exposition of the Holy Gospel According to Saint Luke*, trans. Theodosia Tomkinson (Etna, Calif.: Center for Traditionalist Orthodox Studies, 1998), 81.

14. Cynthia Hahn, "'Joseph Will Perfect, Mary Enlighten and Jesus Save Thee': The Holy Family as Marriage Model in the Mérode Triptych," *Art Bulletin* 68 (1986): 54–66, and "Joseph as Ambrose's 'Artisan of the Soul' in the *Holy Family in Egypt* by Albrecht Dürer," *Zeitschrift für Kunstgeschichte* 47 (1984): 515–22.

15. Marcel Lalonde has summarized the scattered statements of the church fathers on this topic: "La conclusion générale qui se dégage de notre exposé sur l'évolution historique d'une typologie déterminée peut donc se formuler de façon suivante: parce que le mariage des parents de Jésus symbolise les noces virginales du Christ et de l'Eglise, saint Joseph est la figure des prêtres, des évêques et même du Pape qui sont les époux *visibles* de l'Eglise, et surtout il est la figure du Christ lui-même, l'époux *invisible* de l'Eglise" ("La Signification mystique de mariage de Joseph et de Marie," *Cahiers de Joséphologie* 19 [1971]: 562–63).

11. The Dissolution of Distinctions

1. *Ephrem the Syrian: Hymns*, trans. Kathleen E. McVey (New York: Paulist Press, 1989), 131–32.

2. Ibid., 150.

3. *Origen: Contra Celsum,* trans. Henry Chadwick (Cambridge: Cambridge University Press, 1965), bk.1, chap. 17.

4. Jan Assmann, *Moses der Ägypter: Entzifferung einer Gedächtnisspur* (Munich: Hanser, 1998), 75. [This book was originally published in English under the title *Moses the Egyptian: The Memory of Egypt in Western Monotheism* (Cambridge, Mass.: Harvard University Press, 1997). In preparing the German version, however, Assmann made changes to the text. The references here are to passages that are not found in the English edition. *Trans.*]

5. Ibid.

6. Ibid., 77.

7. Marie-Odile Métral, *Le Mariage: Les Hésitations de l'Occident* (Paris: Aubier, 1977), 57, n. 44.

8. Ibid., 72.

9. *Saint Gregory of Nyssa: Ascetical Works,* trans. Virginia Woods Callahan (Washington, D.C.: Catholic University of America Press, 1967), 10.

10. Ibid., 10–11.

11. Anselm of Canterbury says the following in a meditative prayer directed at Mary: "For if you, Lady, are his mother, surely then your sons are his brothers? But who are the brothers and of whom? Shall I speak out of the rejoicing of my heart, or shall I be silent in case it is too high for me to mention? But if I believe and love why should I not confess it with praise? . . . So our judge is our brother, the Saviour of the world is our brother, and finally our God through Mary is our brother" (*The Prayers and Meditations of St. Anselm,* trans. Sister Benedicta Ward [Harmondsworth: Penguin, 1973], 123).

12. Quoted in Franz Courth, *Mariologie* (Graz: Styria, 1991), 185.

13. Kurt Ruh, *Geschichte der abendländischen Mystik,* vol. 2, *Frauenmystik und franziskanische Mystik der Frühzeit* (Munich: Beck, 1993), 245–95.

14. Oskar Panizza, *The Council of Love: A Celestial Tragedy in Five Acts,* trans. Oreste F. Pucciani (New York: Viking, 1973), and *Das Schwein in poetischer, mythologischer und sittengeschichtlicher Beziehung,* ed. R. Düsterberg (Munich: Belleville, 1994).

15. Knut Boeser, ed., *Der Fall Oskar Panizza: Ein deutscher Dichter im Gefängnis: Eine Dokumentation* (Berlin: Hentrich, 1989), 173.

Part II. Theories

1. Juan Eduardo Tesone, "Psychoanalytische Bemerkungen zum Inzest: Das aufgelöste Dreieck?" *Psyche* 50 (1996): 842.

2. Pierre Legendre, *L'Inestimable Objet de la transmission* (Paris: Fayard, 1985).

12. The Family Novel of Religions

1. Jacobus de Voragine, *The Golden Legend: Readings on the Saints,* trans. William Granger Ryan (Princeton, N.J.: Princeton University Press, 1993), 1:167. All subsequent quotations refer to pages 167–68.

2. Sigmund Freud, *Moses and Monotheism*, trans. Katherine Jones (London: Hogarth, 1951), 93.

3. Ibid., 94.

4. Ibid., 84.

5. Josef Hayim Yerushalmi, *Freud's Moses: Judaism Terminable and Interminable* (New Haven, Conn.: Yale University Press, 1991), 83.

6. Jan Assmann, *Moses the Egyptian: The Memory of Egypt in Western Monotheism* (Cambridge, Mass.: Harvard University Press, 1997).

7. Freud, *Moses and Monotheism*, 106.

8. Ibid., 129.

9. Sigmund Freud, *Totem and Taboo*, trans. and ed. James Strachey (New York: Norton, 1989), 176.

10. Freud, *Moses and Monotheism*, 132.

11. Freud, *Totem and Taboo*, 178.

12. Freud, *Moses and Monotheism*, 135.

13. Ibid.

14. Ibid., 179–82, 212–16.

15. Ibid., 138–40.

16. Ibid., 145.

17. Ibid., 214–15.

18. Herbert Marcuse, *Eros and Civilization: A Philosophical Inquiry into Freud* (Boston: Beacon, 1955), 69–70.

19. Ibid., 70.

20. Freud, *Moses and Monotheism*, 142.

21. She still appears in Freud's *Totem and Taboo*, but only as an aside and as the object of a definite break: "In the Christian doctrine, therefore, men were acknowledging in the most undisguised manner their guilty primeval deed, since they found the fullest atonement for it in the sacrifice of this one son. Atonement with the father was all the more complete since the sacrifice was accompanied by a total renunciation of the women on whose account the rebellion against the father was started" (191).

22. Marianne Krüll, *Freud and His Father*, trans. Arnold J. Pomerans (New York: Norton, 1986).

23. Yerushalmi, *Freud's Moses*, 81.

24. Ibid., 90. All subsequent quotations refer to pages 91–94.

25. Ida Magli, *La Madonna* (Milan: Rizzoli, 1987), 15.

13. Beyond Gender

1. René Girard, *Violence and the Sacred*, trans. Patrick Gregory (Baltimore: Johns Hopkins University Press, 1972), 8.

2. Ibid., 135.

3. René Girard, *The Scapegoat*, trans. Yvonne Freccero (Baltimore: Johns Hopkins University Press, 1986), 149–64, and *Things Hidden Since the Foundation of the World*, trans. Stephan Bann and Michael Metteer (Stanford, Calif.: Stanford University Press, 1987).

4. Girard, *Things Hidden Since the Foundation of the World*, 220–21.

5. Peter Brown, *The Body and Society: Men, Women, and Sexual Renunciation in Early Christianity* (New York: Columbia University Press, 1988), 86, see also 18.

6. Saint Gregory of Nyssa, *On Virginity*, in *Saint Gregory of Nyssa: Ascetical Works*, trans. Virginia Woods Callahan (Washington, D.C.: Catholic University of America Press, 1967), 48.

7. Ibid., 49.

8. Ibid., 18.

9. Brown, *Body and Society*, 6.

10. Susanna Elm, *"Virgins of God": The Making of Asceticism in Late Antiquity* (Oxford: Clarendon, 1994).

14. The Question of Power

1. Max Weber, *Economy and Society: An Outline of Interpretive Sociology*, trans. Ephraim Fischoff et al., 2 vols. (Berkeley: University of California Press, 1978), 1:215.

2. Ibid., 2:1113.

3. Ibid., 1113–14.

4. Ibid., 1117.

5. Max Weber, *Schriften zur Soziologie*, ed. Michael Sukale (Stuttgart: Reclam, 1995), 413–17.

6. Weber, *Economy and Society*, 2:1114.

7. John G. Gager, *Kingdom and Community: The Social World of Early Christianity* (Englewood Cliffs, N.J.: Prentice-Hall, 1975), 20–37.

8. Weber, *Economy and Society*, 2:1116–17.

9. Ibid., 1120.

10. Robin Fox, *The Red Lamp of Incest* (New York: Dutton, 1980); *Kinship and Marriage* (Cambridge: Cambridge University Press, 1983); and *Reproduction and Succession: Studies in Anthropology, Law and Society* (New Brunswick, N.J.: Transaction, 1993).

11. Robin Fox, "The Virgin and the Godfather: Kinship versus the State in Greek Tragedy and After," in Paul Benson, ed., *Anthropology and Literature* (Urbana: University of Illinois Press, 1993), 107–50.

12. Ibid., 144.

13. Ibid., 109.

14. Ibid., 109–10.

15. Ibid., 110.

15. Christianity: On the Road to Becoming the Religion of the Empire

1. John G. Gager, *Kingdom and Community: The Social World of Early Christianity* (Englewood Cliffs, N.J.: Prentice-Hall, 1975), 114–42.

2. Ibid., 130.

3. Peter Brown, *Power and Persuasion: Towards a Christian Empire* (Madison: University of Wisconsin Press, 1992), 18.

4. Ibid., 19.

5. Ibid., 93–94.

6. Ibid., 94.
7. Ibid., 95.
8. Ibid., 152.
9. Antonie Wlosok, "Vater und Vatervorstellungen in der römischen Kultur," in Hubertus Tellenbach, ed., *Das Vaterbild im Abendland*, vol. 1, *Rom, Frühes Christentum, Mittelalter, Neuzeit, Gegenwart* (Stuttgart: Kohlhammer, 1978), 18–54.
10. Brown, *Power and Persuasion*, 154.

16. The Church's Marriage Policy in the Middle Ages

1. Claude Lévi-Strauss, *The Elementary Structures of Kinship*, trans. James Harle Bell, John Richard von Sturmer, and Rodney Needham (Boston: Beacon, 1969).
2. Jack Goody, *The Development of the Family and Marriage in Europe* (Cambridge: Cambridge University Press, 1983), 33.
3. Ibid., 32.
4. Ibid., 39–40.
5. Jean-Louis Flandrin, *Families in Former Times*, trans. Richard Southern (Cambridge: Cambridge University Press, 1979), 23–33.
6. André Burguière, Christiane Klapische-Zuber, Martine Segalen, and Françoise Zonabend, eds., *A History of the Family*, vol. 1, *Distant Worlds, Ancient Worlds*, trans. Sarah Hanbury Tenison (Cambridge, Mass.: Harvard University Press, 1996), 133.
7. Ibid.
8. Goody, *Development of the Family*, 137.
9. Ibid., 41–42.
10. Ibid., 76.
11. Ibid., 77.
12. Ibid., 72–73.
13. Ibid., 75.
14. Ibid., 43–44.
15. Ibid., 99.
16. Ibid., 45–46.
17. Ibid., 97.
18. The theological universalism of the church created considerable problems for the Christian mission that was pushing northward from the Mediterranean region. According to Lutz E. von Padberg, "To begin with, the decomposition of the ancient world led to a certain paralysis of the missionary zeal. The concept of Christian universality, which had become an active historical force through the implementation of Christ's commandment to spread the word, suddenly found itself confronted with the tribalism of the Germanic peoples, who did not know what to do with the idea of monotheism. To Christians, Adam was the one father of all humanity through whom sin had come into the world, and Christ was the one through whom all could be redeemed. The pagans did not know such a sense of community: beyond their own world lay strange regions in which they had no interest. If Christianity wanted to continue thinking of itself as the

religion of the ecumene, the collapse of the hitherto ordered relationships put it to the test. It had to overcome tribalism, and it took some time before the church could shift its sights to this undertaking" (*Die Christianisierung Europas im Mittelalter* [Stuttgart: Reclam, 1998], 31–32).

19. Goody, *Development of the Family*, 123.

20. Ibid., 101.

21. Ibid., 151–53.

22. Ibid., 153.

23. Ibid., 154.

24. Ibid., 78.

25. August Franzen, *Zölibat und Priesterehe in der Auseinandersetzung der Reformationszeit und der katholischen Reform des 16. Jahrhunderts* (Münster: Aschendorff, 1969), 10–12.

26. *Codex Justinianus*, ed. G. Härel and F.-M. Kaufmann (Leipzig: Reclam, 1991), 1.3.47, p. 36.

27. Jo Ann McNamara, "Chaste Marriage and Clerical Celibacy," in Vern L. Bullough and James Brundage, eds., *Sexual Practices and the Medieval Church* (Buffalo, N.Y.: Prometheus, 1982), 23.

28. Ibid., 28.

29. Ibid., 30.

30. Georges Duby, *The Knight, the Lady, and the Priest: The Making of Modern Marriage in Medieval France*, trans. Barbara Bray (New York: Pantheon, 1983), 116.

31. Goody, *Development of the Family*, 80.

32. Robin Fox, "The Virgin and the Godfather: Kinship versus the State in Greek Tragedy and After," in Paul Benson, ed., *Anthropology and Literature* (Urbana: University of Illinois Press, 1993), 143.

33. Ibid., 144–45.

34. Duby, *Knight, the Lady, and the Priest*, 185.

35. Georges Duby, *Love and Marriage in the Middle Ages*, trans. Jane Dunnett (Chicago: University of Chicago Press, 1994), 17.

36. Duby, *Knight, the Lady, and the Priest*, 177.

37. Quoted in Marina Warner, *Alone of All Her Sex: The Myth and the Cult of the Virgin Mary* (New York: Knopf, 1976), 184.

38. According to Cynthia Hahn, "Despite its apparent unsuitability as a model for normal matrimony, the virginal marriage of Mary and Joseph was so prized as an image of perfection that it emerged as a vision of holy marriage in the liturgical celebration of matrimony" ("'Joseph Will Perfect, Mary Enlighten and Jesus Save Thee': The Holy Family as Marriage Model in the Mérode Triptych," *Art Bulletin* 68 [1986]: 63).

39. Duby, *Love and Marriage*, 27–28.

40. Ibid., 28–29.

17. The Protestant Holy Family

1. Lyndal Roper, *The Holy Household: Women and Morals in Reformation Augsburg* (Oxford: Oxford University Press, 1989), 232.

2. August Franzen, *Zölibat und Priesterehe in der Auseinandersetzung der Reformationszeit und der katholischen Reform des 16. Jahrhunderts* (Münster: Aschendorff, 1969), 9.

3. Ibid., 65.

4. Heiko A. Oberman, *Luther: Man Between God and the Devil*, trans. Eileen Walliser-Schwarzbart (New Haven, Conn.: Yale University Press, 1989), 278.

5. Martin Luther, "A Marriage Booklet for Simple Pastors," trans. P. Z. Strodach, in *Works of Martin Luther* (Philadelphia: Castle, 1915), 6:217–30.

6. Klaus Suppan, *Die Ehelehre Martin Luthers: Theologische und rechtshistorische Aspekte des reformatorischen Eheverständnisses* (Salzburg: Pustet, 1971), 36–40; Joel F. Harrington, *Reordering Marriage and Society in Reformation Germany* (Cambridge: Cambridge University Press, 1995), 101–66, 273–78.

7. Scholarly opinion diverges on the question of the immediate effects of the Reformation and of the marital reforms it pursued. A fairly recent book on the topic, Harrington's *Reordering Marriage and Society in Reformation Germany*, is rather skeptical on this point. Harrington argues that the situation in Germany was too complicated and regionally too diverse, that the reformer's interest in order was too strong and, in the final analysis, too conservative, and that the influence of the church remained too powerful even among Protestants to allow for a breakdown of the confessions according to the following crude scheme: Catholicism that was focused on the hereafter and the church versus Protestantism that was oriented toward the secular.

8. Martin Greiffenhagen has written: "What it was all about might be described by the two concepts *secularization* and *spiritualization*. These two words signal a certain dialectic, and that, precisely, is what it was about: on the one hand, Luther stripped the world of all the holy magic that had accumulated in Catholic religiosity and church practice. . . . That is the one side: *secularization*. The flip side is called *spiritualization*; to quote Luther's words: 'Let the entire world therefore be full of service to God [*Gottesdienstes*]. Not only in the church but also in the home, the kitchen, the cellar, the workshop, in the field, among burghers and peasants.' . . . Helmuth Plessner has described this religious animation of the world with the felicitous phrase *worldly piety* [*Weltfrömmigkeit*]. Secular affairs, by virtue of being regarded as spheres in which Christian faith could prove itself, were infused with an immense intensity. The Protestant Christian is, so to speak, always in service to God precisely because there no longer is a separate sphere of piety. What matters is making all of life holy" ("Einleitung," in Martin Greiffenhagen, ed., *Das evangelische Pfarrhaus: Eine Kultur- und Sozialgeschichte* [Stuttgart: Kreuz, 1984], 7–8).

9. Wilhelm Baur, *Das deutsche evangelische Pfarrhaus: Seine Gründung, seine Entfaltung und sein Bestand,* 3d ed. (Bremen: Muller, 1884), 73.

10. Julius Hoffmann, *Die "Hausväterliteratur" und die "Predigt über den christlichen Hausstand": Lehre vom Hause und Bildung für das häusliche Leben im 16., 17. und 18. Jahrhundert* (Berlin: Weinheim, 1959).

11. Ibid., 45.

12. André Burguière, Christiane Klapische-Zuber, Martine Segalen, and Françoise Zonabend, eds., *A History of the Family,* vol. 2, *The Impact of Modernity,* trans. Sarah Hanbury Tenison (Cambridge, Mass.: Harvard University Press, 1996), 107.

13. Lawrence Stone, *The Family, Sex and Marriage in England, 1500–1800* (London: Weidenfeld and Nicolson, 1977), 140.

14. Ibid., 142.

15. See, for example, Paul Rebhun, *Haußfried: Was für ursachen den Christlichen Eheleuten zubedencken / den lieben Haußfriede in der Ehe zu erhalten* (Nuremberg, 1605), [23].

16. Ibid., [12]ff.

17. Justus Menius, *Oeconomia Christiana: Von Christlicher Haußhaltung durch Iustum Moenium* (Nuremberg, 1606), chap. 7.

18. Albrecht Schöne, *Säkularisation als sprachbildende Kraft: Studien zur Dichtung deutscher Pfarrerssöhne*, 2d ed. (Göttingen: Vandenhoek & Ruprecht, 1968).

19. Baur, *Das deutsche evangelische Pfarrhaus*, 74.

20. Quoted in Harrington, *Reordering Marriage and Society*, 42.

21. Hoffmann, *Die "Hausväterliteratur,"* 45, referring to Menius's *Oeconomia Christiana* of 1529.

22. Barbara Vinken, "Alle Menschen werden Brüder: Republik, Rhetorik, Differenz der Geschlechter," *Lendemains* 18 (1993): 112–23.

23. Harrington, *Reordering Marriage and Society*, 38–47.

24. *Dr. Martin Luther's Large Catechism*, trans. Dr. Lenker (Minneapolis: Augsburg, 1935), 72.

25. Ibid., 75.

26. Stone, *Family, Sex and Marriage*, 140.

27. Ibid., 134–42.

28. See, in particular, Martin Luther, "The Babylonian Captivity of the Church," trans. A. T. W. Steinhäuser, in *Luther's Works*, ed. Helmut T. Lehmann (Philadelphia: Fortress, 1959), 36:3–126, especially the chapter "Marriage," 92–106.

29. *Code Napoléon: Avec les changemens qui y ont été faits par la loi du 3 septembre 1807 / Gesetzbuch Napoleons* [French–German edition], trans. Gottfried Daniels (Cologne: Pauli, 1807), bk. 1, sec. 163; *Allgemeines Landrecht für die preußischen Staaten*, 2d ed., 3 vols. (Berlin: Keilischen, 1794), pt. 3, sec. 1, § 7–8.

30. The revulsion toward *incest* as such has largely been absorbed by a heightened social sensitivity about *sexual abuse*, especially of children.

31. According to Antonie Wlosok, "As the sole person within the family unit who was a law unto himself and subject to no coercion, the paterfamilias was in charge of all legal and commercial dealings with the outside world, which included relations with the god. . . . What was unusual about his position, and unheard of to modern sensibilities, is the fact that he held the power of life and death—the *vitae necisque potestas*—over all members of his household. By virtue of this power he was also the judge of the family, in which he assumed the place that was tantamount to that of an absolute monarch" ("Vater und Vatervorstellungen in der römischen Kultur," in Hubertus Tellenbach, ed., *Das Vaterbild im Abendland*, vol. 1, *Rom, Frühes Christentum, Mittelalter, Neuzeit, Gegenwart* [Stuttgart: Kohlhammer, 1978], 21). However, this formal legal power was constrained by the *mos maiorum*, "the bonds created by custom" (23). Wlosok's account needs to be corrected on one point: strictly speaking, the Roman paterfamilias was not even part of the family he headed. He was not "a person within the family

unit" but stood *above it*. See David Herlihy, "The Making of the Medieval Family: Symmetry, Structure, and Sentiment," *Journal of Family History* 8 (1983): 118.

32. Harrington, *Reordering Marriage and Society*, 38–47.

33. According to Dieter Lenzen, "The Reformation . . . contributed to the shift of paternal functions to—aside from mothers—the state. The home and the state came to refer to each other. . . . Whether or not Luther intended it that way makes little difference. The fact is that a development is being prepared that, in the age of Absolutism, leads not only to a shift but to a virtual multiplication of functionaries who arrogate to themselves the tasks taken from the fathers" ("Kulturgeschichte der Vaterschaft," in Walter Erhart and Britta Herrmann, eds., *Wann ist der Mann ein Mann? Zur Geschichte der Männlichkeit* [Stuttgart: Metzler, 1997], 105).

34. Stone, *Family, Sex and Marriage*, 202.

35. Ibid.

36. Ever since the work of Marianne Weber, this has been a topos of feminist scholarship: "[A]s a result of the closing of convents and Beguine houses . . . *unmarried* women within Protestantism first lost certain social opportunities, since they had been deprived of the possibility of creating for themselves, precisely by virtue of their virginity, the status of a being of a higher order by entering a convent. Until the independence and dignity of work outside the home gradually became available to them at the end of the [nineteenth] century, these women were now all condemned to lead a dependent familial existence as 'old maids,' and thus already on the outside in terms of social status, in rank below a married woman. As for the married woman, Protestantism deprived her of recourse to a confessor, who, no matter how dubious his support may have been in cases of rough treatment by the husband, had at least given her spiritual backing that lay outside the husband's sphere of authority. The thought of drawing the consequences of this, as far as the woman was concerned—that is to say, to also recognize and protect her moral autonomy and self-responsibility *vis-à-vis* the husband—this thought was very foreign to the Protestantism of that time, as it unfortunately often still is to Protestantism today. To the reformers the man was the natural house priest for wife, children, and domestics, and only the Baptists at least protected the freedom of conscience within the home" (*Ehefrau und Mutter in der Rechtsentwicklung* [Tübingen: Mohr, 1907], 283). Roper has similarly argued that "far from endorsing independent spiritual lives for women, the institutionalized Reformation was most successful when it most insisted on a vision of women's incorporation within the household under the leadership of their husbands"(*Holy Household*), 2.

37. Harrington, *Reordering Marriage and Society*, 78–79.

38. Luisa Accati, "The Larceny of Desire: The Madonna in Seventeenth-century Catholic Europe," in Jim Obelkevich, Lyndal Roper, and Raphael Samuels, eds., *Disciplines of Faith: Studies in Religion, Politics, and Patriarchy* (London: Routledge & Kegan Paul, 1987), 79–80.

39. Wolfgang Kemp, *Rembrandt "Die Heilige Familie" oder die Kunst, eines Vorhang zu lüften* (Frankfurt: Fischer, 1986), 17.

40. Ibid., 57.

41. Andreas Gestrich, "Erziehung im Pfarrhaus: Die sozialgeschichtlichen Grundlagen," in Martin Greiffenhagen, ed., *Das evangelische Pfarrhaus: Eine Kultur- und Sozialgeschichte* (Stuttgart: Kreuz, 1984), 66–67.

42. Albrecht Koschorke, "Inseminationen: Empfängnislehre, Rhetorik und christliche Verkündigung," in Christian Begemann and David Wellbery, eds., *Kunst–Zeugung–Geburt: Theorien und Metaphern ästhetischer Produktion in der Neuzeit* (Freiburg: Rombach, 2002), 89–110.

43. On this point, see Barbara Vinken, *Die deutsche Mutter: Der lange Schatten eines Mythos* (Munich: Piper, 2001).

44. Stephan Buchholz, *Recht, Religion und Ehe: Orientierungswandel und gelehrte Kontroversen im Übergang vom 17. zum 18. Jahrhundert* (Frankfurt am Main: Klostermann, 1988), 417–25. See also Clausdieter Schott, "Preface," in August Wilhelm Hupel, *Vom Zweck der Ehen: Ein Versuch, die Heirat der Kastraten and die Trennung unglücklicher Ehen zu verteidigen* (1771; reprint, Frankfurt am Main: Metzler, 1985).

45. For example, the Joseph role and the father's role as God's representative is split into two phases: the father reserves for himself the rational instruction of the children (sons) who have outgrown the mother's sphere of the nursery.

46. Philippe Ariès, *Centuries of Childhood: A Social History of Family Life*, trans. Robert Baldick (New York: Random House, 1962).

47. Hoffmann, *Die "Hausväterliteratur,"* 151–52.

48. Stone, *Family, Sex and Marriage*, 264.

49. Friedrich Schleiermacher, *Christmas Eve: Dialogue on the Incarnation*, trans. Terrence N. Tice (San Francisco: EM Texts, 1990), 48.

50. Ibid., 84.

51. Gestrich, "Erziehung im Pfarrhaus," 67.

52. Barbara Beuys, *Familienleben in Deutschland: Neue Bilder aus der deutschen Vergangenheit* (Reinbek: Rowohlt, 1984), 234.

53. Of relevance here is the massive study by Schöne, *Säkularisation als sprachbildende Kraft*.

18. The Return of Joseph

1. Jean Gerson, "Considérations sur saint Joseph," in *Oeuvres complètes*, ed. Msgr. [Palémon] Glorieux (Paris: Desclee, 1966), 7:63–99. See also Pal[émon] Glorieux, "Saint Joseph dans l'oeuvre de Gerson," *Cahiers de Joséphologie* 19 (1971): 414–28, and "Saint Joseph dans l'oeuvre de Gerson," *Cahiers de Joséphologie* 23 (1975): 5–22.

2. "Vees doncques quele dignité c'est icy de Joseph que il soit chief et seigneur de la mere du chief et du seigneur de tout le monde" (Gerson, "Considérations," 66).

3. Hildegard Erlemann, *Die Heilige Familie: Ein Tugendvorbild der Gegenreformation im Wandel der Zeit. Kult und Ideologie* (Münster: Ardey, 1993), 131.

4. Ibid., 133ff.

5. Ibid., 172ff.

6. Moritz Meschler, *Das katholische Kirchenjahr*, quoted in Ludwig Soengen, *Der heilige Joseph, der erhabene Beschützer der Kirche; in seiner Größe und Verehrungswürdigkeit dem christlichen Volke dargestellt* (Regensburg, 1910), 118.

7. Erlemann, *Die Heilige Familie*, 170.

8. "Die heilige Familie," quoted in ibid., 170.

9. Ibid., 172.

10. As a Catholic "handbook" in 1892 put it, quoted in ibid., 175.

11. According to Stephan Krass, "Er ist der Zeuge, der nicht zeugen darf" (He is the witness who is not permitted to procreate) ("Der Spätberufene: Anmerkungen zur historischen Josephsfigur," *Neue Zürcher Zeitung*, December 14–15, 1996, 67).The German plays on the words *Zeuge* (witness) and *zeugen* (procreate).

12. Philippe Julien, "Die drei Dimensionen der Vaterschaft in der Psychoanalyse," in Edith Seifert, ed., *Perversion der Philosophie: Lacan und das unmögliche Erbe des Vaters* (Berlin: Tiamat, 1992), 163–65.

13. Jacques Lacan has written: "It is in the *name of the father* that we must recognize the support of the symbolic function which, from the dawn of history, has identified his person with the figure of the law" (*The Language of the Self: The Function of Language in Psychoanalysis*, trans. Anthony Wilden [Baltimore: Johns Hopkins University Press, 1968], 41). See also Lacan's comments on the Christian Father-God in *On Feminine Sexuality: The Limits of Love and Knowledge*, trans. Bruce Fink (New York: Norton, 1998).

14. Lena Lindhoff, *Einführung in die feministische Literaturtheorie* (Stuttgart: Metzler, 1995), 81.

19. Joseph, Abelard, Saint-Preux

1. Jack Goody, *The Development of the Family and Marriage in Europe* (Cambridge: Cambridge University Press, 1983),153–56.

2. Stephan Buchholz, *Recht, Religion und Ehe: Orientierungswandel und gelehrte Kontroversen im Übergang vom 17. zum 18. Jahrhundert* (Frankfurt am Main.: Klostermann, 1988), chap. 5.

3. Niklas Luhmann, *Love as Passion: The Codification of Intimacy*, trans. Jeremy Gaines and Doris L. Jones (Cambridge, Mass.: Harvard University Press, 1986), 129–44.

4. On this point, see Albrecht Koschorke, *Körperströme und Schriftverkehr: Mediologie des 18. Jahrhunderts* (Munich: Fink, 1999).

5. See the detailed account by Etienne Gilson, *Heloise and Abelard*, trans. L. K. Shook (Ann Arbor: University of Michigan Press, 1963).

6. *The Letters of Abelard and Heloise*, trans. and ed. Betty Radice (London: Penguin, 1974), 142.

7. Quoted in Adalbert Podlech, *Abaelard und Heloisa oder die Theologie der Liebe* (Munich: Piper, 1990), 224.

8. *Letters of Abelard and Heloise*, 138.

9. Ibid., 150.

10. The twelfth century is not considered a very productive period in the history of Josephology. Abelard said little about Joseph in explicit terms and nothing that went beyond the patristic teachings. See Aimé Trottier, "Deux maîtres français du 12ᵉ siècle: Abélard et Pierre Comestor," *Cahiers de Joséphologie* 19 (1971): 280–95.

11. *Letters of Abelard and Heloise*, 148.

12. Jean-Jacques Rousseau, *Julie, or The New Heloise: Letters of Two Lovers Who Live in a Small Town at the Foot of the Alps*, trans. Philip Stewart and Jean Vaché (Hanover, N.H.: University Press of New England, 1997), 291–92.

13. Ibid., 294.

14. Ibid.

20. Holy Family, Bourgeois Family

1. Thomas Laqueur, "Orgasm, Generation, and the Politics of Reproductive Biology," *Representations* 14 (1986): 1–41.

2. Albrecht Koschorke, *Körperströme und Schriftverkehr: Mediologie des 18. Jahrhunderts* (Munich: Fink, 1999),15–20, 437–43.

3. Heinrich von Kleist to Wilhelmine von Zenge, May 30, 1800, *Sämtliche Werke und Briefe*, ed. H. Sembdner, 7th ed., 2 vols. (Munich: Hanser, 1987), 2:506.

4. Ibid., 506–7.

5. Karl Gottfried Bauer, *Über die Mittel dem Geschlechtstriebe eine unschädliche Richtung zu geben* (Leipzig, 1791), 75.

6. Ibid., 87.

7. Wilhelm Traugott Krug, *Philosophie der Ehe: Ein Beytrag zur Philosophie des Lebens für beide Geschlechter* (Leipzig: Roch, 1800), 102.

8. Kleist, *Sämtliche Werke*, 2:899–900.

9. Ibid., 1:22.

10. Heinrich von Kleist, *"The Marquise of O——" and Other Stories*, trans. David Luke and Nigel Reeves (London: Penguin, 1978), 68.

11. Ibid., 69–70.

12. Ibid., 79.

13. Ibid., 90–91.

14. Ibid., 74–75.

15. Ibid., 94.

16. Ibid., 96–97. [The English translation by Luke and Reeves reads: "I do not want to hear anything." I have changed this to read: "I do not want to *know* anything." I believe this captures more accurately the whole point that Kleist is attempting to make: the Marquise does not want to know what she knows. *Trans.*]

17. Ibid., 112–13.

18. Barbara Vinken and Anselm Haverkamp, "Die zurechtgelegte Frau: Gottesbegehren und transzendentale Familie in Kleist's *Marquise von O . . .*," in Gerhard Neumann, ed., *Heinrich von Kleist: Kriegsfall, Rechtsfall, Sündenfall* (Freiburg: Rombach, 1994), 127–47.

19. *Briefe der Ninon de Lenclos* (Frankfurt am Main, 1989), letter 27.

21. Christ and Oedipus: Freud's Coup

1. Ludwig Feuerbach, *The Essence of Christianity*, trans. George Eliot (New York: Prometheus, 1989).

2. Theodor Mundt, *Madonna: Unterhaltung mit einer Heiligen* (1835; reprint, Frankfurt am Main: Athenäum, 1973), 261.

3. David Blackbourn, *Volksfrömmigkeit und Fortschrittsglaube im Kulturkampf* (Stuttgart: Steiner, 1988).

4. Barbara Vinken, *Die deutsche Mutter: Der lange Schatten eines Mythos* (Munich: Piper, 2001)

5. Thomas Macho, *Weihnachten: Kindsmord und Zeitenwende* (Munich: Fink, forthcoming).

6. Friedrich Kittler, *Dichter—Mutter—Kind* (Munich: Fink, 1991), 103–18, and *Aufschreibesysteme, 1800/1900* (Munich: Fink, 1985).

7. For example, the travel letters speak of the "indecent [*frivole*] mysticism" of the Catholic girls of Prague and invoke a "distant simoniacal future" and the "happiness of free love" (Mundt, *Madonna*, 297, 325).

8. Gerhart Hauptmann, *Michael Kramer*, trans. Ludwig Lewisohn, in Ludwig Lewisohn, ed., *The Dramatic Works of Gerhart Hauptmann*, vol. 3, *Domestic Dramas* (New York: Huebsch, 1914), 513.

9. Ibid., 537.

10. Walter Hasenclever, *Der Sohn: Ein Drama in fünf Akten* (Stuttgart: Reclam, 1994), act 4, scene 3, p. 94.

11. Ibid., act 2, scene 1, p. 29.

12. The slogan "fatherless society," which had an illustrious career in sociopsychological diagnoses of the twentieth century, was coined in 1919 by Paul Federn. Federn related Freud's analysis of religion to the contemporary political situation after the end of World War I, which was dominated by the collapse of the monarchies in Germany and Austria and by revolutionary activities ("Die vaterlose Gesellschaft," in H. Dahmer, ed., *Analytische Sozialpsychologie* [Frankfurt am Main: Suhrkamp, 1980], 1:65–87).

13. "Now I have the term: We modern German are something like Christ Socialists" (65). "I converse with Christ. I believed I had overcome him, but I have only overcome his idolatrous priests and false servants. Christ is harsh and relentless. He drives the Jewish money-changers out of the temple. A declaration of war against money. . . . We are all sick! Only the fight against corruption can save us again" (38–39) (Joseph Goebbels, *Michael: A Novel*, trans. Joachim Neugroschel [New York: Amok, 1987]).

22. Remnant Families in the Welfare State

1. Lawrence Stone has spoken of a "divorce society" (*Road to Divorce: England, 1530–1987* [Oxford: Oxford University Press, 1990]).

2. Barbara Vinken, *Die deutsche Mutter: Der lange Schatten eines Mythos* (Munich: Piper, 2001).

3. Michael Mitterauer and Reinhard Sieder, *The European Family: Patriarchy to Partnership from the Middle Ages to the Present,* trans. Karla Oosterveen and Manfred Hörzinger (Chicago: University of Chicago Press, 1982), 1–23, 71–92.

4. This circumstance has evoked considerable resentment; take, for example, Dieter Lenzen: "What is left? In many parts of society, the functions of the father appear to be approaching zero. The remaining alimentary function is undoubtedly the most stable one. To be sure, the state is taking vigorous alimentary action . . . concerning a number of situations that qualify for support. But as long as there are others who can be asked to pay, that is what will happen. Fathers, who are even being deprived of their procreative functions by present trends, no longer have any means of power at their disposal to resist. At the moment it is impossible to say whether or not the propagated form of 'new fatherhood,' which at least invokes an emphatic term, will be suitable for achieving a rehabilitation of fatherhood in the areas of support, protection, and guidance. However, the fact that the motivation for this concept is derived not from a reshaping of the father–child relationship but from the need to unburden the mother gives cause for justified doubt" ("Kulturgeschichte der Vaterschaft," in Walter Erhart and Britta Herrmann, eds., *Wann ist der Mann ein Mann? Zur Geschichte der Männlichkeit* [Stuttgart: Metzler, 1997], 110).

5. This apt summary appears on the dust jacket of Philippe Meyer's study *Das Kind und die Staatsräson oder Die Verstaatlichung der Familie* (Reinbek: Rowohlt, 1981).

6. According to Martin Burckhardt, whose "core thesis" is that "our modern technological means of reproduction are technologized theology" ("Muttergottes Weltmaschine: Über den Zusammenhang von unbefleckter Empfängnis und technischer Reproduktion," *Metis,* no. 11 [special issue: *Reinheit*] [1977]: 34).

7. Nicolas Abraham and Maria Torok, *The Wolf Man's Magic Word: A Cryptonymy,* trans. Nicholas Rand (Minneapolis: University of Minnesota Press, 1986). See, especially, the preface by Jacques Derrida.

23. Theology and Family in George Lucas's *Star Wars*

1. Oliver Denker, *Star Wars: Die Filme* (Munich: Heyne, 1997), 50.

2. George Lucas, *Star Wars: Episode I: The Phantom Menace* [illustrated screenplay] (London: Ebury, 1999), 61.

3. Ibid., 64.

4. Ibid., 96.

5. Ibid., 106.

6. Brent Staples, "Shuffling Through the Star Wars," *New York Times,* June 20, 1999, 14.

7. Ibid. In 1999 the Internet was full of Web sites for and against Jar Jar Binks, demanding that he be either "destroyed" or "saved."

8. Patricia J. Williams, "Racial Ventriloquism," *The Nation,* July 5, 1999. Williams was familiar with this caricature from Sander Gilman's book *The Jew's Body* (New York: Routledge, 1991), 45. Gilman, in turn, had taken it from Eduard Fuchs, *Die Juden in der Karikatur: Ein Beitrag zur Kulturgeschichte* (Munich: Langen, 1921), 200. Fuchs provides other anti-Semitic cartoons that one could use for comparison.

9. The Jedi Qui-Gon tries to influence Watto by means of a magical gesture in order to make him favorably disposed to letting Anakin go. But Watto instantly sees through the ruse and rebuffs Qui-Gon's spiritual influence: "Mind tricks don't work on me—only money" (Lucas, *Star Wars*, 45).

10. Ethel Matala de Mazza, *Der verfasste Körper: Zum Projekt einer organischen Gemeinschaft in der politischen Romantik* (Freiburg: Rombach, 1999), 362–88.

11. This is already apparent in a work that marks Goebbels as an inferior imitator of Expressionism: *Michael: A Novel*, trans. Joachim Neugroschel (New York: Amok, 1987). Goebbels's book is the story of an awakening and conversion, whose hero has a preference for seeing himself reflected in the figure of the Christian Redeemer. In the process, Christ is stripped of his Jewish origins and turned into the first anti-Semite: "Christ is the genius of love, as such the most diametrical opposite of Judaism, which is the incarnation of hate. . . . Christ is the first great enemy of the Jews. . . . The idea of sacrifice first gained visible shape in Christ. Sacrifice is intrinsic to socialism. Sacrifice oneself for others. The Jew, however, does not understand this at all" (65–66). This reference is not intended to draw a direct line from German Romanticism to National Socialism and beyond. I am only talking about the tenacity and poly-contextual adaptability of a stereotype that wanders in and out of the culture of the Christian West.